CAPTIVE AUDIENCE

Studies in Modern Drama
Kimball King, *Series Editor*

CAPTIVE AUDIENCE

Prison and Captivity in Contemporary Theater

Edited by
Thomas Fahy and Kimball King

Routledge
Taylor & Francis Group
New York London

Published in 2003 by
Routledge
29 West 35th Street
New York, NY 10001
www.routledge-ny.com

Published in Great Britain by
Routledge
11 New Fetter Lane
London EC4P 4EE
www.routledge.co.uk

Routledge is an imprint of the Taylor & Francis Group.

Printed in the United States of America on acid-free paper.

10   9   8   7   6   5   4   3   2

Library of Congress Cataloging-in-Publication Data

Captive audience : prison and captivity in contemporary theater / edited
   by Thomas Fahy and Kimball King.
      p.   cm.—(Studies in modern drama ; 19)
   Includes bibliographical references and index.
   ISBN 0-415-96580-2 (hardback : alk. paper)
      1. Drama—20th century—History and criticism.   2. Prisons in
literature.   3. Prisoners in literature.   4. Imprisonment in literature.
I. Fahy, Thomas Richard.   II. King, Kimball.   III. Series.

PN1650.P74 C37   2003
809.2′9355—dc21   2003002697

Contents

PART II

General Editor's Note

At the Modern Language Association meetings in Washington, D.C., in 2000, a plethora of scholarly papers were devoted to themes of captivity and imprisonment in all forms of literature. Dramatic literature is a particularly effective genre for conveying a sense of confinement, since the *theater* itself is a mini "prison" for the audience that willingly submits to an artist's vision for the duration of a performance. In the nineteenth century Nathaniel Hawthorne commented satirically that "whatever Utopia of human virtue and happiness they might originally project, the founders of any new colony have recognized among their earliest practical necessities," the allocation of prison sites. So it seems that society is always imperfect and that prisons, while perhaps inevitable, are constant testimonies to its imperfection. Major playwrights have attempted to expose the flaws of modern life by examining the easily forgotten world of the social failures, "misfits," and prisoners whose existence reminds us of our human limitations.

In this volume, Thomas Fahy, a professor at California Polytechnic University at San Luis Obispo (who also collaborated with me on another Routledge volume, *Peering Behind the Curtain: Disability, Illness, and the Extraordinary Body in Contemporary Theater* [2001]), and I have selected essays by important scholars who attempt to examine the enigmatic and paradoxical role of imprisonment themes in contemporary dramatic literature. We are especially grateful that a major playwright such as Harold Pinter has allowed us to print his own assessment of prison conditions in the modern world. Not only essays on Pinter's plays and those of Peter Weiss, William Inge, and Tennessee Williams, but also essays on less-well-known playwrights, often focusing on Hispanic or African-American characters, provide insights into complex and often contradictory social assumptions.

—Kimball King

Captive Audience: An Introduction

THOMAS FAHY

In most mainstream television shows about crime, such as *NYPD Blue, Law and Order,* and *The Practice,* the story ends with either a confession of guilt or a courtroom conviction. At this moment, justice prevails because the criminal is removed from the narrative. With this figure behind bars, order is restored. We can feel safe again. This invisibility is also designed to focus our attention on the crime itself, not the broader social forces behind it. By ending the story here, the criminal vanishes. His or her story is silenced. And with it, the problems of the prison system remain unacknowledged; its deplorable living conditions, inherent racism, and failure to offer training, education, or any substantive rehabilitation can be overlooked more easily.

The theater of imprisonment tries to rectify this invisibility by putting the prison experience into a palpable and confined space (on stage) with real people (actors). It creates an intimacy between audience and actor that forges a personal investment in the topic and can become the starting point for social change. Perhaps it is the space itself that makes this possible. Enclosed within the walls of a theater, it is easy to sympathize with those held captive on stage. The dynamic of live performance creates a sense of obligation and entrapment for the viewer—even if of our own choosing. Barring a coughing fit or crying baby, most people remain in their seats until intermission or the finale. Social assumptions about rudeness and propriety prevent us from leaving early. In this way, we not only share the same room with those on stage, but we share a feeling of captivity.

Regardless of the reason, this sense of confinement (unique to live performance) can be used very powerfully by dramatists. This shared experience makes us aware of both our role as passive observers and our tacit acceptance of the abuses within the prison system. Unlike the television shows and news reports that rely on the "confessional" moment for resolution, this drama individualizes the people held captive by telling their stories, and it raises questions that are typically ignored: How and why are they in prison? What steps can be taken to prevent this outcome? In doing so, these works challenge viewers to recognize the social forces that contribute to crime and, ultimately, to act.

Part I of this collection focuses on stories by and about prison life. Whether through the case of Susan Smith, the works of Cherríe Moraga and Luis Alfaro, or the reviews of Miguel Piñero's *Short Eyes,* these essays explore the ways in which race, gender, and sexuality shape narratives of captivity. Rena Fraden's "The Confessional Voice: Medea's Brutal Imagination" begins by revisiting her work on Rhodessa Jones and the Medea Project—an organization that works with incarcerated and formerly incarcerated women in San Francisco. In reexamining the interviews used in her book *Imagining Medea,* she notices the ways that the confessional moment fails to "liberate" these women. It is not a question of truthfulness but of interrogating "the work the confession was supposed to *do.*" Using Medea's production of *Buried Fire* and the story of Susan Smith, Fraden examines the ways that the confession does not "always tell the whole truth." Social—as well as personal—culpability must be understood, and the confessional moment often distracts us from this truth. It gives us a "comforting" explanation for the crime. One of the ways that the Medea Project engages with this issue is by presenting multiple confessions and perspectives to explore different versions of the truth. "The theater is a space for confessions, but only the kind that are never over. In the ritual of the theater, power is spotlighted, but the truth is never fully revealed."

Tiffany Ana Lopez frames her essay, "Emotional Contraband: Prison as Metaphor and Meaning in U.S. Latina Drama," with a powerful discussion of her experiences visiting her incarcerated brother. She examines prison as a performance space—defined by ritual, a scripted hierarchy, surveillance, and her own role as a witness/visitor. Since prisoners mostly remain invisible in society, how do we get access to their stories? How do we understand how one ends up in prison? And how can the reader/viewer "adopt the role of the visitor, the witness, the agent of social change"? Using the plays of Migdalia Cruz, Cherríe Moraga, and Luis Alfaro, Lopez argues that Latina/o drama engages with these questions through an exploration of violence and captivity. They use the power of critical witnessing—"the commitment to stand at the cultural front lines as an activist-bound viewer of prison theater"—to inspire social change by implicating the viewer "in the fate of the person or persons they are watching."

In "Seeing Ethnicity: The Impact of Race-and Class on the Critical Reception of Miguel Piñero's *Short Eyes,*" Fiona Mills examines the ways that race- and class-based prejudices prevented drama critics from "witnessing" Piñero's play. His portrayal of "interracial fraternity created among inmates despite individual prejudices" has not prevented many prominent critics from attacking Piñero's status as an ex-convict, his lack of formal education, and even the play's audience, which was predominantly Latina/o and African American. They felt that the participatory response of the audience was distracting, "offensive," and "inappropriate" for the theater. From these reviews, Mills raises questions about the role of race and class in American theater and argues that the play's demand for social action and change upset critics. "It is the play's pointed description of life among the lower classes and the visceral response it elicited from its racially diverse audience that disturbed drama critics the most." By using Piñero's play as an example of Latino/a drama more broadly, Mills concludes that the marginalization of this drama reflects ongoing cultural biases against non-Anglo art on Broadway.

Part II begins with Harold Pinter speaking not as a playwright or poet, but as an activist. This brief excerpt from a recent speech presents a number of chilling statistics about the American penal system. Pinter's criticisms not only echo those expressed in Part I, but his own fictional and filmic portrayals of captivity also offer an effective introduction for the critical discussions of drama about prison in this section.

Both Ann C. Hall and Christopher C. Hudgins examine one of the more neglected aspects of Harold Pinter's oeuvre—screenplays. In "Harold Pinter's Prison House: The Screenplay of Kafka's *The Trial*," Ann Hall examines the relationship between spectator and spectacle in this adaptation and argues that Pinter places the audience "in the role of witness and participant." Opening with an examination of Michel Foucault's *Discipline and Punish: The Birth of the Prison,* Hall links this analysis of surveillance as power to Pinter's depiction of society in *The Trial.* It is ultimately Pinter's use of the medium of film—the gaze of the camera itself—that so powerfully renders the tension between captivity and freedom, objectivity and individuality, and justice and oppression. Just as Hall discusses some of the ramifications of the cuts made to this screenplay, Christopher C. Hudgins also addresses the significant differences between the film and the original script for Pinter's adaptation of Margaret Atwood's *The Handmaid's Tale.* He begins by challenging the critics who view Pinter's early works as "nonpolitical," arguing instead that they implicitly attack social conformity, class inequalities, and conformist behavior. Using *The Handmaid's Tale* as his primary example, Hudgins explores the political implications of Pinter's decision to make us identify with the villain and the villain's desire for power. Ultimately, Hudgins believes that Pinter's version focuses "our attention on both the 'evil,' the prison-like society, and the nobility of the courage of resistance."

Pamela Cooper's "'A World of Bodies': Performing Flesh in *Marat/Sade*" examines the contrast between freedom and confinement through the pairing of Jean-Paul Marat and the Marquis de Sade. Playwright Peter Weiss establishes a dialogue between these antagonists to establish and break down binaries. Reading *Marat/Sade* through the lens of Julia Kristeva, Cooper argues that Weiss "experiments with a dramatic vocabulary for abjection." He specifically uses the body in fragments (refuse and corpses) as a metaphor for the waste products of social and political change, and in this way, he politicizes the abject. Robert F. Gross also explores Kristeva's notion of the abject in "*The Disposal:* William Inge's Abject Drama." Unlike Kristeva's focus on the female body, however, Gross looks at the ways in which the male body that does not control abjection is feminized. He specifically investigates the link between abjection and homosexuality, and the implications of "and subversion of, fantasies of male criminality, sexuality, and anality" in *The Disposal*. As the title suggests, abjection is the primary metaphor of the play, and ironically, the play's critical failure makes the work "itself an abject drama." Gross argues that *The Disposal* attempts to counter assumptions about the male homosexual as threatening "the entire project of modern American masculinity." Though it fails to do this convincingly, Inge does argue "for a Christianity and a dramaturgy that can embrace abjection rather than treat it with loathing and exclusion."

Thomas Fahy reads Tennessee Williams's use of prison as a metaphor for art and masculinity in the recently rediscovered *Not about Nightingales*. Williams wrote this play as an impassioned response to the 1938 "Klondike" massacre at the Philadelphia County Prison. In this drama, Williams aligns social action—the need to fight injustice—with both masculine solidarity and artistry. Together, the play suggests that art and fraternity can bring about social change. By presenting community and artistry as masculine virtues, Williams ultimately challenges audiences to recognize art's potential power to inspire social reform and to reconsider popular assumptions about manhood. Claudia Barnett also explores issues of gender in her essay "Physical Prisons: Naomi Wallace's Drama of Captivity." Barnett argues that Wallace's staging of prison "challenges traditional definitions of crime and punishment, victim and abuser." In creating situations where blame is earned by all (regardless of gender), Wallace asks audiences to reevaluate assumptions about women as victims, exploring the ways in which characters are trapped by the past, their own bodies, gender, and class. Her drama—particularly *One Flea Spare*—associates prison with theater, and by "focusing on issues of the passive watcher in her plays, she forces her audience to reexamine its own role in the theater and in society."

Lois Gordon's "*No Exit* and *Waiting for Godot*: Performances in Contrast" concludes the collection. Gordon specifically juxtaposes the ways in which Beckett's characters are trapped by the human condition and Sartre's by bad choices—"condemned by their indifference to the value of life and the power they have in creating a worthy life." This perspective limits Sartre's characters. They cannot see possibilities, only limitations, and they are unable to see the ways in which their actions define who they are. The heroes of *Waiting for Godot*, however, recognize freedoms—even within a "limited universe." For them, art—the act of creating or inventing—makes this perspective possible, and it reassures them of being alive.

All of the works discussed in this collection explore the power that art has to impact perspective. The drama of captivity and prison challenges audiences/readers to examine the silence and invisibility surrounding prison. The works ask us to consider the ways in which we watch without engagement. By giving voice to those who have been hidden and silenced, these works provide a way to begin healing on both personal and cultural levels. They use prison— literally and metaphorically—as well as our sense of entrapment in the theater to raise uncomfortable and difficult questions. And ultimately, they demand change—change that begins with our own sense of social responsibility.

PART I

1

The Confessional Voice: Medea's Brutal Imagination

RENA FRADEN

Indeed there is a dialectic at the heart of the scene of crime—a surplus and a simultaneous dearth of meaning. Looking at the scene of crime we experience an overwhelming presence of meaning, but a sense also of the evanescent, banal, insubstantial.

—PEARSON AND SHANKS

The confession has spread its effects far and wide. It plays a part in justice, medicine, education, family relationships, and love relations, in the most ordinary affairs of everyday life, and in the most solemn rites; one confesses one's crimes, one's sins, one's thoughts and desires, one's illnesses and troubles; one goes about telling, with the greatest precision, whatever is most difficult to tell. . . . One confesses—or is forced to confess. When it is not spontaneous or dictated by some internal imperative, the confession is wrung from a person by violence or threat; it is driven from its hiding place in the soul, or extracted from the body.

—MICHEL FOUCAULT

The first time I heard the director of the Medea Project in San Francisco, Rhodessa Jones, describe how she conducted workshops in jails with incarcerated women, forcing them to see the ways in which they had been abused by men, while their own rage had caused them to abandon their children, I was struck by how brilliantly that classical reference highlighted similarities and differences in their stories. The women in the 1990s were held hostage to men and to drugs, trapped in a victim/victimizer's vicious circle, angry, like the classical Medea, but without any of her skills—her spells and connections to gods and her gift for plotting. It may be enough to remind ourselves briefly that Euripides's Medea never apologizes and never confesses, nor does she

9

ever express guilt. She hesitates, but then she steels herself to be a hero, sends her children off to murder the woman who is to become her husband's new wife, and then moves offstage to kill her own children to punish her husband for deserting her. Euripides might give us cause to think of her as monstrous by the end of his play, and perhaps she is a monster because she feels no remorse. I am not sure.

In Greek tragedy, the violence mostly happens offstage, while the stage becomes the place to make sense of it; there are explanations, though usually not repentance. One of the biggest differences between the classical theater and the modern reenactment of the Medea plot, it has come to seem to me, is the striking absence and then necessary presence of confession. It is easy to forget that Euripides's Medea, in the end, escapes many possible punitive endings, including a definitive social judgment against her. She is not put to death or even imprisoned, but flies off in the sun god's chariot, off to Athens and the future—in which god only knows what she'll do next. Modern Medeas are not such good escape artists. We have trapped them, forced them to confess, to feel guilt, to explain themselves, to seek penance, to say they were crazy, to justify themselves in some way, to seek our forgiveness and our understanding. But the confession weirdly contains something of that dialectic noted above: an overwhelming sense that the confession should mean so much and *do* so much, and an uneasy sense that the confession is never commensurate with the crime.

In my book, *Imagining Medea: Rhodessa Jones and the Theater for Incarcerated Women,* I described a theatrical project that relies principally on exposing the stories of people's lives. The Medea Project works with incarcerated and formerly incarcerated women in the San Francisco jails, shaping their life stories around myths and music and dance, and performing in public for a limited run, with permission from the sheriff to do so. It can be seen as both postmodern in its juxtaposition of styles, of hip-hop and African drumming, of stilt walkers and trapeze artists, of Greek and African myths, and as humanistic in an old-fashioned sense, believing in the free will and the accessibility of truth, the usefulness of expressing the self. In each performance, at certain moments, the swirl of busy dances and musical numbers subsides, and a woman steps forward to deliver a speech, which is both confessional and autobiographical. This moment, in stark contrast to the busy dances and musical numbers, is unadorned and quiet, but also more powerfully arresting, as the movement, literally, stops. It appears dramatically as a separation. The woman, no longer part of the mass group or chorus, breaks free to claim her own space, speak in her own voice, becoming the dramatic equivalent of a star, in the spotlight, featured, an individual, someone we must notice. And how we read this is unmistakable. It is a dramatic moment that proclaims: "This Is the Truth," their truth, her truth, a revelation, a confession.

Much of what drives the Medea Project is the belief in the necessity for a shared confessional moment. Rhodessa Jones, the director of the project, believes that people can't "move on" with their lives until they confront their past and speak it publicly. The confessional moment drives both the workshop and the arc of the public performance. In it, the women reimagine themselves, looking backward and then casting forward. Many of the people involved in the Medea Project—including the sheriff, the guards, and the women themselves—believe that the act of confession is therapeutic, part of the rehabilitation process. A common-sense response is to say, "Of course." *Imagining Medea* contains a healthy chunk of interviews from all the participants. I depended on the interviews for my "evidence" as to how the project worked. But I spent very little time interrogating the interviewees' conceptions of their confessions or analyzing the material the interviewees produced. I didn't press people on gaps in their stories, as I might have if these were purely texts or dead people. Partly this was because I felt honor bound to "believe" them, and partly, I felt the main point of the book was to describe *how* the participants felt they were participating. At the same time, it seemed to me, the more I came to know something about some of the women and the way the project developed, the more complicated and vexed that confessional moment became for me.

Most everyone involved in the project knew that to tell the Medea Project only as an upbeat story of salvation and liberation would not do justice to other plots. The number of women participating over ten years was still very, very small (maybe one hundred of the thousands of women committed in increasing numbers in the jails of San Francisco alone). And many of the women disappeared completely, so it was impossible to know what happened to them next. On the one hand, the power of that confessional moment in workshop and performance, in which the women tried to express not only the shape of the particular crime that landed them in jail, but also their newly created, different, saved self, always elicited the cheers and laughter and hopefulness from spectators, and from me as well. But on the other hand, neither the art of the sort they were involved with in the Medea Project (composing songs, dancing, reenacting myths), nor those confessional revelatory moments performed in workshops and then on stage could ensure literal or figurative freedom from old selves, that they would be sprung, no longer imprisoned or held captive to old stories, bad plots. An ongoing balancing act marked the project between the optimism of the confession and pledge to be different and the skepticism that a confession, even if truly felt, could perform the necessary liberation from horrendous surroundings. Increasingly I came to feel that the one confessional moment was somehow not equal to the complexity of a life—not false exactly, but certainly only partial—and I became suspicious that confessions did not always lead back, whatever the truth status of the confession, to power and liberation.

It wasn't at all the truth of a particular confession I was questioning; I was just trying to figure out what work the confession was supposed to *do*. There is already a way in which the theater contaminates or at least complicates the parameters of sincerity and authenticity, even in a project that depends upon a certain amount of autobiographical transparency. When a soliloquy, for instance, promises to reveal to us a character's true thoughts and real self, it can only do so because of the contrast between the performance the character puts on for others and the performance about to be put on for us. The character is *always* performing for an audience; the audience changes and the form of address may change as well, but a character is never *not* performing versions of the self to others in the theater. They may be said to have designs on us—the audience—as much, if not more, than the adversaries they face on stage. The rhetorical space of the theater, like that of the confession, depends upon a relationship between at least two people: a participant (the confessor, the actor) and a spectator (the person who hears the confession, the audience).[1] Theater, like the confession, must occur in a social space. But what sort of transaction takes place there? How does the theatrical social space with its particular generic conventions shape the work that confession is supposed to do? Who was I as a spectator hearing these confessions? If my role was to absolve and forgive, as a priest would, how literally was I supposed to do this? Or was I in the position of interrogator, an implicit prosecutor? Did my desire to hear confessions, to believe in them, and be swept away by them, drive the production of them? And *why* did I so want to hear them?

Obviously, Foucault's genealogy of confession has helped to confirm my sense that confessions are a historical development, not natural human behavior. (The Catholic Church doesn't deem the confession a sacrament until the thirteenth century, for instance.)[2] We are now, at least in Western culture, what Foucault calls a "confessing animal" (Foucault 59). Whether coerced or spontaneous, confessions are driven from hiding so that every aspect of our life seems revealed to the panoptic gaze. But what is important to Foucault is the way in which the confession is a ritual that exists within a *power* relationship. I quote at length:

> Whence a metamorphosis in literature: we have passed from a pleasure to
> be recounted and heard, centering on the heroic or marvelous narration of
> "trials" of bravery or sainthood, to a literature ordered according to the in-
> finite task of extracting from the depths of oneself, in between the words, a
> truth which the very form of the confession holds out like a shimmering mi-
> rage. Whence too this new way of philosophizing: seeking the fundamental
> relation to the true, not simply in oneself—in some forgotten knowledge, or
> in a certain primal trace—but in the self-examination that yields, through
> a multitude of fleeting impressions, the basic certainties of consciousness.
> The obligation to confess is now relayed through so many different points,
> is so deeply ingrained in us, that we no longer perceive it as the effect of a
> power that constrains us; on the contrary, it seems to us that truth, lodged
> in our most secret nature, "demands" only to surface; that if it fails to do
> so, this is because a constraint holds it in place, the violence of a power
> weighs it down, and it can finally be articulated only at the price of a kind

of liberation. Confession frees, but power reduces one to silence; truth does not belong to the order of power, but shares an original affinity with freedom: traditional themes in philosophy, which a "political history of truth" would have to overturn by showing that truth is not by nature free—nor error servile—but that its production is thoroughly imbued with relations of power. The confession is an example of this. . . .

The confession is a ritual of discourse in which the speaking subject is also the subject of the statement; it is also a ritual that unfolds within a power relationship, for one does not confess without the presence (or virtual presence) of a partner who is not simply the interlocutor but the authority who requires the confession, prescribes and appreciates it, and intervenes in order to judge, punish, forgive, console, and reconcile; a ritual in which the truth is corroborated by the obstacles and resistances it has had to surmount in order to be formulated; and finally, a ritual in which the expression alone, independently of its external consequences, produces intrinsic modifications in the person who articulates it: it exonerates, redeems, and purifies him; it unburdens him of his wrongs, liberates him, and promises him salvation. (Foucault 59–60, 61–62)

Foucault calls attention to two things that seem important to me. One is recognizable: that classical literature is short on confession and that we no longer delight as much in heroic trials as we do in narratives that describe the interior of the heart. But I underscore Foucault's description of modern literature in which the truth of the self becomes a "shimmering mirage"; the truthful self *seems* to be there, but it isn't really, first because it is an *infinite* task, this extracting from the depths of oneself the truth of oneself, and second because the truth does not seem to lie *in* words but rather in *between* the words, so that the form of the confession, which is necessarily in words, is not equal to the task. The second proposition makes strange what seems common sense: Confessions may not be (only) sources of truth; even when they are taken to be true, truth is never free from the effects of power: "[T]ruth is not by nature free—nor error servile. . . ." Modern Medeas are good case studies of the theatrical problematics of the confession: Their extreme crimes strain the descriptive capability of language, and the crimes themselves turn on the exercise of power and the effect of having none.

One of the modern Medeas who was invoked in the Medea Project's fourth production, *Buried Fire,* in 1996, and who appeared as a character in Cornelius Eady's play, *Brutal Imagination,* in 2001–2002, was the historical Susan Smith. In 1994 Smith claimed that she and her children were kidnapped by a black man, only to confess nine days later that she had herself released the emergency brake of her car with her children strapped in their car seats and let it roll into John D. Long Lake in South Carolina. Her handwritten confession, which was published in newspapers, only describes her state of mind the evening she killed her children. It does not give any sort of a back story, no family genealogy. On the one hand, it is very satisfying to be able to read a confession so neatly and definitively delivered. Nine-day mystery solved. Responsibility taken. No loose ends. But on the other hand, the text of this confession is astonishingly clichéd and banal, and Smith is so quick to assign herself forgiveness that it risks our incredulity. What follows is the complete confession:

> When I left my home on Tuesday, Oct. 25, I was very emotionally distraught. I didn't want to live anymore! I felt like things could never get any worse. When I left home, I was going to ride around a little while and then go to my mom's. As I rode and rode and rode, I felt even more anxiety coming upon me about not wanting to live. I felt I couldn't be a good mom anymore, but I didn't want my children to grow up without a mom. I felt I had to end our lives to protect us from any grief or harm. I had never felt so lonely and so sad in my entire life. I was in love with someone very much, but he didn't love me and never would. I had a very difficult time accepting that. But I had hurt him very much, and I could see why he could never love me. When I was at John D. Long Lake, I had never felt so scared and unsure as I did then. I wanted to end my life so bad and was in my car ready to go down that ramp into the water, and I did go part way, but I stopped. I went again and stopped. I then got out of the car and stood by the car a nervous wreck. Why was I feeling this way? Why was everything so bad in my life? I had no answers to these questions. I dropped to the lowest point when I allowed my children to go down that ramp into the water without me. I took off running and screaming, "Oh God! Oh God, no!" What have I done? Why did you let this happen? I wanted to turn around so bad and go back, but I knew it was too late. I was an absolute mental case! I couldn't believe what I had done. I love my children with all my (a picture of a heart). That will never change. I have prayed to them for forgiveness and hope that they will find it in their (a picture of a heart) to forgive me. I never meant to hurt them!! I am sorry for what has happened and I know that I need some help. I don't think I will ever be able to forgive myself for what I have done. My children, Michael and Alex, are with our Heavenly Father now, and I know that they will never be hurt again. As a mom, that means more than words could ever say.
>
> I knew from day one, the truth would prevail, but I was so scared I didn't know what to do. It was very tough emotionally to sit and watch my family hurt like they did. It was time to bring a peace of mind to everyone, including myself. My children deserve to have the best, and now they will. I broke down on Thursday, Nov. 3, and told Sheriff Howard Wells the truth. It wasn't easy, but after the truth was out, I felt like the world was lifted off my shoulders. I know now that it is going to be a tough and long road ahead of me. At this very moment, I don't feel I will be able to handle what's coming, but I have prayed to God that he give me the strength to survive each day and to face those times and situations in my life that will be extremely painful. I have put my total faith in God, and he will take care of me.
>
> SIGNED SUSAN V. SMITH [3]

Her lie, that a black man kidnapped her children, and her confession that it was she who "allowed her children to go down that ramp," finally breaks free from her and becomes the truth she tells. She says she knew all along the truth would "prevail," but she had been frightened. "It wasn't easy," but once she told, the transformation that confession promises begins: exoneration, redemption, purification. She felt unburdened, "The world lifted off my shoulders." God steps in conveniently to take care of her, to ensure that she will be able to "handle what's coming." But the way in which Smith tells the truth is so trite that her confession does not wholly satisfy. The extraction of her self, to resort to Foucault's analogy, seems truncated, incomplete, her truth a "shimmering mirage," in part, at least, because the words do not adequately capture the act performed. Shouldn't the confession have been more of a struggle? The language more intense? Shouldn't she have hurt *more?* Shouldn't there be *more* she could have revealed? To say she had been "very emotionally distraught" that evening must have been an understatement, given what she was about to do; the clichéd nature of the phrases "a nervous wreck," and then the pictures she resorts to of a heart to signify love, only serve to underscore the way in which the confession seems not to get anywhere near the feeling of despair she claims to remember. It could be that there is a very simple explanation for the gap between word and feeling: One might be that she is a liar and pathological, in which case there isn't much to be learned from her; another is that she just isn't very good with words. But it is also clear that she herself doesn't know, or doesn't have the language to know, the answers as to *why* she felt the way she did. "Why was I feeling this way? Why was everything so bad in my life? I had no answers to these questions." But these are the questions that we want answers to. Without knowing why she did what she did, we don't know whether she is a natural principle, like a buried fire, dangerous but preventable, or whether she is an aberration, a horror, pathological.

By the end of her confession, Smith feels she may have a long road ahead but God will take care of her; the sheriff feels satisfied that justice has been done. But the drama is just beginning for the rest of us who witness the Medea Project's *Buried Fire* or Cornelius Eady's *Brutal Imagination*. One way in which the institution of Western theater questions the simplistic equation of confession as truth, and shows the way in which a confession is part of a system of power, is that even when Fate or the gods are players, the drama consists in humans attempting to outwit or defy those otherworldly powers. The theater certainly knows a *deus ex machina* when it sees one. God, whom Smith invokes, may well be up to taking care of her in real life. He may indeed prove to be her liberator. But in the theater, he's just a trick, a machine, an easy way out, an admission that life can't be properly sorted out without an unnatural device from the wings. Neither the Medea Project nor Eady turn to God to help sort out meaning or to serve as a catalyst for social transformation.

Instead they find traces of power, as most Western, secular drama does, in human, social places.

When Susan Smith's story made national news, the Medea Project immediately recognized a fellow Medeaite. In the workshops that led to *Buried Fire*, Rhodessa Jones wanted to explore various sorts of destructive love. The central image was a natural one: a raging forest fire, which, buried but not extinguished, would grow in intensity until igniting in the air. Susan Smith seemed to fit the natural metaphor and the theme of destructive love. Love failed to protect her, and love was what she continually sought. Her father had committed suicide when she was young; her stepfather had sexually abused her when she was a teenager, and though she reported it to various authorities, neither social workers nor her mother did anything about it. Married young, with two toddlers, estranged from her husband, in love with a boss's son who had just written her to break off their affair, Smith had been ignored and abandoned.[4] With a certain kind of terrible economy, just as she had been ignored, so she chose to expunge the lives of her own children. Sean Reynolds, a social worker who had been involved with the project from the beginning, gave a speech about corrupted love in the middle of *Buried Fire*, and used Smith as her example:

> Love corrupted is rageful, out of control. It is the kind of love that corrupted Susan Smith. It is the good versus the evil kind of love. And Susan Smith was certainly not programmed to control.
>
> Everything in her own sorry history taught her to put that kind of out of control love above the love of her children. Susan, at six years old, had been her father's favorite child, but he committed suicide, in the heartbreak of divorce, abandoning his favorite child by this most selfish act. At thirteen, Susan made her own suicide attempt. Psychiatrists recommended she be hospitalized for depression. Now, most of us with common sense know that it would be unthinkable for a mother to kill her own children, but is it no less unthinkable that a mother would reject a chance to help her child who is bent on killing herself? At fifteen her stepfather, a pillar of the community, sexually molested her, but Susan's mother decided not to press charges against him. Instead she was more willing to sacrifice her own daughter's physical integrity, self-esteem, and life to hold onto that man.[5]

The Medea Project made a comprehensive indictment of the entire family and community, which protected the status quo, sacrificing both generations of children. Society's belief in "crazy love," romantic love, was responsible, at least in part, for these desperate acts of suicide and murder. By rejecting the solitary thrust of Smith's confession and ignoring the solution Smith finds of a God who will take care of her, Reynolds forces the audience to figure out what sort of care they should have taken or might take now. The Medea Project had always believed in the power of confessions and continued to build them into each of their productions, but they also saw that the autobiographical confession did not always tell the whole truth. In fact, the way in which a confession conventionally had to be singular and individual—only one signature allowed at the bottom of the sheet—seemed to preclude tracing *social* culpability, power that ran between and among people that caused them to act the way they did.

Generically, Western drama is never satisfied with the singular voice; the static monologue must include other voices within it if it is to read like drama. Western theater always exists in a social space; it depends upon a live audience, and it is born out of a conflict between two actors speaking. We expect debate and conflict in the theater, between literal and figurative different points of view. In the theater, multiple confessions are more dramatically interesting than one. And drama always delays the confession, or refuses to hear it altogether, or interrupts it, or makes some part of it ambiguous to maximize the experience of extraction, testing possible versions of the truth for as long as possible before settling for an ending.

Another theatrical version of Susan Smith's story, *Brutal Imagination* by Cornelius Eady, dramatizes her confession by splitting her voice into her own and the black man she claimed had killed her children. In his two-person play, Eady shows how the power of racial stereotypes allows an implausible story to seem true. *Brutal Imagination* was first conceived as a series of poems, all written in the voice of the black man in a knit cap whom Smith conjured up as the kidnapper of her children. In its first staged incarnation at the Kitchen in New York, Eady himself read all of the poems in his own voice, with some of the poems set to music, but when he was invited by the Vineyard Theatre to workshop it again, he made the decision to turn the series of poems into a narrative, a theater piece:

> In theatricalizing [Eady says], I was trying to give some sort of dimension to that lie. . . . When I was composing the poetry it was all in the imagined voice of the black man, a monologue. In the theater it became two people. It wasn't so much the story that we were interested in. We knew the story. We know the plot. She did it. She confesses. And Joe [Joe Morton, the actor who plays "Mr. Zero," the supposed kidnapper] is released to move on to the next job. What is the action between these two characters? That became our question at the Kitchen and at the Vineyard. When we sat [the actors] down, there were two people. That's the basic truth. There were flesh and bones in front of us. From her point of view, he's real. Once we buy that piece of it, we're in her world. So it becomes not what they're saying, but why are they here? What's about to happen? Who are they? What's their journey?[6]

Eady had begun by imagining the black man who was so familiar a figure that he just naturally appeared on the tip of Smith's tongue when she ran up to a stranger's door to report her children were gone: a kidnapper, a demon, a criminal, a black man had taken them. "Susan Smith has invented me because /

Nobody else in town will do what / She needs me to do."[7] Eady hadn't wanted
to investigate Smith or her family; instead he traced the racial lie she tells about
that black man and how that lie becomes a truth, a flyer handed out, a person
whom people reported having seen. But in the move from poetic monologue to
a dialogue between the black man and Susan Smith, Eady found himself having
to reimagine Smith, and especially to imagine what she and Mr. Zero meant to
each other. As the "I" of Mr. Zero's poetic words becomes divided, such that
sometimes he speaks the lines and sometimes Susan Smith does on stage, the
play dramatizes the weird way in which Mr. Zero exists for real, though we
are constantly reminded that he is only a figment of Smith's imagination, as
well as our own. Physically, we see two people, but the language compresses
the two people on stage into a "we": "Like a bad lover, she has given me a
poisoned heart / It pounds both our ribs, black, angry, nothing / but business"
(Eady 6). She has given him a poisoned heart, but one heart pounds in *both*
bodies: Susan is as black and angry as Mr. Zero, though for different reasons.

When, in the very last part of the play, Eady dramatizes Smith's resistance to confess, the stage direction is: "SUSAN *clutches* MR. ZERO, *as she
desperately tries to hold him close.*" There are three players now, Susan, the
lie she has been telling, and the sheriff who needs her to confess:

SUSAN: There have been days you have almost

Spilled

From me, nearly taken a breath.
Yanked

Yourself clean. You've
Trembled

My coffee cup. You well
Under

My eyes. You've been
Gravel

On my mattress. You are
Not

Gone. You are going to
Worm

> Your way out. You have
> Not
>
> Disappeared. You
> Slide
>
> Between my teeth,
> Double
>
> Me over as I try
> Not
>
> To blurt you out. The
> Closer
>
> The Sheriff inches me
> Toward
>
> This,
>
> MR. ZERO: The
> Louder
>
> He hears
> Me bitch. (Eady 39–40)

The last two words, "Me bitch," spoken by Mr. Zero on stage are utterly ambiguous, either as to whom is being referred to as "me" or whether "bitch" is a subject or a verb. "me" = Mr. Zero, "bitch" = Susan Smith? As in, MR. ZERO: "*Me,* (you bitch)." Or "me" = Mr. Zero is "bitching"? Or when Mr. Zero speaks at this point in the play, since he is about to *stop* speaking because Susan Smith is going to admit that she has been making up his part all along, the "me" could just as easily refer to Susan. I think the audience wants to have the ambiguity resolved, the boundaries of self restored. But the confession that follows and ends the play does not cure, does not liberate, does not redeem either the woman or free the character she has imagined. Eady insists at the beginning and at the close of his play that the brutal imagining of Mr. Zero will continue: "Though it's common belief / That Susan Smith willed me alive / At the moment / Her babies sank into the lake / When called, I come" (Eady 4) He'll come again. Susan's confession, which Eady excerpts from the newspaper account, is inadequate now, not only because the language is so unimaginative, so flatly inexpressive, but because it doesn't even allude to the brutal imagining of Mr. Zero. The confession is not complete, a shallow extraction at best.

> *When I left my home on Tuesday, October 25, I was very emotionally distraught*
> MR. ZERO: I have yet
> To breathe.
>
> I am in the back of her mind,
> Not even a notion.
>
> A scrap of cloth, the way
> A man lopes down a street.
>
> Later, a black woman will say:
> "we knew exactly who she was describing."
>
> At this point, I have no language,
> No tongue, no mouth.
>
> I am not me, yet.
> I am just an understanding.
>
> SUSAN: As I rode and rode and rode, I felt
> Even more anxiety.
>
> MR. ZERO: Susan parks on a bridge,
> And stares over the rail.
> Below her feet, a dark blanket of river,
> She wants to pull over herself,
> Children and all.
>
> I am not the call of the current.
>
> She is heartbroken.
> She gazes down,
> And imagines heaven.
>
> SUSAN: I felt I couldn't be a good mom anymore, but I didn't want
> my children to grow up without a mom.
>
> MR. ZERO; I am not me, yet.
> At the bridge,

One of Susan's kids cries,
So she drives to the lake,
To the boat dock.

I am not yet opportunity.

SUSAN: I had never felt so lonely
And so sad.

When I was at John D. Long Lake
I had never felt so scared
And so unsure.

MR. ZERO: Who shall be a witness?
Bullfrogs, water fowl.

Who will notice?
Moths, dragonflies
Field mice.

SUSAN: I wanted to end my life so bad
And I was in my car ready to
Go down that ramp into
The water.

MR. ZERO: My hand isn't her hand
Panicked on the
Emergency brake.

SUSAN: And I did go part way,
But I stopped.

MR. ZERO: I am not Gravity,
The water lapping against
The gravel.

SUSAN: I went again and stopped.
I then got out of the car.

MR. ZERO: Susan stares at the sinking.
My muscles aren't her muscles,
Burned from pushing.
The lake has no appetite,

But it takes the car slowly,
Swallow by swallow, like a snake.

SUSAN: Why was I feeling this way?
Why was everything so bad
In my life?

MR. ZERO: Susan stares at the taillights
As they slide from here
To hidden.

SUSAN: I have no answers
To these questions.

Susan *places her hands over her ears.*

MR. ZERO: She has only me,
After she removes our hands
From our ears.

SUSAN *uncovers her ears slowly.* MR. ZERO *stares at her, picks up
one of the composite sketch pictures, stares at it, and he slowly exits.
Stage fades to black.* (Eady 41–44)

Because we have no answers, we imagine possibilities; Mr. Zero steps
forward. The theater is the perfect place to reenact the scene of the crime. As the
audience, we do not perform as detectives who believe in the virtues of hard-
core evidence, clues, detection, pathology, nor as priests or gods who wait to
hear confessions and take care by forgiving trespasses. The theatrical audience
is there to imagine what it must have felt like for victim and perpetrator, and
why what happened took place. We are in this Third Space, a place neither
here nor there, one in which people are masked and made up and speak lies.
The theater is a space for confessions, but only the kind that are never over.
In the ritual of the theater, power is spotlighted, but the truth is never fully
revealed. Instead we are treated to infinite extractions. We uncover our ears.

Notes

1. See McAuley who argues that what differentiates the theater from other forms of
   drama is that it takes place "live," "and that it requires the simultaneous presence
   of both performer and spectator" (3).
2. Confession itself, as a sacrament, does not occur in the Christian church until the
   thirteenth century. Peter Brooks argues that it is only then, with the official admission

of confession in church politics and culture, that the modern world begins:

> [Confession] . . . offers articulation of hidden acts and thoughts in a form
> that reveals—perhaps in a sense creates—the inwardness of the person
> confessing, and allows the person's punishment, absolution, rehabilita-
> tion, reintegration. . . . The requirement of confession imposed by the
> Church in the thirteenth century both reflects and instigates the emer-
> gence of the modern sense of selfhood and the individual's responsibility
> for his or her actions, intentions, thoughts—and for the acts of speech
> that lay them bare. With gathering momentum through the Renaissance
> and Romanticism up to our time, confessional speech becomes more and
> more crucial in defining concepts—sincerity, authenticity—that we are
> supposed to live by. (2, 5–6)

3. *Herald-Journal,* Spartanburg, South Carolina. November 22, 1994. (internet:
   http://222.teleplex.net/SHJ/smith/ninedays/ssconf.html.)
4. Reading through local newspaper accounts during the nine days between the "disappearance" and Smith's confession is fascinating, because we know what happened
   and what is to come. We wait for the recognition scene, anticipating how people will react to being lied to. The sheriff says he was suspicious all along, but
   that he was worried that if he pushed Smith too hard she might commit suicide
   and then it would be even longer before they knew, if ever, what had happened.
   See www.crimelibrary.com/fillicide/smith/index.html and also the stories in the
   Herald-Journal, accessed at www.teleplex.net/SHJ/smith/ninedays/urally01.html.
5. From unpublished text, *Buried Fire,* conceived and directed by Rhodessa Jones at
   the Lorraine Hansberry Theater in San Francisco, January 10, 1996.
6. Interview with author, May 15, 2002. Diedre Murray worked with Eady composing
   music for the poems, but they came to feel that the music was interrupting the
   narrative flow of the piece; they decided in the end to use music only as background
   to the words. *Brutal Imagination* ran from December through January 2001–02
   at the Vineyard Theatre in New York City. Joe Morton and Sally Murphy played
   Mr. Zero and Susan Smith; it was directed by Diane Paulus.
7. Cornelius Eady, *Brutal Imagination* 5. All further quotations taken from the unpublished theater script. *Brutal Imagination* has been published as a poem by Putnam
   in 2001, without speaker roles delineated.

Works Cited

McAuley, Gay. *Space in Performance: Making Meaning in the Theatre*. Ann Arbor:
     The University of Michigan Press, 1999.

Brooks, Peter. *Troubling Confessions: Speaking Guilt in Law & Literature*. Chicago:
     The University of Chicago Press, 2000.

Eady, Cornelius. *Brutal Imagination.* New York: G. P. Putnam's Sons, 2001.

————. *Brutal Imagination.* Unpublished Playscript.

Foucault, Michel. *The History of Sexuality Volume 1: An Introduction.* Translated by Robert Hurley. New York: Vintage Books, 1980.

Fraden, Rena. *Imagining Medea: Rhodessa Jones and Theater for Incarcerated Women.* Chapel Hill: The University of North Carolina, 2001.

Jones, Rhodessa. *Buried Fire.* Unpublished Playscript.

Pearsons, Mike and Michael Shanks. *Theatre/Archaeology.* New York: Routledge, 2001.

"Susan Smith Confession." *Herald-Journal, Spartanburg, South Carolina.* 22 Nov. 1994. *http://222.teleplex.net/SHJ/smith/ninedays/ssconf.html. www.crimelibrary. com/fillicide/smith/index.html.*

2

Emotional Contraband: Prison as Metaphor and Meaning in U.S. Latina Drama

TIFFANY ANA LOPEZ

The prison returns my letters, the word "CONTRABAND" emblazoned across the envelope. So far, this has happened three times. The offending contents: writing tablets naively sent in a cardboard box; a comic book with an over-looked cartoon about safe-cracking; a post-office issued packet of fifty one-cent stamps that exceeds the quantity limit of forty full-postage stamps. The charge feels overbearing when the only thing I've attempted to smuggle in are frustratingly small tokens of support, simple reminders of basic human interaction. Consequently, this policing feels more like a brutal assault on emotional outreach than a truly valid concern with safety and security.

Indeed, the prison functions as a high-stakes performance space. Not only mail, but visitors are carefully screened and searched before they can enter this theater of incarceration. It begins with the audition consisting of a full back-ground check. The contraband missives were merely a harbinger of things to come. Once cleared for entry, visitors will be notified of the appropriate cos-tume and swiftly reminded of their scripted place in the hierarchy. Confronted with such an onslaught of petty gestures and directorial surveillance, it takes a lot to remember one has come to perform not for the directors—more point-edly, the overseers—but for an audience of one for whom the visit means the world. For however brief a moment, the most everyday acts performed during our time together (an embrace, the showing of family photographs, the sharing of snacks) will proudly defy the logic of violence that defines imprisonment.

How many of us really know—or even care—what happens in American prisons? Since the 1980s, politicians increasingly insist on prisons represent-ing the harshest domain of punishment possible. On average, incarcerating a single inmate costs $20,000 per year for housing, meals, and security alone. Without vocational training, education, social programs, mental health care, or drug rehabilitation, prisons negatively impact the future. They also pose deeply disturbing questions regarding the history and future of race relations. Built in once-thriving rural communities, prisons offer economic revitalization—but rarely for the communities of color whose members are incarcerated at unprecedented rates. For Anglo guards raised well away from major urban centers, the prison often marks their first interactions with people of color. In California, African Americans and Latinos make up the overwhelming majority of the prison population. Walter Dean Myers's juvenile novel *Monster,* a cross-genre account of a black teenager facing the possibilities of an adult prison sentence, presents the harrowing realities facing today's black and brown youth.

Prisoners are without doubt society's most convenient scapegoats. Migdalia Cruz's beastly heroine Citrona, the caged hirsute in *Fur,* describes the result of this objectifying force: "When you're like me, no one thinks they can betray you because no one takes you seriously, because no one thinks you're human" (Cruz 98). Cruz's play effectively illustrates why prison stands as such a powerful metaphor for women, people of color, and others who perceive themselves as socially disappeared: "I'm the grass that's not suppose to be alive. Like there's concrete covering me up, so people think I'm dead" (Cruz 87). Significantly, the treatment of prisoners provides a litmus test for larger cultural relations. As the editors of *Prison Masculinities* write, "The prison system, though it isolates prisoners from mainstream society, is not an isolated institutional element within that society. It is melded to the social landscape and to the social relations of men and women" (Sabo et al. 5). The recurring dominant narratives that so consistently focus on individualized acts of random violence keep us dangerously distracted from the larger systemic problems that inform the prison industrial complex.

For most, the primary source of information about prison issues still remains television news, popular journalism, and Hollywood film. Through the nightly news, shows like *OZ* and *Law & Order* and films such as *The Shawshank Redemption* and *Minority Report,* media images of crime and criminals abound. Typically, such dominant narratives focus on the crimes committed, the criminals apprehended, the justice served. Yet, despite the frequency of these images, the lives of people in prison remain invisible, their stories largely ignored. At the very moment that social services have been slashed to bits, public sentiment has dramatically shifted from an emphasis on reform to a near obsession with retribution. Recreation, education, and arts programs historically associated with rehabilitation have been cut drastically to emphasize prison as the harshest domain of punishment possible. What does it mean for a society when prison is promoted as an answer for social problems largely associated with poverty? How might the arts, theater in particular, offer alternative visions for the future?

Notably, the Latina/o dramatic works discussed in this essay are hotly charged by the attendant specters of patriarchy, nationalism, colonialism, homophobia, racism, sexism, and gender and class oppression–elements which constitute the deeply woven fibers of the prison industrial complex. The prison industrial complex is the term invoked, most notably by Angela Davis, to describe an entire economy dependent on incarceration. As the editors of the anthology *Prison Masculinities* observe, "Those we perceive as actually having fallen to the bottom—homeless people, single welfare mothers, the disabled, and immigrants—serve this dark purpose [of scapegoating] very well. But the criminal is the best target of all—easily stigmatized and easily disappeared" (Sabo et al., 14). Paradoxically, despite the totalizing frequency of images that comprise the matrix of the prison industrial complex, the actual lives of people in prison remain invisible, their stories virtually ignored. How do people end up in prison? What kind of life paths lead there? How do families survive the violence historically connected to the prison industrial complex, including the forms of domestic violence that operate in tandem with the state violence that threatens to incapacitate an entire people? As an invitational art, how might theater enable the viewer/reader to adopt the role of the visitor, the witness, the agent of social change? These are precisely the questions addressed by the Latina/o plays discussed in this essay.

In order to understand the history that informs the long standing relationship between Latina/o drama and social action, my essay begins first by analyzing the ways that the plays of Migdalia Cruz, Cherríe Moraga, and Luis Alfaro explore violence, imprisonment, and captivity. Following the playwrights' charged engagement with the issues that inform these plays, I employ the term *critical witnessing* to describe the commitment to stand at the cultural front lines as an activism-driven viewer of prison theater or as an advocate and visitor working within the theatrical realm of the prison. To illustrate this practice, I conclude by discussing my own experiences visiting my incarcerated brother.

Representations of Imprisonment, Captivity, and Violence

In her book, *Imagining Medea: Rhodessa Jones and Theater for Incarcerated Women,* Rena Fraden articulates the ultimate goal of any theater that attempts to vigilantly posit itself at the forefront of community building: "to inspire the audience to think of more creative and useful intersections that will help protect and educate everyone who inhabits our worldly public sphere" (Fraden 26). Activist drama teacher Jean Trounstine proclaims a similar mission in her moving pedagogical memoir *Shakespeare behind Bars:* "Shakespeare has said that art is a mirror in which we see ourselves, but art is also a way to envision what we can become" (Trounstine 237). In the 1980s, theater scholar Jorge Huerta coined the term *necessary theater* to describe the activist component of early Chicano movement plays, works explicitly intended to politically mobilize audiences as much as to entertain them. Recently, in the second edition of her *Loving in the War Years,* dramatist Cherríe Moraga questioned the possibilities of this continued vibrant relationship between art and activism.

> The programs and political movements that once fostered the cultivation of artists twenty-five years ago are virtually nonexistent today. The NEA has been butchered and anti-affirmative action in California links arms with Proposition 187 in waging a class war against Raza to ensure that only the most privileged and "American" will be allowed access to the arts and education. There are few cultural centers left, little creative writing, teatro, or visual arts being offered through Chicano/Latino studies programs. Universities across the country may be preparing a cadre of literary critics, political and social scientists, historians and lawyers (lots of lawyers) to negotiate a settlement, but where are our artists to predict the next uprising? (Moraga 149).

In Moraga's home state of California, over the past twenty years, nearly two dozen new prisons have been built but only one university. Funds once insistently earmarked for arts and education are now routed directly and unapologetically toward support of the prison industrial complex. While institutions of higher education find themselves grappling with draconian budget cuts, prison guards receive a pay increase. Black and brown urban youth presently have much greater opportunity for entrance into a state prison than a state university. Moraga's reservations are more than well founded. In the face of an increasingly conservative social climate, U.S. Latina/o drama still very much functions as a necessary theater.

When asked why she doesn't incorporate into her plays more positive "role models," such as doctors or lawyers, Cruz replies that she chooses to write of the members of her community she knows most intimately: poor people, those whose life stories are most often reduced to convenient stereotypes and who, not so coincidentally, also make up the bulk of the prison population. Her current work-in-progress, *El Grito del Bronx* (under commission by the Public Theatre), depicts the life of a Puerto Rican prisoner on death row. The play explores the impact of crime and imprisonment on the incarcerated and his family as well as on the crime victims. This daring play also eloquently illustrates how for most people the experience of crime and violence and the quest for justice and cultural healing are painfully complex. A paradigmatic work, it also represents Cruz's ongoing exploration of the lives of women in situations of captivity, most especially women living in such extreme poverty that their bodies comprise the only object over which they have any sense of control. For example, Cruz's series of monologues, *Telling Tales,* depicts a young girl responding to her neighborhood's horrifying displays of vigilantism in the name of justice; *Fur*, her darkly comic take on *Beauty and the Beast,* centers around a hirsute named Citrona, sold by her mother to a deranged pet shop owner who keeps her locked in a cage in the basement of his store; *Miriam's Flowers* looks at an impoverished young girl who releases her inexpressible feelings of grief over the tragic death of her baby brother through ritual acts of scarification; *Lolita de Lares* portrays the life of outlaw Puerto Rican freedom fighter Lolita Lebron.

While only recently recognized by scholars, Cruz's work has long held the attention of her contemporaries Luis Alfaro and Cherríe Moraga, both of whom praise Cruz for occupying the cutting edge of American theater in her insistent breaking of taboos and bold exploration of the multiple forms of violence that shape Latina/o identity. Cruz studied under the direction of esteemed playwright and writing teacher Maria Irene Fornes at the Hispanic Playwrights Lab at INTAR in New York City. Although she completely distances herself from identity politics, Fornes also writes about the matters of domestic and political violence that so greatly inform Latina life within a prison nation: women's imprisonment within the home space, the strict policing of female/feminized behavior, the collusive power of cultural myths. *Mud, The Conduct of Life,* and *Sarita* all feature women in situations of confinement at the hands of patriarchal authority. Held captive by the traditional limitations set on women, *Sarita* stabs her lover Julio to death and ends up in a mental hospital. One of Fornes's signature plays, *The Conduct of Life* further illustrates how political and domestic violence mutually inform one another. One character, Leticia, clearly understands the mechanisms of terror employed by the state, as evidenced when she plaintively asks, "Why do they leave the bodies in the streets,—how evil, to frighten people" (Fornes 85); yet, she nevertheless remains willfully blind to her husband's torturing a young homeless girl in their basement because she doesn't want to risk losing the comforts of her middle-class life should she expose its awful foundations. In this way, Fornes's work challenges audiences to think about the contradictions that inform the spectrum of social relationships driven by varied mechanisms of power.

Cherríe Moraga's plays have insistently laid bare the comprehensive matrix of the prison industrial complex by showing how family and state power speak in concert. Her first published play, *Giving Up the Ghost,* opens with the lines of a song Moraga's mother would sing to her, "If I had wings like an angel, over these prison walls I would fly" (Moraga 3). Prison represents the feelings of confinement which result from extreme forms of social policing, such as the strict demarcation of gender roles. Throughout her career Cherríe Moraga has insistently posited cultural critique as an act of love. As a Chicana lesbian historically exiled from her own community,[1] Moraga determinedly carves a space for herself within Chicano culture by critically expanding definitions of Chicanismo. Ultimately, family occupies a central role in all of her plays as a space where, "for better or worse, we first learn to love." Her critique of the Chicano family is thus carefully situated within the much larger social histories that direct the broader context of Chicano life. For example, the father's physical abuse of his wife in *Shadow of a Man* is directly linked to his unfulfilled homosocial/homoerotic feelings for his compadre. Such explorations of the dark side of familial relations comprise a critical practice in Moraga's work that scholar Yvonne Yarbro Bejarano describes as "touching the wound in order to heal" (Yarbro Bejarano 48).

In her introduction to *The Hungry Woman,* Moraga writes *"Imagine freedom,* I tell myself. *Write freedom.* And I try to do so by painting pictures of prisoners on the page. They are the surviving codices of our loss" (Moraga, *Hungry Woman* x). This play effectively merges the Medea story with the Aztec myth of the Hungry Woman to unravel the historical threads of racism, sexism, and homophobia that make up the fabric of both Chicana/o history and the prison industrial complex. Throughout this work, Moraga purposefully juxtaposes the borderlands as a criminalized nation-space with other, more invisible, spaces of imprisonment. Moraga's notes designate Phoenix, Arizona as representing this interstitial place: "Phoenix is now a city-in-ruin, the dumping site of every kind of poison and person unwanted by its neighbors. Scenes shift to the 'present,' where MEDEA is an inmate in a prison psychiatric ward, to events in the past leading to MEDEA's incarceration." In Moraga's *Heroes and Saints,* police assault a laborer protesting local growers' lethal use of pesticides. Reporter Ana Perez witnesses the beating: "She's been struck! Amparo Manriquez . . . oh my god! The policeman . . . (He continues to beat her in slow, methodical blows.) 'Stop him! Jesus! No! No! Stop him!'" (Moraga, *Heroes and Saints* 133). Moraga's preface positions this work in direct conversation with Luis Valdez's *The Shunken Head of Pancho Villa;* yet the play also clearly speaks to the wider history of criminalized Chicano social protest, such as the case that originally inspired Teatro de la Esperanza's landmark play *Guadalupe.*

These particular Latina plays powerfully illustrate the problematic ways culture situates women to absorb the damaging effects of patriarchy. Prison represents patriarchal authority writ large. Women not only have to navigate their own survival of multiple forms of violence—physical, emotional, environmental, historical—they also have to deal with the repercussions of the violence men do to one another. Realizing that her father's preference for the company of men seriously emotionally devastated her mother, Moraga writes of the mother's passing on the wound, "every blow you dealt to me was a caress he denied you." Too often women of color find themselves cast in supportive starring roles to the men in their families and communities directed into the hellish depths of the prison industrial complex. Behind every man in prison stands a woman providing his lifeline to humanity in the form of emotional support, organized visits, collect phone calls, letters and packages, even legal aid and research assistance.

Yet, as Moraga illustrates in her writing, it is often these same women who unwittingly groom their sons to so destructively participate in patriarchy. Moraga's *Shadow of a Man* offers one of the most powerful portraits of the complicated dynamics of father-son relationships. Tragically, too many men—but most especially men in prison—can only speak of their relationships with their fathers in negative terms. In their introduction to *Prison Masculinities,* the editors note, "Men's pursuit of masculinity is implicated in their involvement with crime" (Sabo et al. 3). They further observe the connection to other institutions, such as the family, that regulate social behavior, "The prison code is very familiar to men in the United States because it is similar to the male code that reigns outside of prison" (Sabo et al. 10). Like Moraga, Luis Alfaro focuses on family relationships to more fully understand extended social performances, most especially the ways men use violence as form of social glue. Alfaro's plays focus on the lives of women as a means by which to also powerfully examine male gender and sexuality. Alfaro has studied principally under the direction of female mentors. As a result, his work clearly borrows from Latina feminism to develop a dramatic discourse about men and masculinity that focuses on the staging of the male body and cultural expectations for male gender performance.

Throughout Alfaro's landmark solo performance piece, *Downtown,* destructive male behaviors—drinking, physical violence, the abusive wielding of patriarchal authority, the wretched inability to express emotion—are explored as cancerous black spots in the hearts of Latino men, ones which desperately need to be closely examined for the purposes of personal and political healing. In the segment "Roller Derby," Alfaro's dressing in drag represents the feminized role that his father so clearly communicated as abhorrent. But the real drag, what has been pulled along with such difficulty, is the burden imposed by compulsory heterosexuality in conjunction with weighty ideals of Chicano masculinity, cultural expectations for identity performance that are so rigid and constricting they acquire the power to maim and wound. A performance genre devoted to high drama and full body contact, roller derby enacts both the emotional and physical impact of the father's violence, from his actual blows to emotional neglect.

In the conjoining monologue *Pocho Nightmare—A Moo-Moo Approaches,* Alfaro further explores the negative ways the father understands the feminine and how his targets—in this second case, the mother—respond by internalizing abuse to the point of engaging in acts of self-inflicted violence. Alfaro explicitly empathizes with his mother, using his own large and feminized body to illustrate her plight. He removes his protective gear and steps to the side of the stage where a tub of water, two boxes of twinkies and a liter of soda await. While the soundtrack of Alfaro narrating the tale of the Moo Moo, "a story about Mamas and Mexico" plays, he opens a box of Twinkies and begins, one by one, to pop open the plastic packages with an audible BANG from the bursting wrapper; then he crams them into his mouth. At first, the audience laughs at the image of Alfaro gorging himself on Twinkies, a snack food representing at once nostalgia and the transgression of junk food. Quickly, the laughter turns uncomfortable, eventually inappro-priate, as the story progresses, and Alfaro's face contorts with the rapid pace of his stuffing Twinkie after Twinkie after Twinkie, eyes and cheeks bulging, the gag reflex kicking in. The story isn't about nostalgia and sweets at all.

Though subtitled a story about "Mamas and Mexico," this work is actually a cautionary tale about fathers and the United States, about the intersections between classism, racism, sexism, and homophobia that also spill into the terrain of the prison industrial complex. The editors of *Prison Masculinities* speak at length about the dangerous ways seemingly disconnected forms of oppression actually mutually inform one another: "The indignities inflicted on men in prison are part of the larger pattern of a society that permits (and perhaps at some level has come to expect) the abuse of men and the endurance of that abuse in silence. This is the dark side of patriarchy, yet it is one with the toleration of abuse of women" (Sabo et al. 99). Such pointed analytical observations clearly inform *Downtown*. As Alfaro's father figure crosses over and becomes Americanized, he reinterprets his large and culturally solid wife, once perceived as beautiful, as an excessive affront to his evolving sense of what it means to be an American man. The Twinkies she so self-destructively devours emblematize the "pocho," a cultural figure all too willing to internalize the dominant culture's values; the little cakes, tan on the outside and white inside, are a product made in America with their consumption historically marketed as a virtual rite of passage into the popular culture. Absolutely, Twinkies do have iconographic status, signifying class mobility enabled by the disposable income needed to allow such gastronomic luxuries. Twinkies also take on an added dimension as a consumable prop within the prison theater. Junk food is the principle vehicle for social interaction during the average five to seven hour span of a visit. While the vending machines will seldom offer water or fresh fruit, they will always be well stocked with soda and junk food.

Significantly, Twinkies' phallic shape yokes together gender and class oppression. Alfaro's narrative describes the Moo-Moo's gorging as "suicide by hostess," (with all the multiple meanings of "hostess") and connects her fatally internalized emotions directly to the father's rejection of her female body and metonymically to his rejection of the feminized body of Mexico and— referencing back to "Roller Derby"—to his rejections of the feminized son, through the lines: "Once the Moo-Moo threatened to kill a woman on the block, with a nasty disposition, who called the Moo-Moo's son effeminate." Alfaro exposes the destructive impact of the metaphoric feminization of the national body and its ultimate literal toll on actual female bodies. The mother's body in times of need signifies "the abundance of Mexico," but when alliances shift, she then conveniently represents a nightmarish excess. It is this hungry woman's son who then redraws the boundaries by telling the story and establishing a determined political alliance with his mother's body. By hinging together "Roller Derby" and "Pocho Nightmare," Alfaro brilliantly illustrates how homophobia and misogyny work in tandem with nationalism and patriarchy.

The closing line of the original ending to this play, staged at the end of the 1980s is "Are you a friend or a phobe?"

Like many literary works about trauma and violence, these plays ask the viewer to move beyond the page or stage and to step into the larger arena of personal transformation and community building. Clearly, fundamentally poor and disenfranchised people must have their physical and material needs met to break out of the cycle of poverty, violence, and addiction. While not a remedy in and of itself, art definitely plays a powerful role in personal transformation and cultural healing by offering another face in the mirror to whom the subject might tell her story, so that she may learn to critically see herself in a different light. By sharing a story with others, one sees alternative worlds and can thereby envision a life that is not strictly fixed in history.

Cultural critic Elizabeth Alexander reminds us about the taxing burden of being spectators to profoundly disturbing and emotionally difficult artworks dealing with matters of violence and trauma: "Those who receive stories become witnesses once removed but witnesses nonetheless" (Alexander 95). In a similar vein, literary critic Kali Tal affirms, "Bearing witness is an aggressive act. It is born out of a refusal to bow to outside pressure to revise or to repress experience, a decision to embrace conflict rather than conformity, to endure a lifetime of anger and pain rather than to submit to the seductive pull of revision and repression. Its goal is change" (Tal 7). Writers like Cherríe Moraga, Migdalia Cruz, and Luis Alfaro employ the voice of the critical witness by maintaining that very little separates the writer from the person to whom he or she has actively chosen to bear witnesses. The two are intimately bound through violence and spectacle alike. Critical witnesses use their ability to speak and describe the event, however limited this may be, to move the reader to the position of "one who witnesses rather than simply watches" (Alexander 98). As the lead character Alex says to the parole board in Kosmond Russell's haunting prison play, *The Visit:* "I request my freedom so that I might be free to tell my story." For those prisoners given life sentences (or in the case of those who die in prison), the only part of them that ever gets out is their story. Critical witnesses understand themselves to be distinctively implicated in the fate of the person or persons they are watching, their writing characterized by a distinct "sense of collective violation" (Alexander 100). Critical witnessing is, indeed, the mission of the visit, the fiercely committed movement toward what Luis Alfaro terms "an intersection of possibility." It is the transformation of stories of violence into stories of hope. Somewhere, someone listens. This is the alchemy of blood.

Lockdown and Breakout

I want to end this essay with a personal discussion of prison as a theatrical space to further ground my readings of violence, imprisonment and captivity in

Latina drama and my subsequent understanding of the discernable possibilities of theater as a realm for critical witnessing.

In November 1999, my brother brutally killed our father. He is now serving a thirty-year prison sentence. At fifteen, I left home in fear for my life. My sister followed suit. Yet my brother and father never could let go of one another. Every time my brother tried to start a new life for himself, my father would sabotage his efforts. When he tried to join the army, my father claimed my brother had a drug problem. When my brother married, my father visited daily with six packs of beer under his arm, engaging in the bonding my brother had desperately craved his entire life, with the unavoidably toxic results leading to the demise of his marriage. When my brother disappeared for two years following a complete breakdown that landed him homeless, my father hunted him down, promising to finally provide a proper home, complete with the love absent from our growing-up years. Each time, my brother embraced these false promises. As daughters, as females, my sister and I had been taught that our place within the family did not carry the same worth as that occupied by our brother, the lone male, the anointed son. Within two years of that last tragic leap of faith, my father lay dead, my brother gone, too, having traded one prison for another. No one, not my father, not my brother, not us daughters, should be so crushed at the hands of violence. If we refuse to forsake him, my sister and I will spend the next thirty years maintaining correspondence, quarterly packages, and visits to the prison. If my brother makes it that far, we will have to figure out how to address his release. We continue to process our recovery from the violence of our father while now additionally dealing with the violence of the state.

It is easy to temporarily forget the ugly realities of our brother's life, when we live so far away from the prison. Letters alone allow too much room for pretending our brother is simply away on a thirty-year voyage of disappearance, some kind of cruel extended vacation. Certainly, the dominant culture would have us believe such crushing fantasies, as illustrated in the absurd cinematic adaptation of Phillip K. Dick's brilliant short story, *Minority Report* when Stephen Spielberg's narrator describes the release of the wrongly incarcerated after years in straitjacket confinement in a shower-stall sized pod as without any significant damage whatsoever. Our sense of violence and violation is felt most palpably in the live theatrical realm of the prison visit. Prison officials direct our conduct, giving us very specific instructions regarding our costuming and the scripted limits of our behavior. We are carefully screened and physically searched. (My brother will be required to undergo a full cavity body search both before and after the visit.) When we use the restroom, we must ask permission and stand at a door opened only by a guard possessing an almost medieval turnkey. If menstruating, one may not discreetly take in her own brand of tampon; she must notify the guard who will provide prison-approved supplies. There is one good thing: the palpable sense of community in the visiting room. All of us gathered here are highly conscious of what it means to be necessary actors, bound by the experience of forced separation from our family members and the attendant subjection to all the inconveniences, indignities, and humiliations we must endure in order to perform these carefully orchestrated acts of love.

Here, as in other constructed places, form and meaning mutually inform one another. The hours of the visit are limited; the clock moves swiftly. Visiting hours begin at 8 A.M. on the weekends; if you are lucky and arrive at the crack of dawn, you and your inmate will be sitting together by 9:30, 10:30 if the processing staff is slow and the lines are long. One Sunday I arrive at 8:00 A.M. and find my sister and I are the 67th visiting group in line. Visiting hours end promptly at 2:30 P.M. Quiet patience, fatigued silence, and practiced resignation constitute the group dynamic. For these brief but precious hours, many have driven the entire length of the state of California.

At the entrance of the facility are handbooks for visitors, one specifically written for women. The control of women's bodies definitely dictates the tone for the prison visit. This particular prison is located in the desert. Despite temperatures that exceed 100 degrees, sleeveless shirts are strictly forbidden, as are underwire bras. No sports bra on hand in the car? Then you won't see your inmate, because going commando is not an option; underwear is mandatory. If you unwittingly come in the wrong attire, you have to embrace improvisation without shame. Approval of a particular shirt on Friday does not guarantee approval of the same shirt on Sunday. I've learned to always carry an insurance policy of assorted garments in my car, and more than once I have angrily, defiantly, shamelessly changed clear out in the open in the middle of the parking lot. A theatrical gesture intended as a gift to the inmates, a fuck-you to the guards.

The images that have fueled the mental rehearsals leading up to such moments: Fourth of July weekend, I witness an elderly woman in a wheelchair turned away because she wore a summer blouse without the regulated sleeves. The same fate befalls a middle-aged woman wearing a very tasteful sundress. I imagine both of these women spending much time carefully choosing the color and fabric to combat the extreme summer heat, meet a respectable sense of decorum, and visually cheer their incarcerated family member. Like them, I came sleeveless to the visit. In such heat, it didn't even cross my mind that a simple T-shirt might sabotage the visit. The only way I could enter the facility was to change into the sweatshirt I had brought for the evening and endure the heat, a small concession in comparison to the many brutal compromises faced by my brother on a daily basis. I do inquire about the enforcement of this rule on one of the hottest days of summer. The officer explains that there are prisoners serving time for "certain behaviors" that would be aggravated by seeing the flesh of a woman's upper arm and the area under the armpit near the breast. Never mind the fact that nearly every prisoner has access to a television where he can see Victoria's Secret ads, beer commercials, and the like. (Later, a friend informs me that some guards call such clothing "fondling garments.") I take a seat and watch a woman go through processing wearing a longsleeve shirt and a khaki skirt with clearly visible thong panty lines. Without missing a beat, the guards quickly process her through. Nothing at this place makes sense. And I never want it to. I recall Ashe Bandele's reflections on the extreme personal searches she had to endure to have conjugal visits with her husband:

> The first two or three times that happened to me, I felt immodest. I felt shame and embarrassment. Now I feel camaraderie with women who work the peep shows or who lap dance for a living. Except, of course, I don't get paid. But you know I think I should. For every glance that gets held too long, for each time one of those police runs his fingers across my underwear, those motherfuckers owe me, in the very least, cash money (Bandele 47).

Bandele's words viscerally capture how visiting an inmate requires a lot to be checked at the door. Here, critical witnessing necessarily demands that one enter the visiting room as a performance space. You have to remember the larger mission of the visit; you have to determinedly play your role so that you may return home again whole.

It's about a half-mile walk to the unit that houses my brother. Once there, we go through a second round of screening and check-in procedures. A large poster states the ground rules: "Inmates and their visitors shall only embrace and kiss at the beginning and end of each visit; except for holding hands, no other bodily contact shall be permitted." Any additional physical displays may result in the termination of the visit. All parties must sit with their feet firmly planted on the floor and their bodies facing toward the stationed officer at the front of the room. Additionally, "Inmates and their visitors shall refrain from any behavior which would conceivably disturb or offend other visitors or inmates." There's no clarification as to what, precisely, this means. As Foucault reminds us, the panopticon—the prison surveillance model par excellence—succeeds because of this lack of full clarification. Such moments of indeterminate meaning effectively train us to internalize the perspective of those in power. In our fear of the unknown, we imaginatively dwell on the punishment that might result from being caught by the keepers; in time, we find ourselves reflexively compliant and more than willingly doing the right thing for the oppressors without consciousness or question. The challenge, always, is to remain critically engaged and enraged. While there is room for improvisation in the visiting room, one acts first with a clear sense of an assigned role. Each visit, you take careful note of the rules so that you can successfully perform your role and achieve its urgent purpose: to reassure the prisoner there is a world beyond the razor wire, distinct and separate from this punishing place.

The prisoners also enter the visiting space with a keen sense of performance, coming out in the best state-issued clothing they can assemble. I am told there are wardrobe specialists who keep shirts and pants clean and mended, shoes polished, ready to loan out if an inmate is caught unprepared. I witness ingenious expressions of personal style and subtle acts of defiance through the detailing of hair and accessories. One inmate sports buffed down leather panels that make his state issue boots look like hip suede loafers. These men go out of their way to convey the importance of those few precious hours and the individuality that prison tries to squash. Never outside the realm of the prison visiting room (except for television and film) have I seen young men pay such passionate and focused attention to their female visitors. This is a high price for women to pay so that they may be so clearly well regarded. Groups play Scrabble and flip coins into the vending machines, practically convinced we are in a community center in the middle of a city, anywhere. We are, indeed, in a city and space that could be anywhere in the U.S.A. But, there is no real forgetting amidst the physical and emotional scars that mark the air.

In his essay "Scars," prison writer Jarvis Masters theorizes about the role physical abuse plays in grooming men for the prison system:

> I believe that, for many men, institutionalization is a kind of refuge from the devastation of child abuse in their lives. . . . Secretly, we all like it here. This place welcomes a man who is full of rage and violence. Here he is not abnormal or perceived as different. Here rage is nothing new, and for men scarred by child abuse and violent lives, the prison is an extension of inner life. We learn to abuse and reabuse ourselves by moving in and out of places like San Quentin. (Sabo et al. 205)

I suspect this is true for my brother. Tragically, our family is actually closer now that my father no longer lives to terrorize us, now that we are united in empathetic support for my brother. As a family we find ourselves newly defined through active and constructive acts rather than through entirely defensive reactions. I am unable to perceive the world the same way after being so brutally transformed by the rehearsal hall of my family and the cruel theater of prison. Everything eventually comes together on this open stage, this once blank page.

To circle back to the academic thread guiding this essay: I find Latina drama particularly instructive for thinking about the relationship between prison and performance. One sees the historical roots of the prison industrial complex referenced in Moraga's *Giving up the Ghost:* "This *is* Mexico! What are you talking about? It was those gringos that put up those fences between us!" (Moraga, *Heroes and Saints* 17). Migdalia Cruz's *Fur* brilliantly explores incarceration as an enforcing dynamic of romantic relationships: "That cage is the biggest cage you've ever been in–doesn't that tell you a little something about my intentions? About how I feel?" (Cruz 89). Though more subtly, Luis

Alfaro spotlights the long standing visual images that fuel the prison industrial complex: "I turn on the TV. See a Chicano, a beautiful sight, man. A Chicano, a brown Chicano on television. Fijate, hombre. And you know what he's carrying? The same thing he was carrying twenty-five years ago. A gun. A big old pistola" (Alfaro, *Chicanismo*). Plays by such incredibly diverse voices collectively explore violence, imprisonment, and captivity (both literal and metaphoric) in an effort to politicize–and, most optimistically, transform—dominating narratives of violence. These writers position themselves on the front lines of their communities where they witness, among other cultural outrages, helicopters invading barrio space with impunity; police searches and seizures without cause or apology; the kind of ignorance, neglect, or abuse that sets the stage for tracking into the bowels of the prison system.

In the television news, people from these communities are objectified, cast into the role of a stereotype made painfully familiar and then disappeared altogether from the social landscape. The dramas of which I speak in this essay offer potentially revolutionary counternarratives, discourses of love and violence intertwined that magnify all that is usually shrouded in mystery or placed in shadow. They give a name, a face, and—most importantly— a fully human context to those insistently put under erasure. It is through a quite basic sharing of story—tales that reflect, validate, and complicate images usually relegated to the margins—that audiences witness the transformation of embattled communities from stereotypes and statistics into multidimensional and, most importantly, fully humanized people. Plays dealing with prison issues and attendant themes of incarceration have the proven power to motivate audiences to return to the theater as a site of collective mourning, outrage, and organization.[2] Such theater provides a context that invites empathy and understanding and, in turn, fosters the kind of critical witnessing that might ultimately lead to the actual change of social conditions.

Acknowledgements

I want to thank Richard Contreras for his invaluable research assistance and Diana Rendon, Martha Ramirez, Karen Venegas, and Enrique Negrete for their outstanding references and response. Special appreciation goes to Thomas Fahy for his encouragement of this work and to the members of Women and Theater for their feedback on an earlier version delivered as a talk at the 2002 meeting in Irvine. Thank you to Kristen Brunnemer and Cheryl Edelson for their proofreading and comments on final drafts. To Amy Ongiri, my collaborator in pedagogical activism.

Notes

1. In a public letter circulated in response to her glaring exclusion from the recent Chicano Classics Theatre Festival, Cherrie Moraga spoke of the painful nature of her

ongoing struggle against intercultural exclusion rooted in sexism and homophobia: "I am tired of pounding on my own familia's door to get in. . . . I experience these kinds of conflicts with white people all the time and have little trouble just 'writing them off' as ignorant people, not really worth the battle. But with other Chicanos and Chicanas, I remain (for better or worse) engaged. I care. And it is that caring that causes me to feel the rechazo, as from a brother to a sister. For better or worse, I am your hermana. I say this as your peer, as your 'sister in struggle,' where ironically those words (cliche as they may sound) still mean something to me. I do not need your protection, but yes, your defense . . . as I carry weapons daily on your behalf." Moraga's letter sparked an impromptu session led by me devoted to her work and the broader context of her letter within the history of Chicano teatro. This was a historic moment. As many former participants who were actively involved in the Chicano Theater Movement made clear, in the past, the response would have been to walk away and close the door on future conversations and collaborative efforts of community building.

2. Performances of *The Exonerated* at the Actors Gang in Los Angeles (April–June 2002) were accompanied by post-play discussions with activists involved with antideath penalty and prison moratorium groups. In the lobby, audience members had the opportunity to sign various petitions, join mailing lists, gather printed material, or make donations for the recently exonerated whose stories inspired this riveting play. I personally saw the work three times, taking with me a close friend, the ex-prisoner and activist-poet Raul Salinas, and journalist Sasha Abramsky (author of *Prison Blues: How Politics Built a Prison Nation*). Indeed, at each of my visits I recognized a few audience members also returning to the theater to share the play with others. In personal interviews with me, the playwright Kosmond Russell recalled this phenomenon of returning audiences throughout the run of his play *The Visit*, an emotionally wrenching account of an incarcerated black man with AIDS and his final visits with his family. This play inspired an audience member, filmmaker Jordan Walker Pearlman, to translate the story into film (HBO films). At the screening of this work on my campus as part of a course titled "Cultural Studies in a Prison Nation," students openly wept and during the post-film discussion expressed overwhelming feelings of outrage and grief; one student sadly said she had no idea how to begin visiting her incarcerated family members because there were simply so many. Audiences at the recent revival of Carlos Morton's *The Many Deaths of Danny Morales* as part of the Chicano Classics Theater Festival (UCLA, July 25–30, 2002) cried out in empathetic identification during key scenes where police beat the protagonist; they gave the work a standing ovation. At the closing remarks for the festival, student leaders spoke at length about how such plays motivate them to return to their colleges and neighborhoods with resolve to create community based teatro that will "educate our people" and "inspire others to action."

Works Cited

Alexander, Elizabeth. "'Can you be BLACK and look at this?': Reading the Rodney King Video(s)," in *Black Male: Representations of Masculinity in Contemporary American Art*. Ed. Henry Louis Gates Jr. et al. New York: Whitney Museum of American Art, 1994.

Alfaro, Luis. *Downtown,* in *O Solo Homo: The New Queer Performance.* Eds. Holly Hughes and David Roman. New York: Grove Press, 1998.

———. *Chicanismo.* Unpublished manuscript. Provided at the courtesy of the author.

Bandele, Asha. *The Prisoner's Wife: A Memoir.* New York: Simon and Schuster, 1999.

Cruz, Migdalia. *Fur* in *Out of the Fringe: Contemporary Latina/Latino Theatre and Peformance.* Eds. Caridad Svich and Maria Teresa Marrero. New York: Theatre Communications Group, 2000.

Fornes, Maria Irene. *Plays.* New York: Performing Arts Journal Publications, 1986.

Fraden, Rena. *Imagining Medea: Rhodessa Jones and Theater for Incarcerated Women.* Chapel Hill: The University of North Carolina Press, 2001.

Moraga, Cherríe. *Loving in the War Years / lo que nunca paso por sus labios.* Cambridge, Mass.: South End Press, 2000.

———. *Heroes and Saints & Other Plays.* Albuquerque: West End Press, 2000.

———. *The Hungry Woman.* Albuquerque: West End Press, 2001.

Russell, Kosmond. *The Visit.* Unpublished manuscript. Provided at the courtesy of the author.

Sabo, Don, Terry A. Kupers, and Willie London eds. *Prison Masculinities.* Philadelphia: Temple University Press, 2001.

Tal, Kali. *Worlds of Hurt: Reading the Literatures of Trauma.* Cambridge: Cambridge University Press, 1996.

Trounstine, Jean. *Shakespeare behind Bars: The Power of Drama in a Women's Prison.* New York: St. Martin's Press, 2001.

Yarbro-Bejarano, Yvonne. *The Wounded Heart: Writing on Cherrie Moraga.* Austin: University of Texas Press, 2001.

3

Seeing Ethnicity: The Impact of Race and Class on the Critical Reception of Miguel Piñero's *Short Eyes*

FIONA MILLS

If Broadway is to come to terms with its own anachronism and ahistoricity, the only solution for its survival is to redefine itself... and to become more inclusive of regional and minority theater—women's, gay and lesbian, African American, Asian American, and U.S. Latino/a. The existence of these theaters serves as a constant reminder of Broadway's fossilized, white Eurocentric identity, an identity that is captured in its denomination as the Great White Way.
    —ALBERTO SANDOVAL-SÁNCHEZ, *JOSÉ CAN YOU SEE?: LATINOS ON*
                                                            AND OFF BROADWAY

Introduction: You Can Take the Man Out of Prison, but Can You Take the Prison Out of the Man?

In a 1974 interview with Norma Alarcón-McKesson, the late Nuyorican[1] playwright Miguel Piñero discussed his recent status as a critically lauded dramatist—a somewhat unusual position for an ex-convict to embody—and proclaimed that "theater is the only thing that still belongs to the people" (Alarcón-McKesson 56). An extremely talented man with a penchant for trouble, Piñero's story was quite well known in the 1970s due to the immense success, both popular and critical, of his prison drama *Short Eyes*. The play went on to win an Obie, the New York Drama Critics Circle Award as Best American Play of 1973–74, and six Tony nominations, and it earned Piñero the 1973–74 Elizabeth Hull-Kate Warner award from the Dramatists Guild of New York. Upon completing *Short Eyes*, Piñero continued his literary work with the founding of the Nuyorican Poets Café,[2] in conjunction with poet Miguel Algarín, and the publication of several volumes of poetry along with a number of other plays. However, none of his other publications garnered him as much attention as his debut play, and it remains his best-known work.

41

Born in Puerto Rico and later raised in the ghettos of New York City, his was a hard-luck story. Piñero spoke openly about his forays with drugs, time spent in prison, gang days running with the Young Lords, as well as his experiences as a burglar, thief, drug addict, and dope pusher in the hopes of reaching out to young Puerto Ricans and helping them to avoid the troubles he had experienced. Unfortunately, Piñero was never able to outrun his demons. He continued to thieve and con to support his drug habit, ultimately dying of cirrhosis of the liver at the young age of forty-one.[3] However, writing seemed to give him some respite. At the least, it certainly granted him a new lease on life after prison. As he related to many interviewers, writing saved his life and enabled him to avoid subsequent stays in prison. Piñero, though, never forgot where he came from or lost touch with his roots.[4] He drew upon his experiences, and those of his friends, as a member of the oppressed and often despondent underclass for his art. It was his successful portrayal of the raw emotion and vibrancy of prison life realistically rendered on stage that garnered him accolades. His metaphorical use of prison to depict and comment upon life among the underclasses in American society struck a profound chord with critics and audiences alike. Ironically, although his play, whose characters were predominantly Puerto Rican and African American,[5] realistically depicted racial tension and the interracial fraternity created among inmates despite individual prejudices, it was subject to race- and class-based prejudices in its reception by several well-known drama critics. Specifically, several critics refer to Piñero, both directly and indirectly, as ignorant and unsophisticated, implying that, as an uneducated Puerto Rican ex-convict, he was out of his depth on Broadway. More telling, though, is the negative and, at times, outraged critical response to the play's audience, largely composed of Latino/a and African-American persons, and their participatory engagement with the play as it unfolds on stage. This reception, marked by its overt classist and racist overtones, casts aspersions on Piñero's aforementioned proclamation of drama "belonging to the people" and calls into question the relation of ethnicity and class to theater—both the production of non-Anglo drama and the accessibility of theater to those outside of the Anglo American middle and upper classes.

In examining these reviews, one must keep in mind the fact that Piñero's play was written and first produced in 1973–74, with a film adaptation in 1977, and subsequent revivals in the 1980s, prior to the heyday of political correctness and the breakout success on Broadway of such non-Anglo playwrights as African-American dramatist August Wilson, or the frequent production of Latino/a plays such as Milcha Sánchez-Scott's *Roosters* or José Rivera's *Marisol*.[6] However, despite the political correctness of the 1990s and the recent boom in Latino/a culture, very few U.S. Latino/a plays have ever been produced on Broadway—a fact that Alberto Sandoval-Sánchez laments in his contention that "although it may seem impossible, only four Latino plays have ever crossed over: *Short Eyes, Zoot Suit, Cuba and His Teddy Bear,* and, most recently, John Leguizamo's *Freak"* (Sandoval-Sánchez 110). Recently, interest in Piñero has been revived, most likely due to the 2002 biographical film, *Piñero,* starring Benjamin Bratt. Interestingly, both the 1977 film adaptation of *Short Eyes* and the recent biopic received much more favorable reviews, leading one to ponder the acceptability of palpable and spontaneous audience reaction in the theater as well as the firmly entrenched position of theater as a paragon of high art in the United States. These reviews suggest that realistic and unapologetic depictions of the seedy underbelly of America's lower classes are much more acceptable on screen than on stage where a person can observe from the safe position of a voyeur the ethnic and lower class "other," while refraining from actual contact with them.

Although Piñero's play did indeed make it to Broadway,[7] eventually landing at the Vivian Beaumont Theater in Lincoln Center as part of the New York Shakespeare Festival, its reviews imply that the rawness of prison life is unsuitable material for Broadway and better reserved for the big screen, where viewers can maintain some distance from the material at hand. Perhaps it is easier to pretend that the drama unfolding before one's eyes on the big screen is mere fiction or art and unrelated to one's own experience in the world. Theater, on the other hand, due to its immediacy, renders the maintenance of a controlled distance much harder. It is harder to "look away" from real-life actors as presented in a theatrical work, and, consequently, harder to pretend that what is unfolding on stage is completely irrelevant to life in general. Piñero was more than likely aware of this fact; in repeated interviews he urged viewers not to consider the play a mere prison drama but, instead, to view it as a reflection of American society as a whole. In discussing his play's focus on prison, Piñero contended, "Prison is a society within a society. It's a reflection of life in the streets. The jargon may be different, but we think and feel the same as on the streets and we recreate it in prison" (Wahls 1). It is the play's pointed depiction of life among the lower classes and the visceral response it elicited from its racially diverse audience that disturbed drama critics the most. At the very least, it appears that such a realistic representation of race and class relations cut too close to the bone for these critics, used to reviewing high art pieces by Shakespeare and Sophocles.[8]

In his introduction to *Short Eyes,* Marvin Felix Camillo admonishes readers to look beyond the prison setting of this play (as well as Piñero's own incarceration) in order to embrace its universality. He states, "I urge the readers of *Short Eyes* not to search for some great social reform message or to analyze the personal motives of the original cast or to fall into the trap of feeling this play can be done only by ex-inmates or people from a subculture . . . we are witnessing not a prison play but a play about human relationships" (Camillo xii). Camillo makes a valid point when he cautions readers against letting the fact that this play was written by an ex-convict and originally performed by a group of former inmates influence, either negatively or positively, their interpretation of the quality of this play. As Camillo himself contends, "Prison is a society within a society," and, that being true, the small prison world depicted in *Short Eyes* is a microcosm of larger society (Camillo xiii). However, it appears to have been impossible for critics to ignore the deliberate setting of this play in a "house of detention" and the way in which the theme of imprisonment permeates every aspect of it. This backdrop of incarceration greatly impacted the critical reception of Piñero's play both negatively and positively. This essay explores the relation of class and ethnicity to theater in America in regards to the complicated inception and background of Piñero's prison drama, as revealed in the critical reviews of his play.

The Great White Way: The Marginalization of Latino/a Theater on Broadway

Latino/a theater, along with other so-called minority theater, is a relatively new phenomenon on Broadway. Although Latin American and Spanish drama dates back centuries, a specifically Latino/a form of theater, that is, primarily Anglophone plays written by Latino/as living in the United States, has only developed within the past forty years. In regards to the emergence of a specific category of American drama identified as "Latino/a," critic and scholar Alberto Sandoval-Sánchez establishes the beginning of this type of theater in the 1960s:

> Although theatrical productions of Latinos/as can be recovered from an earlier past, I locate the emergence of U.S. Latino theater in the 1960s as the foundational moment of the formation of a U.S. Latino/a ethnic identity. It was specifically in that decade that the presence and visibility of Latino theater began, with the political activism of Chicano/a farmworkers leading to the institutional establishment, in 1965, of Teatro Campesino in California. (Sandoval-Sánchez 105)

This time period is particularly relevant given the fact that at the very same time Chicano Rights activists were gaining momentum, and it implicitly establishes the political nature underlying Latino/a theater from its inception. Such political activism has been readily reflected in the work of Latino/a playwrights. Sandoval-Sánchez notes that one of the first major Latino/a theater groups, Teatro Campesino, dedicated itself to "one-act interlingual performances, created collectively, had well-defined political platforms: 'Actos: inspire the audience to social action. Illuminate specific points about social problems. Satirize the opposition. Show or hint at a solution. Express what people are feeling'" (Sandoval-Sánchez 105). He suggests that an essential element of Latino/a drama is a focus on social action and change. It is imperative that Latino/a theater educate its audience members about a social problem and offer some sort of a solution. Piñero's pointed examination of the impact of race and class on society, as depicted through the interactions of prison inmates, clearly illustrates Latino/a theater's underlying emphasis on addressing social ills or problems.

Miguel Piñero, through his complicated depiction of relations between prison inmates of various ethnic/racial backgrounds in *Short Eyes,* attempted to enlighten his audience about issues of race and class. That he attempted to address these social ills in his play is not surprising, given that he was writing in the early 1970s near the beginning of the Latino/a theater movement. As a Puerto Rican–born immigrant to New York, Piñero's decision to depict issues of race and class, both explicitly and implicitly, in *Short Eyes* reflects a specifically "Nuyorican" ideology. Accordingly, Sandoval-Sánchez asserts that "as a result of an emerging ethnic and racial consciousness instigated by the 1960s civil rights movement and the *lucha* (struggle) against exploitation, racism, and marginalization of people of color, a theater emerged among Nuyoricans that was designed to foment ethnic pride and denounce imperialist oppression" (Sandoval-Sánchez 105). Although Piñero emphasizes ethnic pride, he expands the play's focus to encompass broader issues of humanity through the play's ambiguous ending.[9] With the play's last line, "Your fear of this place stole your spirit," Piñero implores his readers to fiercely protect and display their spirits and not to allow anything—be it life, death or prison—to diminish it. This line holds particular resonance for Piñero's Latino/a audience members, as it is uttered by one Latino, Juan, to another, Cupcakes. Moreover, Juan serves as the model of humanity throughout the play and acts as an older brother/mentor toward the younger, more insecure Cupcakes. Piñero offers a glimpse of Latino/a society in which a brotherhood is created to protect and nurture the younger generation against an often oppressive and racist Anglo-American world. Juan implores Cupcakes to assert his spirit and not let it be taken from him. Piñero, thus, makes the point that Anglo-American society is all too willing to insist on assimilation and to strip the ethnic "other" of his/her identity and cultural spirit. Notably, Piñero, through his depiction of Juan as the most humane character and morally superior to all the others, suggests that Latino/as possess more humanity and stronger ethics than other ethnic/racial groups—an act in keeping with Nuyorican theater's emphasis on promoting ethnic pride. Piñero's broader commentary on humanity is illustrative of Camillo's aforementioned admonishment to readers to be mindful of the fact that they "are witnessing not a prison play but a play about human relationships" (Camillo xii).

Piñero's emphasis on fraternity and community above individual desires and actions is also consistent with the tenets of Latino/a theater of the 1960s, since, according to Sandoval-Sánchez, its focus was on "community building." Longshoe and the other inmates who kill Davis (a middle-class white man accused of child molesting) fail to respect and uphold this sense of community and, to a greater extent, humanity. On the other hand, Juan, who, although he abhors and condemns the actions of Davis demonstrates a deep reverence for human life and brotherhood through his insistence on not participating in the murder. El Raheem, a militant black inmate, exhibits a similar sense of community and brotherhood in his refusal, in the end, to kill a defenseless man in cold blood. He, like Juan, understands the consequences of transgressing communal bonds. His insistence on elevating the black man and exhorting the other African-American inmates to take pride in their cultural heritage is also a commendable example of community building. These examples illustrate Sandoval-Sánchez's contention that Latino/a theater, emerging in the 1960s, was "a collective endeavor" based in "community building" (Sandoval-Sánchez 107–8).

Sandoval-Sánchez repeatedly underscores the heterogeneity and diversity inherent in Latino/a theater. He uses the metaphor of an "octopus with many legs" to describe Latino/a theater's multiplicity. Sandoval-Sánchez argues that Latino/a theater defies stifling labels and stereotypes. Instead, "This theater revels in problematizing and destabilizing the essentialist notion of monolithic Latino experiences, identities, and ways of seeing." He goes on to argue that Latino/a theater is defined by "its difference, its plurality, its heterogeneity, and its contradictions." Such an image appropriately captures the monstrous image many theatergoers and critics projected onto Piñero's largely Latino/a and African-American audience. According to Sandoval-Sánchez, "Latino theater always locates itself within the domain of difference, of hybridity, of monstrosity. . . . It is this image of monstrosity that accurately captures the nature of a U.S. Latino theater that denies all categorization based on superficial resemblances such as labeling and the imposition of rigidly defined and dominant dramatic structures" (Sandoval-Sánchez 108–9). Although on the surface Piñero's play may seem to present monolithic stereotypes of Latino/as,[10] I would argue that, given its depiction of multifaceted and varied characters, *Short Eyes* defies traditional ethnic stereotypes due to its refusal of monolithic representations of Latinidad, Blackness, or stereotypical race relations. On the contrary, Piñero presents a much more realistic and complex depiction of inter- and intraracial relationships within the prison system. Although racial slurs are bandied about at some points, for the most part blacks, whites, and Puerto Ricans coexist peaceably. Significantly, it is neither race nor class that prompts the inmates to kill Davis. Rather, it is the atrocity and horror of his crime that infuriates them and leads to his death—something that many critics seemingly ignore in their questionable reviews of this play.

Despite the recent boom in Latino/a culture in the U.S. music, film, and television industry, Latino/a theater remains on the margins.[11] The lack of attention given to U.S. Latino/a playwrights is related to issues of language, class, and economic status. Significantly, most U.S. Latino/a playwrights are also excluded from the Latin American canon based on similar contentions. Latino/a theater's marginal status within American theater, according to Sandoval-Sánchez, reflects the way Latino/as in the United States are often relegated to the status of ethnic "other." He contends that "although Latino theater is an integral and intricate part of American theater, like African American and Asian American theater it is a minority art form that is continually marginalized or silenced" (Sandoval-Sánchez 107). Interesting here is Sandoval-Sánchez's emphasis on the marginalization of Latino/a theater and the repeated silencing of this art form, which is clearly evident in the critical reception of Piñero's play. In particular, the repeated critical focus on the alleged "inappropriate" and "offensive" behavior of the play's racially diverse audience is an implicit attempt to silence not only those audience members, but also to effectively silence the play or the production of others like it.

In his discussion of the critical bias against non-Anglo art on Broadway, Sandoval-Sánchez contends that, although younger Latino/a playwrights have received recent critical acclaim, these playwrights are most often formally educated and from the middle class. Accordingly, this:

> reflects a priori how Eurocentric artistic values and bourgeois aesthetics dictate the criteria for evaluating works of art. Aesthetics and agitprop, universality and locality, and authenticity and mimesis are always at odds when it comes to recognizing the artistic and political value of Latino, and other minority, theater. The end result is total depreciation and marginalization, as counter-hegemonic politics and ideologies resist and clash with elitist (mis)conceptions of art. Such a biased value system favors U.S. Latino theatrical productions that enchant Anglo American audiences with touches of exoticism through the use of magical realism. (Sandoval-Sánchez 108)

His comments urge scholars to examine the double bind of race and class that impedes the production of Latino/a theater. Illustrating Sandoval-Sánchez's argument, in their reviews of Piñero's play several reviewers commented favorably on the "Latin jam session" in the play, while simultaneously critiquing *Short Eyes* as a whole. The original script calls for Cupcakes, a Puerto Rican inmate, to deliver an impromptu toast/rap as a means of entertaining the other inmates. In the actual production of the play, this toast/rap was expanded into a musical number accompanied by Latin drums and music. Several reviewers proclaim this to be the play's highlight as well as its most enjoyable aspect. For example, critic Douglas Watt states, "Incidentally, a high spot continues to be the impromptu Latin jam session" (259), while reviewer Martin Gottfried refers to this scene as "a phenomenal Spanish musical number" (259). The fact that these reviewers identify a stereotypical Latin musical number, a remarkably insignificant scene, as the play's highlight demonstrates the preference of theatergoers and reviewers for "exoticism"[12] in Latino/a theater. This penchant for the incorporation of exotic island imagery, or stereotypical

Latin rhythms and music à la Carmen Miranda or Ricky Ricardo, reveals the bias of reviewers against Latino/a theater that depicts or presents more complex material. Instead, theatergoers and reviewers alike shun the realistic side of Latino/a theater, preferring the palatable, superficial song and dance numbers to more complex, psychological explorations, as exemplified by the reception of Piñero's prison drama.

Significantly, Sandoval-Sánchez contends that U.S. Latino/a theater, along with other so-called minority theater, possesses the potential to "save" Broadway: "In a multicultural and democratic society that demands the recognition of diversity and difference, 'minority' theater is the ultimate alternative for the revitalization and survival of American theater on Broadway and nationwide, and for returning to the theater its ritualistic function in society" (Sandoval-Sánchez 110). What is significant in this statement is Sandoval-Sánchez's contention that theater, at its core, is ritualistic and that mainstream Anglo-American theater has lost this capacity. However, he maintains that U.S. Latino/a theater, along with other minority theater, is still capable of performing a ritualistic function in American society. Piñero succeeds in effectively incorporating ritualism into *Short Eyes* since, in the end, the play is not about whether or not Davis is guilty of child molestation, but rather about how the prisoners were reduced to animalistic violence in their killing of Davis. Moreover, it is also about the rules of the prison environment, which can be translated to society at large, in much the same way that Greek drama implicitly imparts lessons about morality and ethics to its audience.

Critical Short-Sightedness: Reading Race and Class Biases in New York Theater Reviews

Despite many negative reviews, *Short Eyes,* at times, received significant and impressive critical accolades and awards. Sandoval-Sánchez argues that the play's legacy of incarceration was integral to its Broadway success. He contends, "There is no doubt that, in part, the critical success of the play was motivated by the ideological factor that the actors as well as the playwright were reformed ex-convicts; the show was seen as an inspired rehabilitation effort" (Sandoval-Sánchez 113). His belief is that many critics praised Piñero's play because its author and most of its cast members were ex-convicts. Essentially, Sandoval-Sánchez claims that critics and theatergoers saw this production as a positive example of the rehabilitation of prisoners. I disagree. With the exception of Mel Gussow's review in the *New York Times,* in which he refers to the potential of theater to rehabilitate persons as successfully demonstrated by Piñero and his cast members,[13] there is no evidence in the reviews to indicate such sentiments generally. On the contrary, some of the reviews negatively acknowledge the fact that Piñero and almost the entire original cast are former inmates. Certainly, many reviewers allude to the "unusual" incarceration background of Piñero and his cast. However, none, with the aforementioned exception, praise the play for its rehabilitative success. If anything, several of the reviewers appear to find this background oddly charming in the way that middle- and upper-class persons often find the struggles of the lower classes to be. For example, in the opening paragraphs of her review, Catherine Hughes refers to the play's unusual inception as "if anything, even more intriguing than the play itself. . . . Mr. Pinero himself is an ex-inmate of Sing Sing Prison, and most of the actors, collectively billed as The Family, are also ex-cons (which provides some of the most absorbing 'Who's Who' cast biographies in years)" (Hughes 457). In a similar vein, Gary Jay Williams refers to the play's roots in:

> a prisoner rehabilitation project. . . . [T]he men in The Family have written their own program biographies, and in them one sees what a dramatic contribution they feel their lives have made to this project. The circumstances and this cast are by no means extratheatrical factors; they help account for some of the visceral audience response to the production. (Williams 764)[14]

On the other hand, for critic Stanley Kauffmann, the legacy of imprisonment that permeates this play is neither a source of charm nor a cause for critical praise. Although he notes that "the bio notes in the program are a sharp change from the usual stuff," he contends that "here is a drama cut right out of some urgent social troubles of our time, performed by people (for the most part) who know firsthand what they are talking about. And yet, within the framework of an art, it's defective—even a trifle boring. Occasionally, you feel a twinge of conscience for not capitulating to it. But no . . . theatrically *Short Eyes* is flawed" (Kauffmann 20). Contrary to Sandoval-Sánchez's assertion that critics favored *Short Eyes* because they saw it as a successful rehabilitation project, Kauffmann resolutely refuses to review this play favorably based on empathy for the cast's prior experiences as inmates. Martin Gottfried makes a similar argument in his contention that "making theater may (or may not) be useful therapy"; however "I don't think that social work should be confused with professional theater or that sympathy should be confused with respect" (Gottfried 259). Thus, in general, the legacy of incarceration surrounding *Short Eyes* was more a source of curiosity than a cause for praise.

Rather than finding the real life prison backdrop of Piñero's play to be charming, many critics negatively critiqued the play, its cast members, and, most vociferously, its audiences. These negative reviews, I contend, reflect a larger race and class bias intrinsic to New York theater during the 1970s.[15] Many reviewers attack Piñero personally and suggest that he is ignorant or somehow unaware of the powerful irony inherent in his play. For example, in her review in *America,* Catherine Hughes states that "there is nothing in the least complex about its plot" (Hughes 457). In his review "Inhuman and Human Theater," Gary Jay Williams similarly derides Piñero's intelligence and play-writing ability in his remarks: "Piñero's play is more about these hungers than he yet knows," and "Piñero is not in full control of his play and there is unrealized irony in the degeneracy of the men who kill the degenerate"(Williams 764–65). Stanley Kauffmann echoes these sentiments in his assertion that "Piñero hasn't much skill in the telling. There *is* a strong irony in his play, but I'm not convinced that he's aware of it" (Kauffmann 20). Lastly, Richard Watts contends that "'Short Eyes' is more of an experience for the uninformed than a successful play" (Watts 260). These remarks suggest that many reviewers held Piñero's status as an uneducated, Puerto Rican ex-convict, something heretofore unseen on Broadway, against him.

More disturbing than the racial bias against Piñero are the times critics negatively commented upon the behavior of audience members—an act that appeared significantly out of place in a theatrical review. Several of the reviews took on an almost sociological air as they dissected and evaluated what they deemed the "inappropriate" behavior of the play's largely non-Anglo audience.[16] Obviously, many of these critics were extremely uncomfortable reviewing a play by a Puerto Rican ex-convict featuring a predominantly Latino and African-American cast of ex-convicts in front of a racially diverse audience—most definitely not the norm on Broadway. Their explicit condemnation of the audience's behavior reveals their race and class biases. This is particularly apparent in the overtly racist language they used at times to critique the audience's proclivity for outspoken "call-and-response" patterns during the play. Moreover, their racist and classist denunciation of the audience's behavior reflects an unspoken yet palpable mandate for a specifically middle- to upper-class mode of theatergoing behavior that is decidedly Anglo/Western in its foundation. In a move that underscores the racial ignorance of many reviewers, the *Christian Science Monitor* includes *Short Eyes* in its review of "New York black theater" and refers to it as "black-oriented theater" (Beaufort 260–61). This suggests that this reviewer was extremely uncomfortable reviewing a Latino/a play, a relatively new phenomenon on Broadway, and did not know how to define and categorize it. Although African-American playwrights were still on the margins of American theater, black theater carries a legacy dating back to the early 1920s. For example during the Harlem Renaissance, African-American actors, such as Paul Robeson, and casts featuring mostly black actors were quite popular on Broadway.[17] Thus, although it too was marginalized, black drama was still much more accepted in New York theater circles than Latino/a plays were at the time of Piñero's debut. This further supports Sandoval-Sánchez's assertions about the marginality of Latino/a theater.

More than any other reviews, John Simon's critique of *Short Eyes* exemplifies the race and class biases common to many New York theater critics. Simon bases most of his review not on the actual play but, instead, on the reaction of the audience. He condemns the audience, composed, not insignificantly, "largely of blacks and Puerto Ricans, but containing also a goodly number of more or less hippified whites." He decries their:

> abominable inhumanity. The fact that they talked or shouted back at the stage (a barbarous habit, admired, oddly by such different critics as Brustein and Barnes) is merely uncivilized. It does express involvement, but involvement that makes it impossible for others to hear, and for its exhibitor to stop and think, is imbecile, antisocial, and worthless. What truly appalled me, though, was the unbridled ecstasy with which these audiences savored—pealingly laughed, defeaningly cheered and applauded—the victim's being hung head down in a filthy toilet, threatened with sexual assault, brutally hounded and mauled, and finally slaughtered. Similar ovations greeted other homosexual acts, fist fights, and even the least show of violence. (Simon 76)

Simon is most disturbed by the audience's noisy reaction to the play. His words here, though, also exemplify his own deeply palpable class and race prejudices.[18] He explicitly refers to the audience's outspoken behavior as "merely uncivilized" and contends that they are thrilled by the slightest hint of violence and debauchery. All of these descriptors are racially charged and reflect Simon's prejudiced belief that such persons should not be part of a Broadway theater audience. According to him, they do not know how to behave properly. In essence, Simon implies that there can be no place for non-Anglo audience members on Broadway unless they conform to Anglo standards of behavior.

Simon's remarks are particularly telling in the words he uses to describe the behavior, and by implication, the audience members themselves. He states that the audience members "behave with abominable inhumanity," and their penchant for talking back, "responding," to the actors is "imbecile, antisocial, and worthless." Simon is particularly appalled by the audience's cheers and jeers in reaction to violent and sexual scenes. Such a reaction, according to Simon, is inexcusable: "There is no excusing this on grounds of unsophisticated spontaneity, childlike identification, unconventionalized forthrightness. It is, I am afraid, bestiality." Simon's choice of words here is particularly relevant as he uses inherently racist adjectives to describe the behaviors of the audience. His contention that such behavior evidences the audience's inherent "bestiality" is particularly disturbing due to its racist undertones. He also effectively bars such persons from attending future plays in his contention that "though it [the play] may function also as catharsis, there remains the hideous underlying fact that any society that needs that much catharsis, of so gross a kind, can never get enough of it from the theater or other harmless sources, and is in grave trouble indeed" (76). Although, as he acknowledges, theater can provide a catharsis for an audience, Simon is clearly uncomfortable with Broadway theater serving this function for a primarily Latino/a and African-American audience as evidenced in his contention that such persons "can never get enough of it [catharsis] from the theater." Simon's remarks stand in direct contrast to the underlying tenet of Latino/a theater: to inspire the audience to social action and "illuminate specific points about social problems. Satirize the opposition. Show or hint at a solution. Express what people are feeling" (Sandoval-Sánchez 105). Here again, Simon reveals his ignorance of non-Anglo cultural forms as well as his explicit unwillingness to identify with or accept a predominantly non-Anglo audience.

In his review, Stanley Kauffmann makes similarly racist remarks in his contention that "the interest of the performance . . . comes entirely from the work of the group as group under Camillo: a free-flowing colorful essay in the self-histrionism of the characters, who are perhaps not so terribly distant from the performers—the creation of a kind of jungle of nativity into which Davis comes like a stranger" (Kauffmann 20). With his deliberate blurring of the characters and the performers, Kauffmann refers to the group of mostly black and Latino/a inmates/performers as creating a "jungle of nativity" into which Davis, a white, upper-middle-class man, is thrown. Such a characterization shows the stereotypically racist depiction of non-Anglos as exotic and hailing from the jungle. Thus, for Kauffmann, the prison dayroom becomes reminiscent of the dark reaches of Africa or a tropical island so stereotypically referred to in such Anglo works as Joseph Conrad's *Heart of Darkness* and Shakespeare's *The Tempest*. Kauffmann is not alone in his use of racist language to respond to Piñero's play. Paul Weidner, then director of the Hartford Stage Company, a well-respected theater company located in Hartford, Conn., reveals himself to be similarly uninformed about non-Anglo cultures and uncomfortable with lower-class and racially diverse audiences. In his discussion of the choices he has made in regards to the plays he has produced, he refers to his apprehension about mounting Miguel Piñero's prison drama *Short Eyes,* remarking, "When we decided to present Miguel Piñero's violent and brutal 'Short Eyes,'. . . I worried that the audience might tear the theater down. Instead that play broke the house record" (Frankel CN22). He believed that such audiences would literally "tear the theater down," due to his assumption of their ignorance and incivility, and revert to common bestiality in an audience setting. Undoubtedly, he would not have made similar remarks about Anglo-American theatergoers attending similarly shocking plays by such accepted dramatists as William Shakespeare, David Mamet, or Neil Simon. Weidner's fear that a non-Anglo audience might literally destroy the theater reflects race and class biases against nontraditional, that is, nonwhite and lower-class, theatergoers and playwrights alike.

Perhaps the headline of Walter Kerr's theater review in the *New York Times,* "Life Mixes with Art and We Are Frightened," most explicitly reflects the threat that Piñero and his nonwhite audience members posed to New York theater. He contends that although real life often intermingles with art, "I don't think I have ever seen it crossed so subtly and so frequently, in some ways so frighteningly, as it was at the preview of 'Short Eyes' I attended" (Kerr 4).

His choice of words here is extremely telling as he says that he was literally "frightened" by the audience's reaction to Piñero's play. Seemingly, this play captured reality a little too accurately for his comfort. He is particularly bothered by the behavior of many audience members, which was not in keeping with the rules of traditional theater behavior:

> Approximately half of the audience was deliberately Not Looking. . . . This sort of thing does not normally happen in the theater. . . . Something else was happening here. Instead of responding dramatically to the material set before them, they had been thrown back onto their life-responses; instead of provisionally sharing an emotion on stage in the ordinary way they were testing—maybe attempting to tame—an emotion they would actually have felt at home. The line had been crossed: imagination had surrendered to an actual, and disturbing, possibility. (Kerr 4)

Kerr is clearly offended by the fact that the audience is not responding "dramatically" to the play, but rather that they are personally reacting to the action unfolding before them. The play obviously struck a familiar chord with many in the audience as they, as non-Anglos or members of the lower class, clearly identified with the experiences of the characters set before them. According to Kerr, the fact that, for them, the play is real is out of the ordinary and unacceptable: "The line had been crossed: imagination had surrendered to an actual, and disturbing, possibility." That the play had spoken in a very palpable way to many in the audience frightened Kerr. The audience's visceral response is unheard of in traditional theater and is extremely threatening. The fact that it is primarily non-Anglo audience members that are responding in this way makes this all the more disturbing and exposes Kerr's inherent race and class prejudices. He is further disturbed by the audience's later vocal response to the action on stage:

> The line was crossed in another way, not long after as onstage brutality increased, yet another segment of the audience—perhaps a third of it— began literally to scream engagement, encouragement of the man doing the brutalizing. If an inmate was attempting to rape a boyish newcomer, he was, in effect, cheered on. . . . I don't pretend to be able to identify the portion of the audience that was volubly reversing drama's traditional sympathy for the underdog, or for the "hooked." So far as I could tell, it was composed of pretty much the same racial mix—black, white, Puerto Rican—that stirred restlessly about on stage. . . . [C]onceivably they were among the once-dispossessed themselves, hard-headed survivors intimate with street-law. (Kerr 4)

Significant here is Kerr's contention that this type of vocal call-and-response behavior is clearly inappropriate in a traditional theater setting. Furthermore, he shows his own misguided sympathy for Davis, the white child molester, as he contends that the audience was "volubly reversing drama's traditional sympathy for the underdog" in their encouragement of the brutality onstage. Kerr misunderstands the audience reaction due to his ignorance of non-Anglo cultural forms and the experiences of the dispossessed lower classes. He continues, stating, "Whatever may have prompted their responses, these were once again, not dramatic responses as we have known them; they were more nearly acknowledgements that this is The Way It Is for the unlucky, and let every man guard his own groin. The arena was truly an arena, not a showcase"(4). Here, Kerr remarks that the audience's visceral reaction to the play is inconsistent with traditional dramatic responses. Again, he is basing this judgment on middle-class Anglo standards of behavior, suggesting that there is no room for deviation from the norm in regards to proper theater behavior. With his assertion that "the arena was truly an arena, not a showcase," he ascribes an animalistic or freakish characteristic to the play's audience.

Significantly, later in the review, Kerr praises the audience when they act in accordance with middle-class Anglo standards of behavior by quietly witnessing and absorbing the action unfolding before them instead of vocally responding to the actors. Kerr refers to the play's last act and declares, "This *is* playwriting now: the audience is torn loose from itself and absorbed quite quietly, altogether intently, in the complexity set before it" (Kerr 3–4). It is significant that it is only once the audience is quiet and attentive— behaving dispassionately—that Kerr deems the play to be successful and the audience to be fully engaged with the material presented before them. Kerr, along with aforementioned reviewers, including Kauffmann and Simon, is obviously unfamiliar with the call-and-response pattern[19] prevalent in the African-American and, to some extent, Latino/a communities as evidenced by his vociferous criticism of the audience's verbal responses to the play's action. Such outspoken response is uncharacteristic of typical, middle-class, Anglo-American Broadway audiences who know to keep quiet and sit politely in their seats. This criticism, although seemingly aimed primarily at the audience's outspokenness, reveals a deeper-seated racial and class prejudice. These remarks reveal Kerr's decidedly middle-class and Anglo cultural biases as he completely misinterprets the audience's active and vocal call-and-response pattern during the play. This is not surprising, as he is clearly uncomfortable with their identification with the play. One may rightfully surmise that, as a middle-class, white theater critic, being in the midst of a cheering and jeering crowd consisting primarily of Latino/as and African Americans is an incredibly frightening experience for him. For Kerr, as is true for many other theater critics, the non-Anglo audience members have trespassed in a sacred, traditionally white space—namely, Broadway.[20]

New York theater's implicit bias toward Anglo and middle-class experience is also reflected in the willingness of critics to self-identify with the few white characters in *Short Eyes* and to proclaim them as "good" or morally upstanding although, in actuality, they are meant to be the exact opposite. Hughes, for example, identifies Captain Allard, the white prison captain, as the sole morally upstanding person in the play, ignoring the empathy and virtuousness of Juan, a Latino who epitomizes humane compassion and respect for life. Instead, Hughes claims that Allard "is about as close as we get to a 'good guy,'" despite the fact that Allard covers up Davis's murder even after proclaming Davis's innocence. Other critics curiously sympathize with Davis, naively believing him to be the victim of mistaken identity. Although there is some ambiguity as to whether or not Davis is actually guilty of this current charge against him,[21] earlier in the play he confesses to Juan that he has molested many young girls in the past. Obviously, some critics choose to ignore this important fact as revealed in their characterization of Davis as an innocent man wrongly accused and murdered. Such an interpretation of the play led several reviewers to conclude that the inmates are little more than barbaric animals who kill on command.

Critic John Simon views Davis as being wrongly accused despite his detailed confessions. He states that Davis "is probably innocent of the present charge," although he "is guilty of *some* child molesting" (Simon 76). Curiously, he expresses his identification with Davis, a middle-class white man who is a self-confessed child molester, when he refers to Davis as the play's so-called "victim" and overlooks the fact that the real victims are the innocent little girls, mostly Puerto Rican and African American, whom Davis molested. *National Review* critic Gary Jay Williams similarly believes Davis to be innocent, as evidenced by his contention that "after a token investigation and coverup, the inmates learn that 'Short Eyes' was innocent of this particular molestation" (Williams 764). Critic Richard Watts reveals an analogous bias in his assertion that Davis is "the play's most sympathetic character" (Watts 260). It appears that Simon's own position, and that of Williams and Watts, as a middle-class white male precludes him from identifying with the experiences of the non-Anglo characters. According to Sandoval-Sánchez, Simon exhibits an extreme case of ethnic blindness in his empathy for and designation of Davis as the play's "victim." Sandoval-Sánchez contends that "obviously, Simons does not identify with the play and its 'uncivilized audience,' who, for him, are barbaric and antisocial peoples of color joined by a handful of white liberals. Simon can only identify with the criminal, whom he sees as a 'victim,' when in reality the protagonist is a different criminal, a child molester, who happens to be white" (Sandoval-Sánchez 114). By overlooking Davis's confession to Juan and championing his innocence, these critics deem the other inmates to deserve imprisonment. Accordingly, the stereotype of the violent and beastly non-Anglo male preying upon the innocent, middle-class white man is preserved and promoted. Such an interpretation is rather simplistic and disregards the complexity of Piñero's play. The fact that Juan refuses to reveal the truth about Davis's guilt further demonstrates the sophistication of Piñero's work—a direct counter to Hughes's claim that "there's nothing in the least complex about its plot." In regards to the death of Davis, Camillo maintains that "Clark Davis represents an emotionally disturbed man from an emotionally disturbed society. His death is the result of the rigidity of social values and morals in the prison world" (Camillo xii). As Camillo's contention suggests, rather than being a place of animalistic barbarity, the prison system, as a microcosm of the larger society, is informed by a strict code of morals and values. Davis's actions are in direct conflict with this code and, accordingly, he is killed.

The fact that the inmates struggle with various levels of guilt upon hearing that Davis may have been innocent underscores Piñero's rendering of complex and humane characters who defy simplistic stereotypes. Significantly, El Raheem and Ice, two African-American inmates, acknowledge that they are all guilty, as they all participated, literally and figuratively, in the murder of Davis. Ice states, "Cupcakes, listen to me, you killed him just as much as I did. . . . No, I didn't swing the knife . . . and neither did you, but we're guilty by not stopping it. . . . We sanctioned it. . . . Only Juan is free" (Piñero 119). Ice makes a salient point: only Juan remains free of guilt over the death of Davis, as he is the sole person who tried to stop the murder. The others must live with their guilt over the fact that they may have killed an innocent man. This scene can be read as pertaining to any action within or outside of prison walls. This scene demonstrates the power of a mob mentality—regardless of the ethnicity of its participants. All participated—black, white, and Puerto Rican. Their actions have disrupted their brotherhood. For, up until this point, despite occasional flare-ups, they all got along because they knew brotherhood was what they needed to survive. The intelligence and complexity of these nonwhite characters are repeatedly overlooked in the critical reviews as the critics choose to ignore their virtues and, instead, view the white characters as morally superior to them.

Simon and the other critics are not the only ones who criticize the behavior of Piñero's audience. Many New York theatergoers walked out in the middle of the play or expressed outrage in the press. For example, in a letter to the editor of the *New York Times,* S. Jay Levin, a fellow theatergoer, responds to Kerr's article and concurs with his inherently racist critique of the audience. Levin claims that he was so appalled by the behavior of the audience that he was "moved to leave the theater before the play ended." The audience's reaction, he claims, "is a frightening commentary on our festering American civilization." His assertion can be read as implicitly decrying the racial diversification of the United States. Analogous to Kerr's comments, Levin implies that non-Anglo persons have intruded on Broadway—a traditionally white space. Levin's comments can also be read metaphorically to refer to what he sees as the encroachment of non-Anglo persons in the United States. Levin continues, contending that the audience "pathological[ly] watched and cheered with cannibalistic relish the brutalization and murder of a wracked and tormented young soul. Mr. Kerr called this stage an arena. I would add that its players were as actors in a bull ring, the picador with his crippling torture of the animal, the toreador moving in for the kill" (Levin 127). Similar to other reviewers' stereotypical, categorizations of Piñero's audience, Levin's references to the "cannibalistic relish" of the audience members and the play's appearance of a "bull ring" are overtly racist remarks alluding to the well-worn stereotype of dark-skinned persons being cannibals, animalistic, and inherently violent. Levin's letter demonstrates that theatergoers were equally critical of the behavior of Piñero's audience. In a telling remark, when asked if any theatergoers ever walk out in the middle of *Short Eyes,* an usher at Joseph Papp's Public Theater downtown where Piñero's play was running, responded by saying, "Oh yes, usually at matinees. And they're always middle-aged or elderly white people who don't quite see this play as 'culture.' Hell, some of them don't so much walk out as run out" (Hentoff 8). The willingness of theatergoers and critics alike to deride Piñero as ignorant and to condemn the behavior of his racially diverse audience serves as a testament to the racism and classism intrinsic to New York theater.

Breaking Through/Moving Past Stereotypes:
The Legacy of Miguel Piñero

The often overtly racist reaction of critics and theatergoers to *Short Eyes* may cause one to wonder why Piñero would want or allow his play to be produced on Broadway, since many of his audience members appeared to be completely out of touch with the material presented before them. This line of thought leads to the question: What is the place of non-Anglo works on Broadway? Should they be presented on Broadway or should they be left, instead, to be produced in relative obscurity in off-Broadway community theaters? Alberto Sandoval-Sánchez asks, "To what extent do race and class worldviews shape and determine theatrical productions and critical reviews?" (114). In answering this question, one must take into consideration the fact that most of those who saw *Short Eyes* were African American and Latino/a. Thus, Piñero was, in fact, able to address his non-Anglo peers. The racial diversity of his audience also testifies to the fact that non-Anglo persons are interested in theater and will come out in droves in support of a fellow non-Anglo playwright. Piñero's material obviously spoke to them due to its realistic depiction of Latino/a and African-American life and in its employment of a majority of non-Anglo actors, most of them ex-convicts—a heretofore unseen occurrence on Broadway. This alone testifies to the need for the production of Latino/a, and other so-called minority theater, for it serves a valuable purpose as a cultural outlet for non-Anglo Americans.

In considering the place of a play like *Short Eyes,* it is useful to bear in mind Sandoval-Sánchez's discussion of Nuyorican theater's emphasis on "community building" and the "ritualistic function" that it serves. Sandoval-Sánchez further contends that another key component of Nuyorican theater of the 1960s and 70s was "to mobilize and raise consciousness among working-class audiences in urban barrios and migrant communities in rural areas" (105–6). Piñero's play was designed to do just that. This is particularly evident in the play's concluding act, during which the prisoners, after having killed the white inmate and supposed child molester Davis, are told by the prison captain that the man was innocent. Upon receiving this news, the prisoners grapple with their guilt, or lack thereof. As Cupcakes is leaving, Juan relents and decides to offer him some advice, although he never reveals his own thoughts about Davis's guilt or innocence. Juan states, "I'll give you something . . . cuz you're leaving this place . . . and only becuz of that, I can't give you no life-style pearls . . . no cues . . . becuz you, like the rest of us . . . became a part of the walls . . . an extra bar in the gate . . . to remain a number for the rest of your life in the street world." Juan tells Cupcakes that he has become a part of the system and that he will always remain a part of the prison even after he returns to the street world. Prison has left its indelible mark on Cupcakes, as it has on all of the inmates. Juan continues, saying, "Cupcake, you went past the money and blew it . . . and you blew it becuz you placed yourself above understanding" (Piñero 120). Here, Juan berates Cupcakes for failing to attempt to understand Davis's plight; for not treating him more humanely with understanding. He tacitly condemns Cupcakes for his implicit participation in Davis's murder. He then offers Cupcakes one last piece of advice: "Oye, espera, no corra, just one thing, brother, your fear of this place stole your spirit. . . . And this ain't no pawnshop" (121). Juan condemns Cupcakes for allowing prison to change him, to break his spirit. His advice here can easily be applied to the Latino/a community in general as he implores Cupcakes to remain true to himself and not be afraid of his own convictions, for had he done so, Davis might still be alive. Notably, Piñero ends his play without revealing the truth about Davis's actions. The audience is left to come to its own conclusion as to whether or not Davis was innocent. In the end, it really doesn't matter whether or not Davis is innocent or guilty. The point is the action undertaken by the inmates and their unwillingness to treat him fairly; their desire to stand in judgment of him and to mete out their own punishment as they saw fit; and how this action, and their subsequent guilt, now affects them. However, Juan does indeed know the actual truth about Davis's guilt. Yet he refuses to share this information with his fellow inmates. Ironically, his possession of this knowledge renders him the one with the biggest cause to want to maim or kill Davis, yet he is the one who refuses to participate in the murder and begs his fellow inmates to do the same. With this irony, Piñero further elevates Juan, a Latino, to a morally superior status in comparison with all of the other inmates. In doing so, he explicitly refutes prevailing negative stereotypes of Latino/as. Piñero particularly relishes the ability of his play to do just that as evidenced by his remark that *Short Eyes* "adds a dimension to the roles thus far portrayed by

Puerto Ricans. . . . [W]e Puerto Ricans are behind blacks. We seldom get to play roles other than junkies or janitors. Although my characters are in jail, I think they come off as human beings—not caricatures" (Kent 56). It is the ability of Piñero's play, and subsequently those of other Latino/a playwrights, to inspire ethnic pride in Latino/a audiences as well as to shatter stereotypical representations of Latino/as for middle-class Anglo-American theatergoers that renders it an important and essential part of American theater.

Ironically, Piñero was well aware of the off-putting nature of his play for members of the middle and upper classes. In an interview with Nat Hentoff of the *New York Times,* Piñero acknowledged their strained and, at times, vociferous condemnation of his play. He remarked that:

> I'm glad you're here, it's the people who read *The Times* that I really try to hit in what I write. You go on the subway, you know, you see a guy reading *The Times,* and you always feel this guy must be doing something great in life. Then he goes home, turns on the TV, watches Cronkite or "Eyewitness News," and he says, "Oh, how shocking, how *shocking!* Would you fix me a martini, please, Myra?" (Hentoff 8)

Piñero admitted that part of his project was to reach members of the middle and upper classes and make them think about issues of race and class—something that he would most likely have been unable to do if his play had not been presented on Broadway. In keeping with Latino/a theater's mandate to "illuminate specific points about social problems," Piñero also discussed the responsibility of society at large to care for all of its members. He argued that

> *everybody* is responsible for what he does, including those people who have power, who are not poor. I told that to a lady at the Public Theater. She had just walked out on my play. "It's so *brutal,*" she was saying. "It's so disgusting!" "Listen," I told her, "you're responsible for it, you know. You pay taxes." I mean, a lot of the people who come to see the play, they're citizens, taxpaying citizens. But except for April 15, they don't consider themselves citizens with a responsibility to know what's going on in the government, in the school district. To try to find out why kids are beaten up by teachers, why there's so much dope in school. It's *their* money that's causing Attica, Auburn, all the prisons and what goes on inside them. (Hentoff 8)

In this way, Piñero took pride in the ability of his play to educate traditional theatergoers about issues of race and class. Accordingly, Latino/a theater's capacity to educate and inform audiences—in particular, middle-class Anglo-American audiences—about social issues also renders it a necessary and important part of the American theater tradition.

Years after Piñero's Broadway debut, theater critics, directors, and producers readily acknowledge his contribution to American theater as an innovator and leader of the Nuyorican and Latino/a communities. Upon Piñero's death, *New York Times* theater critic Mel Gussow reflected upon his ability to push the envelope in regard to ethnic/racial depictions on the Broadway stage, contending that

> "Short Eyes" was a breakthrough, not only in personal terms, but as a harbinger of the art that is coming from the Hispanic-American community. In that sense, it served a purpose not unlike that of [African-American playwright] John Osbourne's "Look Back in Anger," challenging theatrical tradition and preconceptions. "Short Eyes" opened the door to urban reality and among them who entered was Reinaldo Povod, one of a number of emerging young artists who studied with Mr. Piñero. (Gussow, "From the City Streets" H8)

Noted New York theater director Joseph Papp, who was responsible for bringing *Short Eyes* to Lincoln Center, similarly identified the important work that Piñero did in breaking through traditional racial barriers and laying the foundation for future non-Anglo works to be produced on Broadway, specifically through Piñero's position as a mentor for other Latino/a writers:

> Miguel Piñero was the first Puerto Rican to really break through and be accepted as a major writer for the stage. He was an extraordinarily original talent, and he became a mentor and a hero for people like Reinaldo Povod, who wrote "Cuba and His Teddy Bear." The fact that Miguel was successful made it possible for Ray to write. All over the Lower East Side, Miguel was considered someone who had broken through. But in addition to being a symbol, he was a first-class playwright. (Bennets 11)

Sadly, it was only after his death that Piñero's critics fully acknowledged and appreciated his breakthrough talent. Moreover, despite such praise, Latino/a theater is far from becoming an entrenched staple of American theater. Sandoval-Sánchez aptly summarizes the position of Latino/a theater, concluding that "in spite of the occasional gendered, black, or Asian presence on Broadway, U.S. Latino theater is still *absent* on the Great White Way" (117). Although *Short Eyes* was first produced in 1973, as Sandoval-Sánchez contends in his 1999 study, American theater has yet to significantly progress in its critical reception of Latino/a theater productions. Perhaps, until Broadway loses its designation as the Great White Way, American theater will remain forever imprisoned by its race and class prejudices.

Notes

1. Persons either born in Puerto Rico and immigrants to New York City or those born in the United States of Puerto Rican descent and living in New York City.

2. A collaboration that led to the publication of a renowned anthology, *Nuyorican Poetry: An Anthology of Puerto Rican Words and Feelings,* co-edited with Miguel Algarín in 1975, showcasing the works of up-and-coming Nuyorican writers. See Miguel Algarín and Miguel Piñero, eds. *Nuyorican Poetry: An Anthology of Puerto Rican Words and Feelings* (New York: Morrow, 1975).

3. For detailed articles on Piñero's life see: Wahls 1; Knight 1; Hentoff 8; Gussow, "From Prison" 68; Bennets 11; Gussow, "From the City Streets" H8; and Dominguez K3313.

4. Piñero reveals his determination to remain connected to those on the streets in an interview with Nat Hentoff in which he stated, "My being a writer, now, of a successful play doesn't, in any way, make me feel above the other brothers. We're very close. We're all responsible to and for each other" (Hentoff 8).

5. With the exception of a couple of white prison guards and captains along with two white inmates.

6. See Sandoval-Sánchez 108.

7. *Short Eyes* first opened at the Theater of the Riverside Church, where Piñero was playwright in residence. It was seen there by Joseph Papp, legendary director of the New York Public Theater and the Vivian Beaumont Theater at Lincoln Center. After seeing the play, Papp presented *Short Eyes* at both of his theaters. The fact that Piñero's play received such critical reviews is, most likely, linked to its position of prominence in the aforementioned renowned theaters. This connection further underscores the purpose of this study: to analyze the connection between race and class in relation to New York theater.

8. Notably, several negative reviews of this play make inappropriate, yet telling, comparisons between *Short Eyes* and such canonical drama as Shakespeare, Oscar Wilde, and classical Greek tragedy. For example, in his review Stanley Kaufmann refers to the play's inability to hold his attention and notes that it is "odd how infrequently that sort of wandering occurs at *Oedipus Rex*." He also makes the tellingly classist remark that some of the play's "clumsy" passages were "written on a rusty typewriter"(20). John Simon makes a similar remark in his review of *Short Eyes* in regards to what he deems to be Piñero's shortcomings by stating that "we should not blame him overmuch for not having reached at 27, the deeper insight of an Oscar Wilde in *De Profundis*"(76). The fact that critics uphold these Anglo works as the barometer of what is supposedly good theater shows the class- and race-based prejudices prevalent in New York theater of the 1970s.

9. The play ends with the death of Davis, a white inmate who has been accused of child molestation, at the hands of all of the inmates except Juan, who refused to take part in the murder. The ambiguity arises with a debate over Davis's innocence, as proclaimed by the prison captain upon hearing of the murder. However, Davis previously confided his sexual experiences with young girls and, consequently, his guilt to Juan. The inmates pressure Juan to reveal whether or not Davis was in fact guilty. Juan, however, refuses to give in to their demands and remains mum about Davis's confession. His omission leads the inmates to question their murderous actions and their varying degrees of guilt.

10. This is exemplified by José Rivera's reference to "Piñero's heroin addicts" (6) when discussing common stereotypes in Latino/a drama.

11. As Sandoval-Sánchez aptly puts it: "It is undeniable that three Latino plays on Broadway do not constitute the acceptance and mainstream success of U.S. Latino theater" (115).

12. This penchant for exoticism has been similarly expressed by American theatergoers in regards to African-American theater and music—in particular, during the time of the Harlem Renaissance, when Anglo audience members often demanded exotic depictions of Africa and jungle rhythms in African-American art, music, and theater.

13. In his review, Gussow states, "If the team of Mr. Piñero and Mr. Camillo could be utilized in America's prisons, they would probably work wonders of rehabilitation. This production is significant not only as a theatrical event but also as an act of social redemption" (Gussow, "Short Eyes" 168).

14. See also Barnes 45; Watt 258; Watts 260; Beaufort 260–61; Kroll 81; Kerr II:1:4; and Simon 76.

15. In regards to the racial bias that still surfaces in theater reviews of Latino/a plays, Sandoval-Sánchez cites the Latina dramatist Dolores Prida who "has continually denounced Anglo-American theater critics for their lack of Hispanic cultural knowledge and understanding in their reviews of Latino theatrical productions. . . . Prida questions the exclusion of U.S. Latino plays from Anglo-American theater spaces, and thus questions the institutional ethnocentrism and inherent racism inscribed in the official critical response to Latino plays in the mainstream" (117).

16. One notable exception to this is theater reviewer Clive Barnes's admission that "I saw the Lincoln Center 'Short Eyes' at a final matinee with a largely black and Puerto Rico audience. I never quite decided whether I loved the play more than I loved the audience's response to it" Barnes 21.

17. Examples of the critical success of dramas by and about African Americans prior to this time period include Eugene O'Neill's *The King and I,* featuring Paul Robeson, and Lorraine Hansberry's *A Raisin in the Sun,* which won the Drama Critics' Circle Award for 1958–59.

18. Sandoval-Sánchez contends, "For the critic, the characters as well as the audiences have trespassed on Broadway. Simon seems to have experienced only sanitized bourgeois theatrical productions with 'civilized' white audiences" (114). Sandoval-Sánchez uses a telling choice of words in his contention that, according to the visceral reaction evident in Simon's review, the non-Anglo characters as well as audience members have seemingly "trespassed on Broadway." The fact that Sandoval-Sánchez uses the word "trespassed" to describe the position of non-Anglo characters and audiences in relation to Broadway—"The Great White Way"—reveals the discriminatory viewpoints held by many New York theater critics.

19. According to *The Oxford Companion to African American Literature,* "African American oratory is rooted in the vernacular and develops stylistically through a call-response interaction between the speaker and his/her audience." See Andrews, Foster, and Harris 553.

20. In a telling contrast, Kerr includes some brief but favorable remarks about an African-American drama, "Les Femmes Noires," at the end of his review of

Short Eyes. He favors this "short, essentially lyrical journey through black streets,
black homes, (most often middle-class), and black minds" that is "evocatively
played by an exceptionally handsome company of 18" (Kerr 3–4). It is not coinci-
dental that Kerr prefers Edgar White's play about the black middle class with its
attractive and elegant cast members to that of Piñero's unapologetic and, at times,
violent depiction of prison life and its cast composed mainly of ex-convicts. Such
favoritism reveals Kerr's inherent class biases.

21. After the inmates kill Davis, Captain Allard proclaims Davis innocent and admonishes them by saying, "I would like to state that I and Clark Davis' parents hold
you all morally guilty. . . . If you had taken some time out of your own problems
to help this poor man that was placed in here because of mistaken identity. . . . No,
Mr. Davis was not a drug addict. In fact, he was a very well liked and respected
member of his community . . . a working man with a wife and child. . . . Mr. Davis
was an innocent victim of circumstances. . . . Innocent" (Pínero 116–17).

Works Cited

Alarcón-McKesson, Norma. "An Interview with Miguel Piñero," *Revista Chicano-
Riqueña* 4 (1974): 55–7.

Andrews, William L., Frances Smith Foster, and Trudier Harris, eds. *The Oxford
Companion to African American Literature.* New York: Oxford University Press,
1997.

Barnes, Clive. "Theater: 'Short Eyes,' Prison Drama," *New York Times* March 14,
1974: 45.

———. " 'Short Eyes' Moves to the Beaumont." *New York Times* May 24, 1974: 21.

John Beaufort. "N.Y. Black Theater: Grim, Shocking 'Short Eyes.'" *Christian Science
Monitor* March 22, 1974: 260–61.

Bennets, Leslie. "Miguel Pinero, Whose Plays Dealt with Life in Prison, Is Dead at
41." *New York Times* June 18, 1988: 11.

Dominguez, Robert. "Street-life Poet Miguel Pinero was a hard-living Latin Icon."
New York Daily News Jan. 21, 2002: K3313.

Frankel, Haskel. "American Accent in Hartford." *New York Times* Oct 23, 1977:
CN22.

Gottfried, Martin. " 'Short Eyes.' " *Women's Wear Daily* (March 14, 1974): 259.

Gussow, Mel. "From Prison, 'Nowhere Being Nobody,' A Young Playwright Emerges
to Fame." *The New York Times* March 27, 1974: 68.

————. " '*Short Eyes*' Talent and Authenticity in Play of Prison Life." *New York Times Theater Reviews, 1973–4*: 168.

————. "From the City Streets, A Poet of the Stage." *New York Times* July 3, 1988: H8.

Hentoff, Nat. "Piñero: 'I Wanted to Survive.' " *New York Times* May 5, 1974: 8

Hughes, Catherine. " 'Short Eyes'—and 'Scapino' " *America* June 8, 1974: 457.

Kauffmann, Stanley. "Stanley Kauffman on Theater." *New Republic* April 20, 1974: 20.

Kent, Leticia. "Playwright Miguel Piñero brings His 'Eyes' to the Tombs." *New York Times* Jan. 23, 1977: 55–8.

Kerr, Walter. "Life Mixes with Art and We Are Frightened." *New York Times* March 24, 1974: II:1:4.

Knight, Leticia. "Playwright Miguel Pinero Brings His 'Eyes' to the Tombs." *New York Times* Jan. 23, 1977: 1.

Kroll, Jack. "Theater." *Newsweek* April 8, 1974: 81.

Levin, S. Jay Letter to the Editor. *New York Times* May 19, 1974: 127.

Piñero, Miguel. *Short Eyes*. New York: Farrar, Straus and Giroux, 1975.

Román, David. "An Interview with José Rivera." *Performing Arts* 31, no. 6 (1997): 6.

Sandoval-Sánchez, Alberto. *José Can You See?: Latinos On and Off Broadway.* Madison University of Wisconsin Press, 1999.

Simon, John. "De Quasi-Profundis." *New York* June 10, 1974: 76.

Wahls, Robert. "Pinero: Prison, Parole & a Prize." *Sunday News* June 2, 1974: 1.

Watt, Douglas. " 'Short Eyes' a Compelling Drama," *New York Daily News* May 27, 1974: 259.

Watts, Richard. "In a House of Detention." *New York Times Theater Reviews, 1973–4*: 260.

Williams, Gary Jay. "Human and Inhuman Theaters." *National Review* July 5, 1974: 764–5.

PART II

4

On Prisons in the United States: Extract from a Speech Delivered to the Confederation of Analytical Psychologists, London, 25 June 1999

HAROLD PINTER

There are two million people in prison in the United States.

These are some of the devices used in these prisons.

The restraint chair is a steel-framed chair in which the prisoner is immobilized with four-point restraints securing both arms and legs and straps which are tightened across the shoulders and chest. The prisoner's arms are pulled down towards his ankles and padlocked and his legs secured in metal shackles. Prisoners are often left strapped in restraint chairs for extended periods in their own urine and excrement.

A stun gun is a hand-held weapon with two metal prongs which emits an electrical shock of roughly 50,000 volts. The use of stun guns and stun belts is widespread. The belt on the prisoner is activated by a button on the stun gun held by a prison guard. The shock causes severe pain and instant incapacitation. This has been described as torture by remote control.

Mentally disturbed prisoners have been bound, spread-eagled on boards for prolonged periods in four-point restraints without medical authorization or supervision. It is common practice for prisoners to be shackled during transportation by leg irons or chains. Pregnant women are not excluded. Sexual abuse and rape by guards and inmates in these prisons are commonplace.

In 1997 thirty-six states operated fifty-seven "supermax" facilities housing 13,000 prisoners. More are under construction. These are super maximum security facilities. They are designed for isolation of dangerous prisoners but in fact prisoners may be assigned to "supermax" units for relatively minor disciplinary infractions, such as insolence towards staff or, in the case of both men and women, complaints about sexual abuse. Severely disturbed prisoners are held within these facilities receiving neither appropriate evaluation or treatment.

Prisoners spend between 22 and 24 hours a day in claustrophobic and unhealthy conditions. The concrete cells have no natural light. The doors are solid steel. There is no view of and no contact with the outside world.

United Nations Human Rights Committee stated in 1995 that conditions in these prisons were "incompatible" with international standards. The UN special Rapporteur on torture declared them inhumane in 1996.

Thirty-eight states out of fifty employ the death penalty. Lethal injection is the most popular method, followed by electrocution, the gas chamber, hanging and the firing squad. Lethal injection is regarded as the most humane method. But in fact some of the case histories of injections that go wrong are as grotesque as they are grisly.

Mental deficients and people under eighteen do not escape the death penalty. However, the assistant attorney general of Alabama did make the following observation: "Under Alabama law you cannot execute someone who is insane. You have to send him to an asylum, cure him up real good, then execute him."

Amnesty International stated that all these practices constitute cruel, inhuman and degrading treatment. But the "International Community" has not been invited to comment on a system at one and the same time highly sophisticated and primitive, shaped in every respect to undermine the dignity of man.

5

Harold Pinter's Prison House: The Screenplay of Kafka's *The Trial*

ANN C. HALL

Harold Pinter's 1993 screenplay of Franz Kafka's masterpiece, *The Trial,* creates a nightmarish metaphor for modern existence: a naive and apparently innocent man is accused of a crime, but he is never given the trial promised by the title of the novel and the film, never permitted to tell his version of the events, never introduced to his accusers, and, ultimately, killed as a result of a crime we never see him commit. For those familiar with the work of British playwright Harold Pinter such a scenario seems common enough in the Pinter canon. Pinter himself admits that Kafka in general and *The Trial* in particular influenced his career, and it is easy enough to find critics to document the influence of the great Czechoslovakian writer from the beginning of Pinter's career in plays such as *The Birthday Party* (1958) to *Moonlight* (1993).[1] For the purposes of this collection, one of the most significant absences in both the novel and the screenplay is the prison. Characters are threatened with the judicial, not the penal process in order to illustrate the lack of distinction between imprisonment and freedom. In both, there is no difference: the accused, the witnesses, the lawyers, and the executioners are all incarcerated, ironically by their own belief in some external arbiter of justice.

What makes Pinter's adaptation so masterful is not that he radically revises the text and its naturalistic setting. As a matter of fact, Pinter wished to avoid the expressionistic techniques of, for example, Orson Welles (Billington 349), and remained "extraordinarily faithful to Kafka's text in what he includes, in the order of events, and even the language itself" (Gillen 138). Instead, what makes Pinter's work so brilliant is his focus on the spectacular nature of the novel and the issues Kafka presents, a focus that cannot be fully developed in the genre of the novel but can be fully developed in the genre of film.[2] The main character, K., is under constant surveillance throughout the novel. On the one hand, he is crushed by this observation; on the other, he seeks a witness, a transcendent eye, the same external force that all the other characters wish to appeal to for vindication and affirmation. And it is through this complex relationship between spectator and spectacle that Pinter wrests the audience from its passive position as spectator, places them in the role of witness and participant, and, ultimately, places them in the same prison house that Kafka's Herr K. inhabits.

Before examining the screenplay, it is important to discuss the relationship between surveillance, crime, and punishment in the Western tradition, best exemplified in Michel Foucault's *Discipline and Punish: The Birth of the Prison*.[3] As Foucault argues, up until the eighteenth century, crimes were punished publicly. Communities may not have had the details regarding court cases, but they certainly saw the results of various punishments, among the worst being drawing and quartering, hanging, and the pyre (Foucault 3–7). According to Foucault, such spectacles were designed to show subjects the power of their monarchies. The ruling classes had the power and used it swiftly and brutally. Part of the problem with these public executions, however, was that they frequently did not achieve this goal; prisoners might take extended periods of time to die, which would make the governing body appear cruel, neither powerful nor just. Or, with their dying words, prisoners might be tempted to rally crowds against the ruling elite.

In addition to the uncertainties of public execution, governing bodies also became increasingly uncomfortable in their role as executioners. According to Foucault, punishment became less a case of the ruling class's power and more a case of the government merely bending to a natural or higher law. One of the most noticeable changes as a result of this shift in penal philosophy was the emphasis not on execution but on the trial, the process of justice. Briefly, the attitude toward punishment shifted in the eighteenth and nineteenth century from retribution to rehabilitation. Prisoners were ill, misdirected. They were social problems; the prisons, the solution.

Surveillance was the newest and most popular way to effect a cure, and this cure was embodied in the prison architecture and philosophy of Jeremy Bentham, the creator of the Panopticon. Simply put, the Panopticon was a building that afforded the greatest possible opportunity for surveillance:

> All that is needed, then, is to place a supervisor in a central tower and to shut up in each cell a madman, a patient, a condemned man, a worker or a schoolboy.... In short, it reverses the principle of the dungeon; or rather of its first three functions—to enclose, to deprive of light, and to hide— it preserves only the first and eliminates the other two.... Visibility is a trap.... He [the prisoner] is seen, but he does not see. (200–201)

This method of control was thought to be so successful that it was used as a model for schools, hospitals, and insane asylums; many of Bentham's practices remain with us today. The goal of the observatories, of course, was not just incarceration but transformation: criminals would become law-abiding; the ill, well; the mad, sane; and the student, productive. Success would be determined by how successfully the prisoner internalized the external surveillance. As Foucault notes, the prisoner eventually "inscribes in himself the power relation in which he simultaneously plays both roles; he becomes the principle of his own subjection" (202–3). But the method is even more insidious because, as Foucault notes, the tower need not be manned. Bentham's principle of power "should be visible and unverifiable. Visible: the inmate will constantly have before his eyes the tall outline of the central tower from which he is spied upon. Unverifiable: the inmate must never know whether he is being looked at at any moment; but he must be sure that he may always be so" (201). No one needs to watch; the merest hint of supervision is enough to elicit control. The Panopticon "arranges things in such a way that the exercise of power is not added on from the outside, like a rigid constraint, to the functions it invests, but is so subtly present in them as to increase their efficiency by itself increasing its own points of contact" (206). Such effective methods of control, of course, could yield abuse, but as Foucault explains, the Panopticon's creators constructed safeguards against such events by opening the institutions to visitors who would, in effect, guard the guards.

> Modern culture is entirely dependent: not on spectacle but surveillance.... [I]t is not that the beautiful totality of the individual is amputated, repressed, altered by our social order, it is rather that the individual is carefully fabricated in it, according to a whole technique of forces and bodies. We are neither in the amphitheater nor on the stage, but in the panoptic machine, invested by its effects of power, which we bring to ourselves since we are part of the mechanism. (217)

And this is precisely the kind of society Pinter creates in his screenplay of *The Trial,* a "spectacular," paranoid house of mirrors. Like the prisoners in the Panopticon, we learn, as K. does, that there are people viewing us at all times, but that there is, in fact, no one in the tower–no ultimate judge, earthly or divine. The ultimate supervisor is absent, but this supervisor, at least in the case of *The Trial,* is created mythically through obfuscation, a confusing hierarchy of judges, legal myths, and court legends. For the creators of the Panopticon, such obfuscation occurs in the criminal justice system to make the punishment appear to be the natural response of the society, not the demonstration of power by a ruler (Foucault 73–104). But in the Kafka novel and the Pinter screenplay, the chain of command is deliberately mystified by a legal system determined to keep its citizenry oppressed and by a society that has lost its God, the ultimate guard in the tower. The results, however, are the same: Herr K. is overcome by actual and imagined surveillance; he internalizes the watchful eye, participates in his own objectification, and finally, looks for a "spectacular" protector, finds there is none, and dies "like a dog."

The opening of the screenplay leaves no doubt that K. is being watched. Camera movements during the opening credits highlight the omnipresence of film technology and the surveillance that Pinter's screenplay underscores. The camera, in fact, is omnipresent, and it may represent the closest entity to God available to the Kafkaesque, modern world. We are clearly privy to a high level of observation on K.'s life, but at the same time, we are as much in the dark as he is about the voices that whisper outside his door and the old woman who peers into his room from her window in the apartment across the street. Moments after seeing him sleeping, oblivious to the events about to transpire, we discover that K. is under arrest. In retrospect we see that the camera movements, the whisperings, and his elderly neighbor all have K. as their subject. He is under suspicion and observation. When, for example, a second man joins the elderly woman at the window, K. does not see them; but they see him, and we see them watching him. He is under a watch, whether he is aware of it of not, and our perceptions are being directed by the camera, which may or may not provide us with complete information.

During a scene with the inspector, yet another person joins the people in the window; this time K. confronts them, and they immediately move away. K. appears to have succeeded, though from our position in the room K. may have frightened the nosy neighbors, he is still under the scrutiny of the inspector, the other men in the room, and us.

One of the more unfortunate deletions in the film from Pinter's screenplay is the character of Frau Grubach, and though Pinter agreed to the cuts, another level of oppression is missing as a result of these deletions. In the novel and the screenplay, Grubach is the warden of the rooming house. She knows everything about her "guests," and she warns K. about Frau Burstner, another tenant with whom K. is enamored. But Grubach is also poor, and she has a nephew who needs a room, so no matter what she may think of K. or how much she may need the money he continues to lend her, it is not difficult to imagine that she would betray him or anyone else in the house if the price were right, thereby heightening the corrupt and oppressive atmosphere of the house and K.'s world.

K.'s interest in Frau Burstner, despite the warnings from Frau Grubach, reflects both his ignorance of and disdain for this world. And it is this kind of behavior that leads many critics to conclude that K. is egotistical, a tragic flaw that many argue he shares with other great tragic figures such as Oedipus and Lear.[4] Frank Gillen, moreover, links this character flaw to the visual: "Through the images of eyes and looking, through dramatizing some of K.'s feelings of superiority to others, his treatment of them as objects, and his lack of concern with anything other than his own fate, Pinter's screenplay shows K. finally as a victim differing only in kind and degree but not in essence from those who destroy him" (Gillen 147). At this point anyway, K. still believes that he can, as an individual, effect changes. One of his first defenses when he is accused, for example, is to find his "identity papers," as if who he is will somehow protect him from accusations. According to Pinter, one of the reasons he admires K. is that he continues to give "them hell" and resist. According to Pinter, then, he is a rebel (Gussow 89). But in the screenplay and the film, K., though sympathetic, likeable, and rebellious, frequently teeters between two emotional extremes: egotism and naivete. In both instances, however, he has no idea how powerful and pervasive the court system is, how he is in fact already imprisoned by the threat of the trial, not the actual trial or its results.

K. is so secure in his power as an individual that he volunteers to perform the details of his arrest for Frau Burstner, for example. He casts himself into the role of the object-to-be-viewed because he assumes that he can take on or discard the role at will. He does not realize that he is already the object of the court's gaze, and he does not realize that Frau Burstner is not impartial. She mentions in passing, for example, that she is "joining a law firm next month" even though she knows nothing of the law (Pinter 11–12). While K. is not suspicious, the screenplay suggests that he should be. Her behavior, after all, is consistent with the other court representatives. In a court system, in which image is all, Burstner only reacts to the invasion of her privacy when she discovers that her photos have been rearranged. She is clearly part of the system in some way—it is the image that touches her, not the actual event. K., moreover, is so willing to relinquish his power to her, unwilling to gaze at her critically, and continually objectifying himself for her. Burstner, perhaps because of her understanding of the court system, tries to help K. out of this objectified role. "Look" she tells him, encouraging him to be more aware of his surroundings (14). K. cannot. He buries himself in her neck, kissing her passionately, blind, completely at the mercy of the gaze.

At this point, K.'s behavior indicates that he may have already internalized the gaze of the court. As an accused criminal, he immediately becomes oppressed, imprisoned, an object-to-be-viewed. Further, his unwillingness to "look" could indicate his ignorance as well. He does not want to take responsibility for his actions; he wants the observing eye, this time embodied in the maternal figure of Burstner, to protect and care for him. Kafka's novel makes it clear that at one time K. participated in the role of the viewer, frequenting shows (seventeen), but in the Pinter version, K. is always objectified by a gaze, ours or the court's, and he seems particularly reluctant to acknowledge the court's relationship to spectacle, even though his experiences indicate otherwise. Here, for example, he ignores Burstner's explicit cautions about the culture of surveillance they inhabit.

Once he leaves Burstner, K. enters a judicial version of a funhouse, and Pinter's screenplay makes the most of his absurd situation. He is called to a hearing, but the caller does not give him the time. He takes circuitous routes, with intricate passageways and secret code names. When K. knocks on the door of one apartment hoping to find the court, people respond from a door several apartments away. Nothing is as it appears to be, but appearance is all; the court is everywhere and nowhere. These are the truisms of K.'s world and the Pinter screenplay, but K. does not heed them.

When K. finally finds the court, he is shocked—it is chaotic and behind the home of a washerwoman. The symbolism is clear: the mundane is illusory; all is the court. Or, in Pinter's words, "The nightmare of that world is precisely in its ordinariness" (qtd. in Gussow 88). K. does not make such connections. He assumes that the court is separate and reasonable. When he is told that he is late, he challenges the court, its weaknesses and contradictions. He gains the applause of those he presumes are his well-wishers. Of course, K. has completely misjudged the situation. His speech does nothing to change the absurd and arbitrary nature of the proceedings. In fact, he is viewed as a form of entertainment, not the leader of a rebellion. If we were tempted to judge K. harshly before this scene, it is difficult to judge him so now. Like us, he has made incorrect assumptions about his situation. To underscore this conclusion, Kafka and Pinter interrupt K.'s speech with the public lovemaking of the law student and the washerwoman. Nothing K. can say will make a change; there are only new diversions. The magistrate who also lusts after the washerwoman concludes the scene by telling K. that he has lost all "the advantages that a hearing can afford an arrested man" (Pinter 21). K. tells them all to go to hell, but his gesture is impotent.

Undaunted and still secure in his belief that he can control his own destiny, K. returns to view the law books, to "look" for himself, an activity the washerwoman says is forbidden. K. is clearly objectified, incapable of subjectivity, but he forces his way into the courtroom and discovers that the books are filled with pornography. Such a choice underscores the court's ability to objectify people, for pornography is one of the most powerful forms of oppression available to us. In both the Kafka text and the Pinter screenplay, the law is image, and these images are perverse. In the process of his discussions with the washerwoman, she attempts to seduce him, but in a truly absurd scene, she is interrupted and transfixed by the Svengali-like presence of the student. Here, Pinter's screenplay highlights the court's powerful ability to objectify through speculation. The Washerwoman is overcome by a gaze, and K., who appears to be viewing the scene and thereby occupying a position of power, is in fact being watched by the student, objectified. The student even comments that K. has been given too much freedom (25), thus establishing his knowledge of court proceedings that K. does not have access to.

At this point, K.'s future does not look promising. After this scene, he meets the usher, the husband of the washerwoman, and the usher tells K. that he could take revenge on the student and magistrate because he has "nothing to lose" (27). And when the usher provides K. with a tour of the court offices, K. sees Magritte-like figures lining the hall, devoid of expression or the will to live. Those waiting for news of their cases are completely passive, objectified.

Initially K. is upset with their docility, but moments later, he is like them, suffocated by the court atmosphere. The usher, who was helpful, suddenly becomes sadistic and throws him down a flight of stairs. K.'s egotism, his assumption that he is somehow different from the other accused, is quickly dispelled.

And, as the next scene so painfully illustrates, he is really no different from the court representatives. As he is leaving from work, he hears screams of pain. In a closet of the bank, again underscoring the pervasiveness of the court culture, he finds the two warders he complained about being flogged. The court representatives beg K. to help stop the flogging, but K. cannot: "It's my job to flog people I'm told to flog and that's what I'm going to do" (32). K. literally turns a blind eye to the two men, and when asked about the noise by bank colleagues, he says that it was just a dog howling (32). The canine imagery is similar to his final line in the screenplay.

This scene, however, is important, because here K. no longer attempts to change the system. When faced with the flogger's absurd logic, K. does nothing, like everyone else in the screenplay. He is becoming nothing, and he does nothing. The film does not show the darker side of K.'s apathy; however, Pinter's screenplay does. After witnessing the flogging, K. returns home and, in a camera shot reminiscent of the opening scene, we see K. on the bed, this time with his eyes wide open. He is still a spectacle, but perhaps not quite such an innocent one as at the beginning of the film. The next morning, he checks the closet and finds the men still being flogged. Rather than attempting to stop the flogging, K. shuts the door and tells one of his clerks to clean out the closet because if they do not, "We're going to be smothered in filth" (33). K., like other members of this culture, is fearful, apathetic, and overwhelmed by the power of the court. Though some would argue that K. has been this way all along, it is difficult to ignore the fact that during his speech to the court about its abuses, he argued for reform, not just for himself but for others who were also victimized by the process. It would appear, then, that K. has undergone a transformation as a result of this process and observation. He is no longer capable of eliciting change; the system has changed him.

Surprisingly, K. still seems unaware of the court's power and pervasiveness. When his uncle, for example, takes him to Huld, the advocate, he is shocked to find out that people are discussing his case. More disturbing still is the mysterious appearance of a court representative while Huld and he discuss strategy. At this critical moment in his case, his first meeting with his lawyer and the court representative, K. does not stay, perhaps in an attempt to escape the gaze of the court. He leaves the room and is subsequently seduced by Huld's voluptuous caretaker, Leni. Whether he realizes it or not, his escape has led him back to the court once again. Leni, who seduces all accused men, proclaims triumphantly, "Now you belong to me" (39).

When he returns the next day, he finds that his case, according to Huld, is "moderately cheering" (41), but K. is still under the illusion that he can control the outcome. He tells Huld that he will settle the entire case by writing a "short account" of his life as a defense (41). In no uncertain terms, Huld dismisses this suggestion: "What you say is madness. . . . Absolute madness" (41). Individuals, identity, personality do not matter. K. has been completely objectified by observation as a result of his participation in this absurd justice system. He wishes to tell his own story, but he does not realize that as an accused man there is no story to tell.

In an effort to help K.'s case, Leni sends him to the court painter, Titorelli, who further illustrates the court's relationship to spectacle. Not only is K. subjected to the gaze of Titorelli's prostitutes, Titorelli tells him that there is no real escape from the court, only variations on the level of enslavement. When Titorelli is finished, he shows K. an alternative exit from the studio, but it leads to the court. Echoing Kafka's text, the screenplay has Titorelli ask the significant question, "Why are you so surprised?" (48).

K. still does not understand the hopelessness of his situation and decides to fire Huld and make his case without a lawyer. During his visit to Huld, he not only realizes that Leni is as much a part of the court as Titorelli's prostitutes, he also meets Bloch, an accused man whose trial has been going on for five years. Bloch tells him that the people in the court stood when K. entered because they could tell by the shape of his lips that he was a condemned man: "So we didn't think you were arrogant, we thought you were deluded. And so we felt pity for you" (50). And to a certain extent they are correct. K. is deluded. He expects logic from the court, but in the end superstition and obfuscation is all there is. What is surprising is that K. takes so long to learn this; he firmly clings to a faith in the law and its order, its logic. Despite his arrest with no charge, his discovery that the law books are filled with pornography, and his meeting with Titorelli, who tells him there are no full acquittals, K. believes that logical confrontation can change this system. He soon learns that not only has he been deluded about the law, but he is also deluded by Leni. The film merely suggests that Bloch and Leni are having an affair, but in Pinter's screenplay, the relationship is made much more explicit. As Huld tells K., he is not different: his relationship with Leni is not special; it is defined by the court:

> She just finds accused men wildly attractive. She can't help running after
> them. She falls in love with them all and indeed they all seem to fall in love
> with her. Even that miserable worm Bloch she finds attractive–just because
> he's an accused man. (52)

Any illusions K. has about his individuality are shattered during this meeting with Huld, Leni, and Bloch.

To make matters worse, Leni and Huld offer a performance for K. at Bloch's expense in order to create a court morality for K., to show him what the life of an accused man is really like. Bloch is the servile and fawning accused to Huld's inscrutability. In the end, Huld tells Bloch that after all his hard work and years of waiting, his trial has not even begun. K. sees. Deliberate cruelty is all that is in store for him, and though he is shown this spectacle, he is not in any position of power, for Bloch is his future.

Following this performance, K. is called to take a visiting Italian client "sightseeing" at the cathedral, and in the Pinter screenplay, K. once again remains awake, eyes open, on the night before his tour (56). In the cathedral he meets a priest, not an Italian banker, and he seeks solace.... Despite all the recent evidence to the contrary—Leni, Bloch, Titorelli, and others—K. presumes that the priest is an ally. He also still thinks of justice as available, something just and fair above the law and the culture he inhabits. The Priest is quick to say, "Don't delude yourself ... about the Court.... The Court doesn't want anything from you. It receives you when you come and it dismisses you when you go" (60–63). To highlight this point, he tells K. the preface to the Law, a story about a man who seeks the law, is afraid to enter without permission, and realizes, too late, that all he needed to do was ask permission to enter. Before the priest tells the parable, however, he says, "In the writings that preface the Law it says about this delusion" (60). The phrasing is unusual, and it is very easy to read the line as, "It says this about delusion," but this wording is much more ambiguous, making the subsequent parable even more difficult to interpret. If the phrase were, "It says this about delusion," it might be easy to interpret the parable as an example of what happens when one is deluded by oneself or someone else, but as it stands, the wording does not offer any interpretive hints. Is the man who seeks the law blinded by fear? Is the doorkeeper merely waiting for further instructions, or is he a sadist, as K. thinks?

Volumes have been written on this hauntingly ambiguous moment in the novel. What is so refreshing about the Pinter version is that it appears to be as balanced as it would in the novel. Either interpretation could be possible, and either interpretation could lead to unforeseen interpretive consequences. What is striking about this moment in the screenplay is the priest's unwillingness to explain his interpretation of the parable. The only explanation Kafka and Pinter offer is through the priest who says, "But you've missed the point. The scripture is unalterable" (63). He then tells K. that he means nothing to him. He is, after all, a member of the court. At the very least, the parable offers a microcosm of the screenplay's entire court system: it is confusing; there are no guides to interpretation, and the ones that are there are inscrutable. At the same time, it is "unalterable," unchanging, and powerful. It is, like the symbol of justice, blind and in the balance.

In the final scene, K. is led to his death, and with it comes another array of images regarding spectacle and speculation, objectivity and subjectivity, oppression and power. According to Pinter, in *The Trial*:

> Kafka obviously employs the whole idea of how a bureaucratic system works
> but he's also looking at something quite different. And that is—I have to use
> the term—religious identity. One of the captions I would put on *The Trial* is
> simply: "What kind of game is God playing?" That's what [. . .] K. is really
> asking. And the only answer he gets is a pretty brutal one. (qtd. in Billington
> 349)

This statement is as close to an interpretation that Pinter offers. It is also the
one that most influences the final scene and the placement of the viewers'
and K.'s gazes. Initially, K. resists his executioners, but after he sees Frau
Burstner, he decides to keep his "mind calm and discriminating," in effect, to
face death nobly. If this were a Shakespeare play, and if K. were a Lear or
Hamlet, the glimpse into the abyss—death—would afford the tragic character
a moment, at least, of nobility, insight, and subjectivity; however, Kafka is
no Shakespeare. For if we recall Burstner's earlier statements, her poise and
serenity are not based on nobility, but on fear and passivity: "I'm never angry
with anyone," she tells K. as she is about to show him how Grubach spies on
her lodgers. Once again K. is viewing himself and his situation incorrectly,
but here we cannot fault him entirely, for his desire to make sense of his
death and life is a desire we all share. In the Kafka universe, however, such
expectations are not only unattainable, they are absurd. In Kafka's novel and
Pinter's screenplay, there is another false clue that leads us and K. to assume
there is meaning, there is redemption, there is something above and beyond
K.'s petty trial. As K. looks from the rocks to a window, this time he sees a
beatific vision, perhaps a glimpse of paradise. Since he is the viewer, it also
appears that he is in a position of power. He sees a vision of transcendence, a
way out, the ultimate eye in the sky. Pinter's screenplay and Kafka's text do not
offer much solace, for at this moment, K.'s vision is interrupted by the peering
faces of the two executioners who block his glimpse into paradise. Further, K.
is clearly objectified by their gazes. He is a spectacle once again, a "dog" (66).

With this visual image, Pinter communicates the last lines of the Kafka
novel and most effectively concludes the screenplay's illustration regarding
spectacle, speculation, and imprisonment. K. is not redeemed at the end of the
film, because there is no transcendent viewer, only film audiences to witness
his sufferings. Just as there are no guards in the watchtower, there is no divine,
transcendent being above the court culture. Instead, there are only human
beings oppressing one another and creating, through the sum total of their
parts, the illusion that there is a God, a final judge, justice. The culture of the
Kafka novel and of the film, a culture that Pinter captures brilliantly through
the emphasis on the visual technology of film, is, in Foucault's words regarding
prisons and spectacle, "a machine for altering minds" (125). And Pinter's use
of such machinery in his screenplay will perhaps alter our own, prompting us
to think differently about imprisonment and freedom.

Ironically several years after Pinter's screenplay made its debut, a part-time drama teacher at a prison in Leicestershire tried to produce three of Pinter's plays, *Mountain Language* (1988) about political prisoners, *One for the Road* (1985) about a terrorist who tortures a family for their political views, and *Victoria Station* (1982) about two taxi drivers who are lost both literally and figuratively. According to Alan Travis, the governor of the prison thought the plays were not "best suited to 'preparing inmates for a good and useful life on release,' " because they contained subjects of torture, rape, and murder (190). The drama teacher resigned, and the plays were banned.

Notes

1. Depending on which interview you believe, Pinter has been reading *The Trial* since he was seventeen (Marks 22), eighteen (Gussow 88), or fifteen ("Pinter's Czech Mate"). Whatever his age, Pinter was profoundly affected. Marks reports that it "determined him to be a writer" (22). And Kafka's influence was great: "*The Trial* seeped into many people's subconscious, including mine. It had an undeniable influence on my early writing. *The Birthday Party* is a play which owes a lot to Kafka" (Pinter qtd. in Burley).
2. Pinter's expertise in film and screenplays has been demonstrated through works such as *The French Lieutenant's Woman* (1981), *Turtle Diary* (1985), and *The Comfort of Strangers* (1990). Joanne Klein notes, "Like the camera Pinter manipulates not reality, but the mechanisms through which we glimpse it" (qtd. in Gillen 138). And on *The Comfort of Strangers* Katherine Burkman concludes that by consciously using the camera, Pinter foregrounds "its potential for destructiveness (exposing the complicity between film and power)" which "invites us to interrogate our own role as audience" (44). In my own essay on *Mountain Language*, I argue that not only does Pinter bring his stage expertise to the film, he also brings his film expertise to the stage. In this case, he employs the filmic technique of the voice-over to strengthen the political play.
3. In an essay soon to be published by the Missouri Philological Association, "Discipline, Self-Regulation, and Silence in Pinter's *The Dumb Waiter*," Charles Grimes uses Foucault's work to examine *The Dumb Waiter*. Because he offered me a copy of the essay prior to publication, I took greater care in reading Foucault's discussion of the visible and unverifiable.
4. In the notes to *The New Trial*, the play he had been working on at the time of his death, Peter Weiss claims that his K., a member of a corporate conglomerate who is shot by a stray bullet at the end of the play, is "neither hero nor victim; he is a marginal figure, exploited for others' purposes and discarded when he is no longer needed. He is *not a tragic figure* (107, Weiss's italics).

Works Cited

Billington, Michael. *The Life and Work of Harold Pinter*. London: Faber and Faber, 1996.

Burkman, Katherine. "Harold Pinter's Death in Venice: *The Comfort of Strangers.*" *The Pinter Review Annual Essays 1992–93.* Eds. Francis Gillen and Steven Gale. Tampa: University of Tampa Press, 1993, 38–45.

Burley, Leo. "The Jury is Still out on Joseph K." *The Independent* (London). 23 April 1993. *Lexis-Nexis.* 24 May 2000.

Foucault, Michel. *Discipline and Punish: The Birth of the Prison.* Trans. Alan Sheridan. New York: Vintage Books, 1995.

Gillen, Francis. "From Novel to Film: Harold Pinter's Adaptation of *The Trial.*" *Pinter at Sixty.* Eds. Katherine Burkman and John Kundert-Gibbs. Bloomington: Indiana University Press, 1993, 136–148.

Grimes, Charles. "Discipline, Self-Regulation, and Silence in Harold Pinter's *The Dumb Waiter.*" Unpublished Essay. 19 August 2000.

Gussow, Mel. *Conversations with Harold Pinter.* London: Nick Hern Books, 1994.

———. "Voices in the Dark: The Disembodied Voice in Harold Pinter's *Mountain Language.*" *The Pinter Review: Annual Essays 1991.* Eds. Francis Gillen and Steven Gale. Tampa: University of Tampa Press, 1991, 17–22.

Marks, Louis. "Producing Pinter." *Pinter at Sixty.* Eds. Katherine Burkman and John L. Kundert-Gibbs. Bloomington: Indiana University Press, 1993, 18–26.

Pinter, Harold. *The Trial.* Boston: Faber and Faber, 1993.

Travis, Alan. "Pinter: Too Rude for Convicts." *Harold Pinter, Various Voices: Prose, Poetry, Politics.* New York: Grove, 1998, 190.

Weiss, Peter. *The New Trial.* Trans. James Rolleston and Kai Evers. Durham, N.C.: Duke University Press, 2001.

6

Harold Pinter's *The Handmaid's Tale:* Freedom, Prison, and a Hijacked Script

CHRISTOPHER C. HUDGINS

> Marat
> these cells of the inner self
> are worse than the deepest stone dungeon
> and as long as they are locked
> all your revolution remains
> only a prison mutiny
> to be put down
> by corrupted fellow prisoners
> —PETER WEISS, *Marat/Sade*

The vehemence of the moral outrage that bursts from the extract of Harold Pinter's speech about American prisons, which Kimball King and Thomas Fahy have included in this book, may surprise readers unfamiliar with Pinter's political statements or with his plays and films that deal with political themes. Pinter's ringing indictment of the U.S. penal system is especially relevant to his filmscript for *The Handmaid's Tale* (Feb. 1987), adapted from Margaret Atwood's novel (1985). His concluding line, that the United States "system [is] at one and the same time highly sophisticated and primitive, shaped in every respect to undermine the dignity of man," describes in its essence the dystopia he so convincingly evokes in his filmscript adaptation. In effect, the horror of political systems and governments that undermine the dignity of man is at the core of Pinter's political statements and vision.

Pinter scholars frequently write about his political plays as if they represent a major shift in his thematic focus, which is also reflected in his choice of directing assignments and his choice of novels to adapt for the cinema. On a basic level, Pinter's work in the 1980s is indeed about different subject matter from all those wondrous characters of his who are confined in their rooms, threatened by the outside world, challenged by the complexities of personal relationships. Pinter himself says that his growing involvement in politics and international affairs "came to a crux ... with the military coup in Chile in 1973" (Billington 287). Plays such as the brilliant *One for the Road* (1984), *Mountain Language* (1988), and *Party Time* (1991) certainly concentrate on political themes in more direct ways than, for example, *The Birthday Party* (1959). In a conversation with Mel Gussow in 1988, Pinter comments on the three "political films" he's worked on in the last two years, *The Handmaid's Tale* (1987), *Reunion* (1987), and *The Heat of the Day* (1988) (72). In that same interview, though, Pinter discusses the connections between his more overtly political works and his earlier work, which was occasionally castigated for its lack of social commitment. He describes his refusal to write a letter of clarification for Peter Wood, the director of *The Birthday Party,* but adds, "Between you and me, the play showed how the bastards ... how religious forces ruin our lives." The interrogation scene where Goldberg and McCann brainwash Stanley, the young man who has attempted to isolate himself in a shoddy house in a beachfront community, makes him over into a conforming, socially acceptable stereotype, evoking images of torture and "reeducation." Pinter concludes that the play implicitly calls for a revolt from such socially oppressive forces, especially in Petey's lines at the conclusion: "As Stan is taken away, Petey says, 'Stan, don't let them tell you what to do.' I've lived that line all my damn life. Never more than now" (70).

In short, Pinter's early "nonpolitical" work includes political implications, commentary about class, criticism of cowardly or escapist behavior, implicit criticism of social or governmental efforts to enforce conformity, and a good many other political themes—they just aren't so explicit. His political work in the 1980s also depends on his continuing subtle portrayal of character—it is not simple-mindedly polemical or shallow propaganda. Even in *One for the Road,* Pinter portrays the figure of the torturer in rich complexity. In conversation with Michael Billington, Pinter says, "It's difficult to write about something to which you know the answer. If you know that a brutal dictatorship is a bad thing, what are you going to do? Are you simply going to say, 'A brutal dictatorship is a bad thing'? I think that what I was finally able to do in *One for the Road* was to examine the psychology of a man who was an interrogator, a torturer, the head of an organisation, but was also a convinced passionate man of considerable faith; in other words, who believed in a number of things and fought for those ... was able to subject his victims to any amount of horror and humiliation for a just cause as he saw it. I believe that reflects, as you know, situations all over the world ... the question of a just cause" (294).

Pinter's "political works" are every bit as character centered as his earlier works; he dramatizes the negative political situation in more explicit ways, but he forces his audience to respond to the political horror with a new degree of understanding through his portrayal of the "villain" in such a way that we can understand, and perhaps even identify with, him or her and the temptation or thrill of all that power. That, of course, relates to his portrait of the Commander in *The Handmaid's Tale*. In the 1988 interview with Mel Gussow, Pinter comments, "There's a connection between all these concerns in the end, 'even in the very personal *Turtle Diary* and its lonely people'. . . . I feel the question of how power is used and how violence is used, how you terrorize somebody, how you subjugate somebody, has always been alive in my work" (73). The criticism of the governmental or social power structure, more explicit in the work of the 1980s, then, grows out of the personal from Pinter's characters, and there is either an explicit or implied admiration for those who resist, who choose to act courageously.

During a two-hour interview on October 26, 1994, Pinter spoke with Steven H. Gale and me about how pleased he was with his filmscript and the resulting film, *Reunion* (released 1989). He spoke about how the film included a much more personal emphasis than *Schindler's List,* clearly suggesting that he thought it among his best. Based on Fred Uhlman's 1971 novel, the film tells the story of a friendship between a young Jewish boy and an aristocratic German from the perspective of the old man that the Jewish lad has become (Jason Robards). Hans Strauss, we discover, has been sent to New York to live with an uncle; on his departure, rather than face the growing Nazi horror, his parents commit suicide by opening the gas jets in their home. Strauss, now aged, returns to Germany for the first time to try to discover what has happened to his friend, Konradin Von Lohenburg. Alternating between the old man's directly portrayed memories of his youthful friendship, and of Konraden's grudging sympathy with the Nazis, and Strauss's present attempts to discover what has happened to his friend in a Germany clearly not interested in dealing fully with its past, the film chillingly concludes with Strauss's discovery that his friend was one of the men whom Hitler hanged with piano wire after their attempt to assassinate him. Beginning with a mysterious shot of the prison execution chamber, Pinter's script is a subtle, brilliant adaptation of the novel, which fully captures its spirit while transforming it for the film medium, especially in terms of its structure and a complex alternation between past or memory time and present time. Pinter told Gale and me that in this film he thinks he manages to show the effects of a period of horrific, important history through the personal vision of one man whose life has been destroyed by those historical forces and by too many of his fellow citizens failures to resist them. Konraden, whose resistance has proved fatal, we understand as a man of moral courage, of a nobility that is spine-tingling in its selflessness and rightness.

All of Pinter's political works, including his script for *The Handmaid's Tale,* derive a worldview from the central perspective of one individual rather than attempting a more epic, sweeping vision. They are all the more effective because of that personalization, and they avoid the most serious aesthetic defect of "social" works of art, overt didacticism and self-satisfied superiority or condescension. Michael Billington dates this new political interest in Pinter's artistic work to his writing the filmscript for the unproduced *Victory,* based on Joseph Conrad's beautiful novel.[1] Brought to him by Richard Lester, Conrad's tale is not an explicitly political work, but, as Billington observes, "it deals with the dangers of human isolation and detachment from society" (289). Comparing the central thrust of the novel to *The Birthday Party,* Billington concludes that Pinter strips Conrad's story of its romantic rhetoric, exposing its themes more effectively: "as always in adapting another writer's work, Pinter reveals his own obsessions. . . . In showing the collapse of isolationist dreams in the face of human evil, he extends his own vision of the world: retreat into one's own private Eden is, he implies, no longer a possibility" (290).

Lena, in Conrad's novel and in Pinter's filmscript, is the most courageous character, the character who, in Paul Tillich's wonderful phrase, has "the courage to be." Kate, in *The Handmaid's Tale,* a prisoner in many different ways in a fascist, patriarchal, and theocratic society, gradually develops a similar courage in both novel and screenplay, but the Pinter version structures the story more effectively than does the novel to focus our attention on both the "evil"—the prison-like society—and the nobility of the courage to resist. Faithful to the spirit of the novel, he invents a new ending, evocatively portraying just how far his prisoner figure has evolved. In my first interview with Pinter, on May 15, 1984, he told me that in his script for L. P. Hartley's novel *The Go-Between* (1971), he thought that he had managed to remain true to the spirit of the novel despite his various changes in structure and emphases, and that he thought of the first-person narrator's visit to the young man at the end of the film as a courageous act, one that came, as in the novel, after a struggle for self-knowledge. In a good many of Pinter's films, he admires those characters who display a strength of will, the courage to resist forces of conformity or indoctrination, the self-assurance and strength to resist domination. And a good many such figures are women.

In the films, this includes Susan in his first film, *The Servant* (1963), and Jo in *The Pumpkin Eater* (1964). There is a grudging admiration for Marian in *The Go-Between,* who at least for a while violates her culture's dictates against sexual mingling with the lower classes. Even more markedly, Pinter admires Sarah's successful struggle in *The French Lieutenant's Woman* to overcome her Victorian society's dictates about class and sexuality; as he told me in our 1994 interview, he understands Mary in *The Comfort of Strangers* (1990), especially at its conclusion, to demonstrate a kind of courage in response to the horrors that have taken place in Venice. While Pinter also on occasion depicts his male characters responding with strength against oppression of various sorts, he shows a very clear pattern of choosing novels that embody tales of women's struggle against male or societal oppression, religious oppression, or simply their existential dilemma, and often of their triumph. No Pollyanna existentialist or Freudian mystic about that confrontation with death or the dark side, however, Pinter depicts his central figures, even when courageous, as often returning to subservience, failing, or perishing, as does the young German aristocrat in *Reunion,* or even Humbert Humbert in Pinter's unpublished script for *Lolita* (1994), despite their revolts or struggle for moral growth.[2] I find Pinter's summary line about his filmscript for Kafka's *The Trial* perhaps the most revealing as context for his central figure in *The Handmaid's Tale.* The thing he admires about Kafka's Josef K., is "The important thing . . . that he fights like hell all the way along the line" (Gussow 73).

In Atwood's novel and Pinter's adaptation, Kate exhibits some of that same courage. In the novel much of her struggle to find it emerges through internal monologues; in Pinter's script he invents imaginative equivalents for that internal voice and focuses on the horrors of Atwood's dystopia with specific reference to our own culture, society, and governance. Unfortunately, during the "collaborative" filmmaking process, the director and others jettisoned or revised large chunks of Pinter's script and its beautifully structured depiction of Kate's struggle toward courage and revolt from the prison of her society. When Faber and Faber published its three-volume collection of Harold Pinter's screenplays in the fall of 2000, Pinter chose to include among the sixteen scripts even *Langrishe, Go Down* (1978) and *The Heat of the Day* (1989); these had only been broadcast on television at the time of publication.[3] But Pinter chose not to publish his scripts for *The Handmaid's Tale, The Remains of the Day,* or *Lolita,* and three interesting tales lie behind those decisions.[4] Pinter very kindly provided me with a copy of *The Handmaid's Tale* script in its final typescript form, dated February 1987.[5] During our two-hour 1994 interview, Pinter told me that writing the script for *The Handmaid's Tale* had been a long and arduous project. With a number of other tasks to pursue in the spring of 1987, Pinter let go of the project, telling director Volker Schlondorf that he did not have the energy or the time to do more with the script. He suggested that Schlondorf consult with Margaret Atwood about any changes or revisions the director felt necessary. He intensely regretted granting that directorial *carte blanche,* though at the time, he thought, "After all, the author of the novel is not going to fuck up her own work." In 1992, he told much the same story to Mel Gussow: "What [Volker] Schlondorff really did was to get the actors to write a lot of it" (145). And in the Billington biography he says that "the thing became a hotchpotch. . . . I worked with Karel Reisz [*The French Lieutenant's Woman*] for about a year. There are big public scenes in the story and Karel wanted to do them with thousands of people" (299). The budget people refused, and Reisz withdrew. Pinter told Steve Gale and me that he was particularly displeased with the new conclusion for his script. Pinter said even then that he was so dissatisfied with the final product that he would not publish the screenplay.[6]

That Pinter's filmscript for *The Handmaid's Tale* is not readily available has dictated that very little has been written about it, for the film itself is not very good.[7] Both novel and film earned, at best, mixed reviews. Peter S. Prescott's review of the novel labeled its plot formulaic with regard to both its portrayal of sex and the resistance movement" (70). In a more recent article occasioned by the release of a new opera, *The Handmaid's Tale* by Danish composer Poul Ruders, Anthony Tommasini writes that the opera frees the novel from its sermonizing by concentrating on the dramatic situations and the internal struggle of the characters, not so much on the politics. He concludes that the film adaptation did not do that. Ironically, Pinter's script did, as we will see.

In 1986, Daniel Wilson, who hired Pinter to write the screenplay and the soon-to-depart Karel Riesz to direct, wrote that they would not make this typical science fiction: "we're not going to focus on the hardware. . . . The script will be concerned with people, emotions, characters" (*Daily Variety,* n.p.). But after the film was made with the much-revised script, which reviewers *thought* Pinter had written, a number of extremely ironic reviews appeared. The *Rolling Stone* review suggested that "The movie plays even sillier than it sounds." The reviewer goes on to write, "It's hard to believe that playwright Pinter could have come up with this bilge" (*Rolling Stone* 36). Jack Kroll wrote that the film "contains most of the defects of Margaret Atwood's 1985 anti-utopian novel and almost none of the virtues." He suggests that the book's stream of consciousness at least lets us get to know the heroine, concluding, "Astonishingly, Harold Pinter's screenplay becomes a tissue of absurdities" (Kroll 54). And Stanley Kauffman finds no chill in the film "because the consistency is thin and the imagination isn't vivid, even though the screenplay is by Harold Pinter." He finally notes that Pinter, at times a genius in his scriptwriting, could have "raised [Atwood's novel] out of sexy futurist soap opera. Instead, almost lazily, Pinter has merely trailed after Atwood and produced garish science fiction" (Kauffman 26–27).

Unfairly, the script the reviewers blamed on Pinter wasn't his, but an uneven structural and pedestrian disaster put together by a committee of the director, the actors, and Margaret Atwood herself. Where Pinter had honed and restructured for the medium, inventing dramatically rendered scenes to replace or work toward the effect of the internal monologues in the novel, Atwood goes back and replaces some of Pinter's inventions with her own scenes and reinserts some of the material he had excised. Perhaps that's a natural tendency on the author's part, but it destroyed the structural cohesiveness of the Pinter script and obliterates much of our understanding of Kate's moral or identity-seeking journey, as well as our sympathy for her. The final scenes that the "collaborative process" in the film provide, at the expense of Pinter's coherent ending, add a layer of melodrama and claptrap, which is even antifeminist, and which destroys any possibility of considering the film seriously. And a good bit of that has to do with the actors' ham-handed improvising, especially Robert Duvall, whom the director desperately needed to bring to heel.

In the May 17, 1989, *New York Times,* Myra Forsberg writes that Du-vall, unlike some of the cast, finds Pinter's language "'elusive.'" Duvall opines, "'It's limbo language; he doesn't really know American. So I change it sometimes—I just do it. We had big arguments on the set of *Lonesome Dove* about changing the script,' he says, smiling. As for the novel, 'I only read a few pages and then gave up on it.'" His girlfriend hated it, he notes, and he goes on to praise many fundamentalists in the United States (Forsberg H-1, 13). Film buffs may well remember Duvall's obsession with his project *The Apostle* as they ponder this remarkable display of hubris. Forsberg also cites director Schlondorff saying that we "felt that we had to expand Pinter's script, explain how the Republic of Gilead came to happen, things like that. . . . But during rehearsals, we eliminated everything we had incorporated because we felt it was our job to tell the story—not explain the premise. Now the script is as straight and lean as Pinter's original draft" (13). Well, no.

In Gerald Peary's *LA Times* article on the film, he implicitly makes clear in his interview with Atwood why the revision of Pinter's script fails so miserably. Peary cites Atwood as having talked to Pinter a great deal before he wrote the screenplay, but also writes that she had "some reservations about compacting past and present time in Pinter's script" (Peary 39). She doesn't clarify that she revised or eliminated many of these past-time or memory sequences, which provide, subtly and in filmically effective ways, the material that her own stream-of-consciousness musings in the novel did. Pinter's metaphors for Atwood's stream of consciousness allow us both to sympathize more warmly with Kate and to recognize her moral growth. An interview with director Volker Schlondorff by David Denicola makes clear the centrality of Atwood's role in the post-Pinter revisions: Pinter talked with Atwood a lot, says Schlondorff. And then, by implication later in the process, "Oh yes, Margaret Atwood worked more on this picture than Pinter did (Denicola n.p.).

Karel Reisz's initial involvement with the project was a central reason for Pinter's attraction to the novel as an adaptation project, along with the increasing political emphasis in the 1980s in both his personal/social and artistic life. Billington writes that Pinter's "wrestling with a script based on a nightmare vision of America" was entirely complementary to his "attacks on American foreign policy in the real world," particularly his increasing involvement in the defense of human rights in Nicaragua against the U.S.–backed Contras, who, Pinter wrote, "'murdered and mutilated . . . thousands of Nicaraguan men, women and children. . . . They have been raped, skinned, beheaded and castrated'" (Billington 304–5). The brilliant potential of the re-pairing of Reisz and Pinter that producer Daniel Wilson arranged, the duo that brought *The French Lieutenant's Woman* to the screen, had it continued, would perhaps have produced another masterpiece. The strength of *The French Lieutenant's Woman,* in part, lies in Pinter's script managing to tell movingly an epic tale, nothing less than a culture's transition from the premodern to the modern. Through an individual's, Sarah's, very moving, mysterious, and wondrous history, and set against the revealing backdrop of her age, Pinter's script contrasts that earlier culture with the modern culture of the movie crew, which is filming the nineteenth-century story of Sarah's courageous search for an identity beyond her particular type of social prison. Like *French Lieutenant,* Pinter's script for *The Handmaid's Tale,* in contrast to the film itself, is brilliantly evocative in its picture of a culture, this one in the very near future, in its linking of Atwood's dystopic society, which is a multicelled prison, to elements of our contemporary culture. It moves us with its portrait of a woman who gradually rediscovers her courage and perhaps helps to change her world.

The Harold Pinter Archive at the British Library includes three boxes of materials related to *The Handmaid's Tale,* boxes 62, 63, and 64.[8] The boxes are very randomly organized, but box 63 includes a collection of clippings from various newspapers and magazines that Pinter has collected. These substantiate his vision that the abuses Atwood details in her novel, and that he images in his adaptation, are reflective of our world today: that we comfortable folk who aren't immediately affected simply ignore the obvious, an indictment that rings particularly harshly given parallels to the "good Germans" of Nazi Germany and to our own willful ignorance of our outlandishly horrifying criminal justice and penal system. A good many of both Pinter's (and Atwood's) references are clearly meant to remind us of the horror of the Nazi era, but without the hysteria that frequently accompanies such associations. The film, in my opinion, moves toward the simplistic in this area, unlike both novel and original Pinter script. For example, one of the articles from the clippings file describes the spread of the practice of surrogate motherhood, with its overtones of the wealthy elite hiring social inferiors (*New York Times,* Oct. 6, '86); another discusses an Islamic law allowing "temporary" marriages, often with prisoners (*London Times,* June 2, 1986); a third describes abductions of politically errant women and their children in Argentina; a fourth describes the Nazi practice of allowing the elite to father children on "volunteers" (the *lebensborn*) and encouraging SS married men without children to find additional partners. Perhaps most horrifying, one article describes the torture of women prisoners in Iran, with a special emphasis on flaying their feet and on requiring women to torture or execute others to demonstrate repentance. Two articles detail Christian right-wing anti-Semitism in the United States, and another article on torture of women prisoners in Iran includes a very disturbing portrait of their being forced to view a hanging and its aftermath. Finally, Pinter includes an article on fundamentalist Pat Roberts seeking the American presidency. All of these practices are reflected in Pinter's script, less melodramatically than in the film itself, where, for example, the "B-grade" music is offensive in its didactic obviousness and heavy-handedness in underlying these horrors.

The second major reason for Pinter's attraction to the novel as a suitable adaptation project surely involves Atwood's depiction of Kate's wrestling with her reactions to her new status as prisoner and concubine, as "handmaid" to the oppressive forces that have taken over her world. Atwood essentially describes Kate's thoughts vacillating between despair and its ultimate consequence, suicide, as opposed to revolt, which can range from minor to major actions, assertions, or refusals of despair in a situation that would seem to call for it. Atwood also movingly shows Kate weakening at times, refusing either despair or revolt, hoping, in a very human way, simply to survive. In the novel, Kate progresses through many stages, one step backward, two steps forward, like the inmates at the finale of *Marat/Sade,* as she contemplates her present imprisoned situation in contrast to her past freedom, as she guiltily contemplates some of her actions or her failures to act, as she thinks about her surrender to her metaphoric jailers *and* of her potential for revolt. Much of her progression toward courage springs from her memories of her daughter and of her husband, who in the novel may not be dead but literally imprisoned as a "political," in danger of being hanged on "the wall." Kate's hunger for love, though, her wish to move beyond her horrible isolation, is also central to her growth in the novel. This is the kernel of interest, the spirit of the novel, it seems to me, that Pinter says he must always find, through which he can proceed to work on an adaptation, the something that moves him beyond the rather pedestrian notion that patriarchal theocracies and dictatorships are bad.

For example, the novel opens in the training center where the potential handmaidens are conditioned for their roles as surrogate mothers for elite couples. (Because of environmental catastrophe, these elite couples are sterile, although they never test the men, of course.) Kate muses, "We yearned for the future," and they would have been willing to trade their bodies to the guards for a chance at escape. "How did we learn it, this talent for insatiability?" This lust for freedom, she tells us, was in the air. And, by implication, it is one characteristic response of prisoners to the destruction of their freedom, at least at first (Atwood 4). But there are many options for dealing with incarceration, with the reduction by one's society to the status of a nonperson without the ability to choose. The suicide of the Commander's former handmaid is a constantly recurring motif in the novel, but that's balanced, in Kate's thinking, by a chair, sunlight, flowers: "These are not to be dismissed. I am alive. I live, I breathe" (10). At this early stage, Kate concludes, I won't think. "Thinking can hurt your chances, and I intend to last" (10).

The motives for such surrender, of course, are the constraints, the limits of the choices this patriarchal theocracy imposes on her. The system of the handmaids, very loosely based on—or justified by—the very strange Biblical tale of Jacob and Rachel (*Genesis* 30) is enforced by the "alternatives," by what will happen to these young, fertile women if they refuse this service to the state's elite. Kate can commit suicide, or she can resist in various ways that might result in torture, execution, or in going to "the colonies," places where slave laborers are reduced to skin and bones in the midst of environmental mayhem that destroys one's body in a matter of months. (Early on in the novel, there are various hints—such as black market cigarettes—of a revolutionary community, another alternative, the possibility of trading something for something else that is illicit. These hints finally build to the revelation of the "Mayday" group.) And in contrast to these various, almost equally unacceptable alternatives, Atwood gives us Kate's memories of freedom, the life before imprisonment, life with her job, her husband, Luke, and her child, Jill, both captured, in the novel, in their attempt to escape Gilead, to cross the border into Canada. As we discover that the theocracy has made it illegal for women to work, to read, or to own property or money, novel we "hear" Kate remembering her and Luke's dream of buying a big old house to fix up: "Such freedom now seems almost weightless" (32).

Though she continues to meditate on alternatives, the constraints of Kate's situation in the novel have lulled her into guilty inaction; she's guilty about passivity, about going along. But in the closet, one day, she discovers scratched into the floor, "*Nolite te bastardes carborundorum,*" written by her predecessor, the Commander and his wife's former Handmaid who has committed suicide by hanging herself from her light fixture. The phrase means, "Don't let the bastards grind you down." But Kate learns this translation from the Commander in his study, where he has insisted she secretly and regularly join him in defiance of the rules of this "prison," and she concludes that her predecessor must have learned the Latin phrase in this room, from the Commander—and that his wife, the evangelist Serena Joy, simply replaced her, like a dead dog, when she discovered such treason (243). Understandably, Kate wavers. "If my life is bearable, maybe what they're doing is right after all," she thinks. But she *also* recognizes that she has something on the Commander: his illicit behavior and the possibility of her own death and his guilt; this gives her something to trade, some level of power, however ultimately impotent (243). Such pittances, such crumbs, though, are not enough, not given that insatiable urge for freedom, which ebbs and swells throughout the novel.

In essence, on the one hand, *through Kate's musings* Atwood emphasizes the horrific punishment and the efficient indoctrination—hanging for one's "crimes" as an example for the others, torture of various forms, brainwashing, stun guns, the colonies—as a set of cultural tools to keep these "prisoners" under control as "nonpersons"; and on the other hand, through Kate's musings we see several motives, rationales, for not yielding, for revolt, or hope. One is the very human nature, the lust for freedom, for free will, that Atwood describes as the novel opens, however limited or even destructive. A second motive is the example of others braver than oneself who violate the system, who risk everything for escape or power. Here, Moira is Kate's touchstone, in both novel and filmscript, though in the novel she is much more thoroughly developed as Kate's longtime friend. A third motive for going beyond mere endurance, of course, is Kate's longing for her daughter, who in the novel has been captured during the escape attempt and adopted by one of the elite families. And a fourth reason to refuse surrender of self is her need for love, which takes a number of different forms. These areas, in effect, provide a rationale for living under horrific conditions; always tempted to despair, Kate still lusts for freedom, for life itself; she hungers for friendships that are exemplary, inspiring, comforting; she longs for family; and she is desperate for love. In the novel, this last is complicated by both the fact that her husband may well be alive, imprisoned as a "political," and by her consequent guilt at yielding both to the role of handmaid and to loving Nick, the Commander's aide-de-camp, desperate for physical affection, closeness. In her musings, too, we see Kate's attraction to the power of the captor, who provides relief from her boredom and who seems to treat her at times almost as an individual, and to flout the rules himself.

In sum, Atwood's portrait of Kate as she struggles with her imprisonment, with her loss of freedom, family, and lover/husband, is a complex one, realistic in its portrayal of wavering strength and weakness under unbearable conditions and the constant threat of torture or execution. In the novel, such wavering continues until the very end. Serena Joy has discovered that the Commander has been seeing Kate in his study, violating what she regards as his sacred marriage vows, which the regime supposedly upholds and views as essential to the patriarchy, *and* that he has taken Kate to the luxurious and illicit sex club for the elite, staffed by other politicals and undesirables of various sorts, including Moira, whose escape attempt has failed. After recognizing her love for Nick, Kate finds this disaster of Serena Joy's discovery nearly unbearable. She also discovers in the novel that her other friend Ofglen, a member of the Mayday resistance, has hanged herself when her rebel status was discovered. Kate declares to herself, "It was better," as she waits for the guardian's van to arrive (366). But at the same time, she feels great relief: "She has died that I may live," she muses, knowing that under torture Ofglen would have given up her name as a Mayday sympathizer. Now, she determines to repent, renounce, forget about others. Counter to our expectations, she renounces her progress, her drive for rebellious friendship and love; she goes up to her room, sits, and waits for her punishment, convinced that Serena Joy has turned her in (367–69). But then Kate begins to think again, coming out of her fog. She contemplates all kinds of action: suicide, escape, begging the Commander, attacking Serena Joy, going to Nick's room to plead for shelter (373–75). But she does none of these things, waiting, with Beckett-like overtones. Just as she is leaning once more toward suicide, she hears the black van arrive and muses, "I've been wasting my time. I should have taken things into my own hands while I had the chance. I should have stolen a knife from the kitchen, found some way to the sewing scissors. There were the garden shears, the knitting needles; the world is full of weapons if you're looking for them. I should have paid attention" (376).

This ambiguous passage can certainly be read in a variety of ways, but, in context, I understand it to suggest that Kate wishes that she had commandeered any of these weapons to use against her oppressors, that she has learned that inaction is ignoble and self-defeating, the knowledge, near tragically, apparently coming too late. One might also understand the lines to suggest that she wishes she had committed suicide before the worse punishment she expects descends on her. But the more positive reading certainly serves as one impetus for several of Pinter's decisions in his adaptation, his invention of the scene where she kills the Commander. Suddenly, though, in the novel, it is Nick at the door, urging her to trust him, telling her that the black van is really the Mayday resistance coming to rescue her. And, even near despair, she "snatch[es] at this offer. It's all I'm left with" (377). So, as the book concludes, a still-passive Kate is swept out the door, rescued by the menfolk and her true love, feeling sorry for her henpecked Commander, who thinks she is really being arrested and may rat on his illicit activities, though Serena Joy, wanting that baby, has *not* turned her in, ironically. As Kate steps into the van, irresolute to the end but still grasping at courage and life, she muses to herself, "Whether this is my end or a new beginning I have no way of knowing: I have given myself over into the hands of strangers, because it can't be helped. And so I step up into the darkness within; or else the light" (378).

Ignoring the extremely facile, awkward, satiric coda in the novel—an academic conference attempting to evaluate the document of the "Handmaid's Tale" and the Gilead period—what we have here, in bare bones essence, is a fairy-tale ending in Atwood's novel, where a prince in shining armor rescues the helpless lady fair. It's a surprising ending for a writer of Atwood's feminist reputation, and a very weak one. In his filmscript Pinter improves upon it considerably and manages to capture the spirit of the novel as a whole, which—I would suggest—Atwood's ending to the film weakens considerably.

Pinter's restructuring of the novel's chronology, his filmic equivalents for Kate's stream-of-consciousness meditations, and his important inventions, in addition to his subtle choices about what not to include in his script, make of this dystopia what potentially would have been a much more aesthetically pleasing and emotionally moving film than the one we have. The most important of the inventions: (1) in Pinter's version, Jill, Kate's and Luke's child, has escaped capture as her family has attempted to cross the border into Canada, though Luke has been killed; (2) Pinter invents several scenes with Nick and Kate that emphasize that their love, growing far beyond their physical need, is the result of their free choice, not merely their obeying Serena Joy's dictate that they join with her in plotting to get Kate pregnant, since it is clear that the Commander is sterile; (3) in Pinter's script, and in the final film, Kate finally *acts,* no longer waiting, and kills the Commander in his study using a knife hidden in her room by the Mayday resistance movement. Unfortunately, in keeping this ending, the script-by-committee also reverts to Atwood's initial notion that the child has been adopted by the elite and adds one of the soppiest voice-over endings of the rescued lady fair I've ever endured. Both of these decisions undermine the much more subtle, emotional conclusion that Pinter provides and, again, make Kate appear weak and unsympathetic, living for the purposes of the men of the rebellion. In effect she's just changed her jailers.

Pinter's radical revision of the novel's ending and of the results of the meditations of its central figure might seem, at first glance, to violate the "spirit of the novel" which Pinter always pays homage to. I would argue that Pinter's version is more true to the spirit of the novel as a whole than Atwood's own ending, which has the feel of being tacked on, unresolved, somewhat like Mark Twain's concluding chapters for *Huckleberry Finn.* Pinter's restructuring of the novel for the film medium strengthens the work.

In his 1996 conversation with Michael Billington at the National Film Theatre, Pinter says: "I simply told the story [of Robin Maugham's novella *The Servant*], but it emerged with a slightly different perspective. It's also a lot to do with your interpretation. Other people could take the author's original interpretation, but I want to make it absolutely clear that the only point of doing a screenplay of a novel is to be faithful to the intentions of the book *as I understand it*" (my emphasis, Pinter, in Billington, *Various Voices* 56). When Billington asks Pinter about his invention of the rape scene in *Accident,* based on Nicholas Mosley's fine novel, Pinter responds, "I just felt it was a logical progression from two points of view. One is the emotion which is unleashed in the light of the accident; and the second in relation to power. I felt that . . . Stephen chose to exercise the power which he actually possessed at that moment." He goes on to comment that Mosley saw the logic of the change and finally agrees with Billington's comment, that, as an adapter, "the story becomes yours. . . . " Pinter replies, "I think that's inevitable. But as long as you are expressing the nut of the whole thing—the core of it—I do believe you're keeping faith with it. If you respect it—and there's no other way of writing a screenplay adaptation of a novel—then you can't do it down, you can't be false to it." In effect, he concludes, I try to find "the inner world of the novel" (56).

To some purists of literal adaptation that may sound like heresy, but Pinter's scripts, in the opinion of many critics and reviewers, often improve on the original novels, in aesthetic integrity, unity, *quiditas,* especially the weaker ones he's adapted. I would include in that category *The Servant, The Quiller Memorandum,* and a few others as well as *The Handmaid's Tale.* Even with these, Pinter finds that kernel, the spirit of the novel as it moves him, and he struggles to produce a screenplay that is a work of art, that satisfies his rigorous demands upon himself. After careful review of the myriad boxes of materials on the films in the Pinter Archive, it becomes clear that Pinter approaches the task of adaptation with repeated intensely close readings of the novels, and that he does considerable research on sources for the novel's period, reception, background, whatever he feels necessary. In the case of *The French*

Lieutenant's Woman, for example, the relevant boxes include many of Pinter's notes on this close reading process; I'm especially impressed with his lists of the literary quotations, often pairs of literary quotations, with which John Fowles begins his chapters. Pinter includes the ones he finds most important in his notes, and he has clearly used those references as he structures his radical adaptation. In this instance, where Fowles's novel includes the observations of a twentieth-century narrator looking back upon the nineteenth century and commenting on the radical differences between the two eras, and on the radical silliness of some stereotypes about the two eras, Pinter invents a second strand for the novel, the story of the film crew making a movie about the nineteenth-century tale. This modern plot line, with its parallel love stories and betrayals, provides a filmic equivalent for the narrator's twentieth-century voice that is far less artificial than a voice-over would have been. In other words, Pinter's solution to this problem of how to incorporate the spirit of the novel, to project it on to the screen through dramatic equivalencies and inventions, is so suited to the medium that he is working in, film, as to be a brilliant parallel to Fowles's device, in which a narrator commenting on a tale from an earlier period becomes a twentieth-century frame story commenting on the tale from an earlier period. The irony in the film form or genre is of course more indirect, more dramatic, in its commentary and thematic implications than the original, but that is the very nature of the form, its dependence on imagery and on the audience making plot and thematic connections. Fowles wrote, in his famous introduction to the published version of the script: "I do not think of the present script as a mere 'version' of my novel; but as the blueprint ... of a brilliant metaphor for it. . . . I am sure that viable transitions from the one medium to the other need just such an imaginative leap" (xii). Fowles also comments that Pinter's "genius has a further string, and that seems to me to be his truly remarkable gift for reducing the long and complex without distortion" (xi).

In Pinter's adaptation of *The Handmaid's Tale,* both talents—the imaginative leaps of invention and the gift for compression—resulted in a script that is a wonderful metaphor for the spirit of Atwood's novel, one more pleasingly structured in this instance than the original and more powerful in its delivery of the central thematic emphases as they relate to the character of the central figure. The contrast with the film that emerged is simply startling.

Steven Gale has long argued that when Pinter writes a screenplay, "he creates a unique work of art, different from its source and capable of standing on its own as a work of art" (85), and he continues to do so in his wonderful new book on the screenplays, in press as I write. "Structure," of course, is a hugely complex word, referring not only to the plot, the "ordering of events," but to how plot relates to character, how image patterns comment on character and theme, how repeated motifs unify the work and draw straight or ironic parallels, even how ambiguity may be resolved through a vision of the whole. Pinter's discipline, his structuring of all of his works, is not obvious or stilted; it is organic, for want of a better word, and beautiful in its subtlety. The central challenge in adapting *The Handmaid's Tale* is to deal with the interior voice of the novel and the relationship of its central figure to events in her past, but to do so for the screen. To start with the ordering of events, Atwood begins her narrative as Kate comments on life in the indoctrination center for handmaid candidates and then leaps to a scene much later at the Commander's home as Kate, now called Offred (of Fred, the Commander), contemplates her cell-like room and her new life as glorified concubine in a patriarchal theocracy. In the novel, these musings over past events—and they're all past events since the narrator reveals early on that she has escaped to write this narrative—jump around in an achronological fashion. That's certainly a legitimate, even pleasing, novelistic structuring of events, and Pinter has successfully followed such a path in other screenplays. Here, though, he revises that basic arrangement, making the narrative chronological but achieving the equivalence of the stream-of-consciousness musings with flashes of memory from Kate's perspective at crucial moments in her story. The film itself keeps the basic chronological structure but omits many of the memory sequences, which destroys the unity of Pinter's solution.

A few examples from the Pinter script of how this restructuring of the novel's events works in conjunction with the memory sequences in Pinter's script should suffice to clarify how the various elements of the adaptation fit together so beautifully and unobtrusively. The filmscript begins with Kate and Luke's attempt to escape across the border into Canada. The first eight pages of his script include no dialogue except the warnings from the border patrol thugs and the prison guards, that is, the "Aunts" or "wardresses," and the oppressed women speaking as a group of indoctrinated puppets. Pinter's detailed camera and scene directions specify that the film opens with a shot of an empty valley, a billboard in the foreground with "Fly American Airlines," telling us where we are. The only caption in his script is "A Few Years From Now," as opposed to the film's fairy-tale-cute labeling, "Once upon a time / in the recent future / a country went wrong. / The Country was called / The Republic of Gilead"—which undercuts from the beginning the tension developed in Pinter's script. In Pinter's version, we see, at first in long shot, Luke, Kate, and Jill, age five, get out of a Volkswagen, carrying rucksacks and skis, not the pathetic plastic sled of the film; the sled diminishes our opinion of their intelligence and preparation and strength. As the family trudges through the woods in Pinter's script, we see them "THROUGH BINOCULARS," which makes the tension level mount, of course, as we watch Luke attach Jill's skis to her feet. We cut to the border patrolman looking through the binoculars, then back to the family coming out of the woods, as border patrol's voice booms out from an electric megaphone, warning them to turn back or be shot.

Pinter continues this classic cutting as we watch Luke suddenly come out of the woods, beginning to ski down the left side of the valley. The nowmobile pursues him, as a patrolman stays behind with a rifle. We cut to Kate and Jill on the ridge, back to Luke being pursued by the nowmobile, back to Kate and Jill skiing down the right side of the valley, Luke skiing, and Kate skiing. As we're focused on Kate, we hear a shot ring out; her head jerks around, which causes her to lose her balance, and she twists and falls. We focus on Jill, gliding, slowing, stopping, and looking back up the hill. We cut to the patrolman with Luke's dead body; we see Kate and Jill through binoculars, Kate grimacing with pain in the snow, Jill beyond her, looking up; Kate tries to stand, holds her leg, screaming, and collapses; Jill moves up the hill, but Kate "signals frantically to her, pointing down the hill." And Jill "turns and skis down the valley," as we cut to the nowmobile crossing the valley and watch the patrolman take aim at Jill and shoot. The final cut, telling us what we so desperately want to know, is to a shot of Jill escaping, skiing down the valley. And we fade out. Pinter details this action as fifteen shots, in what I've labeled Scene Sequence I, in the Pinter script.

The film has kept Pinter's basic idea of beginning with the capture of the family but mars its economy and invents scandalously bad dialogue to boot, destroying Pinter's elevated tension and our intense sympathy for these three victims. We don't see the American Airlines billboard, but we get an expanded picture of the family journeying up to the valley in a spiffy SUV; we see the group walking through the woods with the little girl whining that she's tired, which undercuts the admiration for her courage that Pinter develops. Flashing lights are our first indicator of trouble in the film, as opposed to the more sinister binocular shot in the script, which suggests something like "Big Brother is watching" almost subliminally, and incidentally echoes a similar technique in Pinter's *The Comfort of Strangers* script. And where Pinter's script lets the audience draw the conclusion that Luke is bravely distracting the border patrol from his wife and child, the film has him say, "I'll keep 'em busy," a pathetic line that distrusts the audience's interpretive abilities and could have come from a B-grade Western. In the film version, as in the novel, Jill is apparently captured; Kate manages to rush after Jill in the film as we see and hear her crying "NO!!" at both Luke's death and her daughter's capture.

The effect of the Pinter version is to underline the courage of all three; in the film version, all three come across as a bit silly and weak by comparison. In Pinter's script, we're especially impressed with young Jill's calm strength and in her discipline at following her mother's wishes, courageously skiing off alone down the valley. The tension in the Pinter version is horrific; it's Kate's love for her husband, as she twists her head around to see what has happened to him, that causes her to fall, ironically; and the fact that the patrolman shoots at Jill underlines his inhumanity, as does the border patrol's willingness to abandon a helpless child to the wilderness, as one apparently useless for their purposes. The film does keep the Pinter invention of Luke's death, but then melodramatic music blares out as we cut to the prison compound. In Pinter's version, the only dialogue we hear from the future handmaids is their mechanically following Aunt Lydia's dictates as they respond, in unison, "We are very well, Aunt Lydia," and, "We are the lucky ones," their wills already sapped.

Both film and Pinter's script cut to the bus taking the "lucky ones" from the prison to the almost equally restrictive handmaid center, but in Pinter's script the institution and its furnishings are much scruffier than in the designer-perfect world of the film. The depiction of the oppression is both more economic and less melodramatic, and we see the first memory sequence as Kate peers at her image in the bus window on the way to her new and unknown destiny. Her memory flash is represented by a shot of Kate and Luke walking down a street in summer, Jill on Luke's shoulders, all laughing, free. And that bus ride, in Pinter's script, is interrupted by a roadblock where we learn that there is terrorist activity in the neighborhood. In short, we are notified of alternatives, of resistance, of hope beyond the walls, much earlier in the Pinter script than in the film, which provides additional context both for our understanding of Kate's actions and for our understanding of subtle indicators in the film that there is a subculture of resistance – especially given Pinter's emphasis in shot 25 of Kate, watching the soldier from the roadblock leaving the bus, fascinated with the idea of the resistance movement. Pinter's second memory sequence is again clearly connected to the action of the "real-time" scene. The women are repeating Aunt Lydia's prayer, at her command, "Oh God make us fruitful," in shot 27, when we cut to a memory flash in shot 28 of Jill skiing down the valley. Over this we hear a sudden scream from real time, and we cut to shot 29, two aunts dragging a girl out who has been caught masturbating and is clearly to be tortured.

In the Pinter script, then, the memory flashes let us know that Kate longs for the freedom that she has had with husband and daughter, is contemplative and mourning the loss of her husband, and is frightened but hopeful about the fate of her escaping daughter—a touchstone, a structural element that will characterize her actions and her vacillation from now on. The film includes far fewer memory sequences, and the first one is not linked effectively to real-time events; it follows the melodramatic sequence of women being herded into livestock trucks and is represented by a shot of Jill wandering in the snow calling out for her mother. Again, this shot underlines Jill's weakness, not her strength as in Pinter's version, and it seemingly contradicts the notion that Kate finds out about Jill's capture in the film only later, when Serena Joy reveals her adoption into the elite family. The decision to "invent" this shot in place of Pinter's more subtly patterned memories was perhaps meant to underline that Kate doesn't know what happened to Jill, but with the concurrent decision to revert back to the novel's emphasis that she's been adopted, it obviates Pinter's very strong ending, which involves Kate's remarkable reunion with her daughter across the border in Canada. In short, the film omits a good many of the Pinter memory sequences, almost all of the ones involving

Luke, and thus loses the Pinter script's very subtle emphasis on Kate's thought processes.

Pinter begins his script with the scene of the capture both because this relatively straightforward chronology of real-time events will support his more adventurous structuring of the memory sequences; by making the chronology clear, he can be assured that the audience is not too bewildered by his interspersing Kate's memory flashes with the real-time plot of the film. More subtly, the decision is structural in the broader sense, in that his version underlines the courage of all three members of the family and emphasizes how important their familial and sexual love has been to them—and by extension, just how much Jill values freedom and hates the oppressive regime. That decision, in turn, works cohesively with his decision to conclude his script with the invented scene of Kate's successfully crossing the border and finding Jill, in an absolutely gorgeous reunion scene.

In his script, after Kate has been rescued by Mayday, Pinter provides a three-part coda. First we see a shot of the underground railroad, represented by a house in the country, at dawn, a new beginning. Kate gets out of an anonymous car as it pulls up, dressed in a short leather jacket and skirt. We see and hear the owners of the house tell Kate that it's set for tomorrow at dawn, and we watch a television broadcast about Nick's successfully fooling the authorities and going on with his undercover work for Mayday. Shot 179 begins the second part of the coda, a recitative of the first scene of the film, as we watch Kate standing on a ridge with a man who is fitting skis to her feet while the helicopters buzz in the background. She declares, "I haven't skied in . . . years," a typical Pinter pause suggesting both fear of ineptitude and joy at a return to some form of normalcy, and she sets off across the valley. Our tension, of course, is palpable, given the first scene. And part three of the coda begins with shot 180, a Canadian country street, an ice cream wagon, girls in short skirts, boys riding bicycles. In the midst of this scene of normalcy, we hear "Sounds of children" as Kate arrives at a school fence and looks through, where, with her, we focus on Jill, playing a ball game with other children, unaware of her mother. Shot 182 shows Kate gazing at Jill through the wire, evocatively emblematic, of course, of her past imprisonment, and walking along the side of the fence, and going into the school. The last line in Pinter's script, as Kate goes into the building to reunite with her daughter, is: "The laughter of children."

Now, that's a powerful scene sequence, imagistically suggesting Kate's continuing courage and will to action, her willingness to risk capture again to regain her daughter, *and* the fact that she does this on her own, not as the recipient of a man's largesse. The ending is balanced, though, not doctrinaire: a man helps her, after all, part of the family who runs that underground railroad effort, but she manages the escape on her own, with her own strength and courage. The laughter of children, a sound we never hear in the Republic of Gilead, the normal play activities, ice cream, short skirts, are all images that contradict the restrictive, imprisoning puritanism we have seen carried to such horrific extremes. And the fact that the underground railroad and the Mayday resistance movement are still operating gives us cause for hope that the laughter of children may once again be heard south of this snowy border. This is very similar to the image that ends Pinter's unpublished script for *Lolita,* and to the invented but finally unpublished scenes with which he ends his manuscript final draft for *The Comfort of Strangers* (British Archive ms. version). All three images carry with them the tenor, the suggestion, of the profound growth of a central character and a heartfelt, perhaps surprising to some, paean to "normalcy," the joy of family and of children, freely pursuing their own interests, without undue intrusion from oppressive forces, be they sexual, social, religious, or governmental. In this instance, too, the image "makes the wheel round" by establishing a pleasing formal unity with the film's beginning image and by completing a subtly presented pattern of suggestions that Kate has achieved a type of growth, a renewal of moral courage in spite of adversity, that no longer leaves her "waiting" or despairing.

In marked contrast, the film version of *The Handmaid's Tale* ends with Kate pleading with Nick that she wants to go with him after heavy-handed scenes in the escape van, and with her crying out her need—to Nick—to find her daughter. As she repeats that she wants to come with him, "Please don't leave me," Nick promises to find her later, reiterating that he must stay in the field. The scene shifts to televison propaganda telling us that the rebels are isolated and will be defeated and a statement from the now-dead Commander promising victory. Now that last is ironic, of course, but after the announcer describes house-to-house searches in pursuit of Offred. We watch the film's perfectly straight conclusion, prefaced by gentle piano music. As she gets water from a campfire outside her silver Airstream trailer, Kate says, "I don't know whether this is the end for me or a new beginning." That's very, very close to Atwood's language in the last paragraphs of the novel; it returns us to seeing Kate as weak and indecisive. In the film she concludes, "But I'm safe here in the mountains, held by the rebels," a dog wagging its tail as she goes inside. "They bring me food and sometimes a message from Nick. And so I wait. I wait for my baby to be born into a different world." None of this is Pinter language, and it's so soppy I think that Natasha Richardson has a hard time delivering it. In the film, Kate concludes this saccharin monologue: "I still dream about Jill. About them telling her I don't exist," as the music gets more somber, "or that I never existed." With the music positively glowing now, she adds, "But I know we're going to find her. She will remember me," Kate's eyes shining, as we focus on her face, in beautiful sunset lighting. The thing is positively amateurish, ending a film—a medium or genre ideally based on images—with a voice-over, a sunset rather than a dawn, and an empty-sounding promise to act, which Kate delivers while still waiting for a man, in an Airstream trailer, isolated in the mountains, beyond the fighting, immobile.

The British archive includes at least four versions of the concluding scenes or coda from the Pinter script, some of them quite different from each other; he clearly worked hard to establish the appropriate tone for his well-structured, echoing conclusion. He also labored over his second major invention, that is Kate murdering the Commander, which goes through multiple revisions. Once more, this scene in the Pinter script brilliantly fits into its overall structure, which depends on Pinter's revision of Kate's relationship with Nick.

In the novel, after their initial scenes, Nick comes upon Offred in the sitting room where she's gone to try to steal something; she'd like a knife from the kitchen but isn't quite ready for that. They kiss, at his urging, and she starts to reach for his fly, but they both think it too risky. He finally reveals that the Commander has told him to come looking for her to deliver the message that he wants to see her in his office the next evening. Melodramatically, Atwood notes that they "were pulled towards each other by a force, current, pulled apart also by hands equally strong" (126–28). Frightened of that second force, they refuse to yield to love or even lust, remaining passive. After she has begun seeing the Commander in his study, playing Scrabble and lightly kissing, Kate begins to make friends with Ofglen, who turns out to be with Mayday, of course; she continues lusting for Nick, despite her guilt about Luke and her fear. But with a quick allusion to Hamlet, Atwood again shows us Kate's indecision, the fear that saps her will. Finally, though, Serena Joy proposes that Kate use Nick to get her pregnant, since it's clear that the Commander is having no luck in the ridiculous ceremonial couplings; that order from one of her many "guards" sends Kate flying to Nick's bed. Now, clearly Kate is still in danger. The Commander, should he find out, could have her executed; one of the vicious doctors might discover the subterfuge and betray her; Nick himself might sell her down the pike at some point. Atwood's Kate does risk, then, she does grow, she does become more human.

Pinter's filmscript, though, makes her growth and courage more emphatic and more sympathetic. In Pinter's version of their first serious encounter, Offred is lying in her bed in the dark, we see a memory flash of Jill skiing down the valley, and a figure slips in. It's Nick, and she tumbles out of bed as Nick delivers his message that the Commander wants to see her the next night (shot 81). Hugely different from the novel's sitting room scene, they make love feverishly, both reaching for the other, neither in control of the other; it is their doing, not Serena Joy's. And at the end, after Offred has murmured softly, "Jesus," she tells Nick she won't go to the Commander. Nick says she must, though a pause ambiguously suggests he does *not* like the idea, because he's a Commander, but he promises to see her (shot 82). In the Pinter version, shot 83 follows this lovemaking scene: Serena Joy, like the Commander, has sent for her, proposing that she think about other ways to get pregnant. After the scene where the doctor offers to fuck her (shot 94), and after she has discovered the photo of Jill, now age eight, that Serena Joy has promised to get, Kate bounds up the stairs to Nick's room to announce the news that her daughter is alive in Canada. They kiss, as Nick tells her, twice, with her lying on top of him and kissing him, "That's good." The image, a couple communicating their heartfelt emotions, beyond the control of the keepers, might as well be in slave quarters, but it's their own action, their own loving, once more.

In Pinter's script, Offred tells Ofglen the news that her daughter is alive in Canada the next day; *she* takes the first risk of speaking as if to a friend, not to a potential betrayer. This leads Ofglen to communicate that her name is Susan, and that Mayday may need Kate to watch and study the Commander. Again, Pinter's structure and invented scenes strengthen his central figure, make her less of a victim. And in the Pinter script, after another scene in the study and the second of the "ceremony" scenes, where we see where the Commander get out of line by touching Kate's face (in the film, predictably, a breast), she challenges the Commander on his actions at the ceremony, *and* begins to pry, helping Mayday, acting, in several senses. Not until after Pinter's version of the birthing scene does he show Serena Joy urging Kate to cheat with Nick, which of course, is tremendously, even comically, ironic; the inmates are getting away with something that one of the guards actually wants them to do, again, though, acting on their own wills, for all the world like "yessin' 'em to death." The placing of Serena Joy's suggestion in Pinter's structure (shot 123), then, again underlines Kate's developing courage, enabled by love and hope. And at the end of that birthing celebration Ofglen tells Offred that Mayday may want to kill Fred, the commander, since he's a "real bastard," in charge of security for the state. Ofglen suggests that she can help them by making the Commander trust her (shot 120).

So, as we watch Kate's courage and willingness to grow, Pinter's version of the murder scene—again, his invention—makes more structural and thematic sense than it does in the film itself, which so ineffectively rearranges Pinter's structure, often returning to that of the novel while leaving now jarring parts of Pinter's script as is. We watch Kate, in Pinter's version, continue to pry and make herself agreeable to the Commander; we see Kate and Nick making love again, with great good humor and camraderie and balance, Serena Joy ironically thinking it's for the first time and at her behest. In Pinter's structure, the outlandish scene where Nick has to drive the Commander and Kate on their "date" follows this joyous lovemaking. The evening at the club in Pinter's version emerges as yet another reason for Kate to hate the Commander, not only over what he does to her, but what they have done to Moira and other habitués of the club, and over the terrible emotions his actions cause Nick.

After the ball, in shot 146, Kate again runs to Nick's room, where Nick, no longer positing the "no romance" idea, is clearly jealous. Kate is the realistic one this time: "I got through it. I faked it." And in reply to his petulance, she says, "Oh for God's sake! What did you want me to do, spit in his face and end up shovelling shit in the Colonies?" But again, she has grown, as

Pinter suggests with her lines, "Do you think we'll ever get out?" and, after his silence, "Do you want to get out? Could we get out together?" Once more, Kate is the one taking the initiative, risking in spite of the danger. As Nick says, "Maybe," he goes to her, touches her, repeats, "Maybe." Offred says, "I'm cold. Hold me." And he does.

This is a wonderfully balanced scene, an emblem of a type of sexual love that is not controlling, not imprisoning with power one over the other, a structural contrast to all of the sexual relationships we've seen in the film, including the Commander's marriage. The film version adds the cliché of Nick clutching the Commander's bottle in his jealous anger and the hackneyed line of wondering if the earth moved. More importantly, it omits the Pinter lines where Kate initiates the idea of their escaping together. These come later in the film, after she tells Nick that she's pregnant. Even in the film, then, she suggests the escape, but it's weakened with the notion of doing this action, not for herself, but largely for Nick and his child.

Pinter's filmscript, though, cuts from this scene of balanced, noncontrolling love in the time of oppression, to the "Women's Salvaging and Male Particicution," scene, which the film places much earlier. Perhaps that decision on the filmmaker's part was because Pinter has two scenes of executions that the handmaids must witness, both of them much more graphic than the prettied up, phony images we get in the film, complete with the handmaids' hoisting up a woman by gently pulling on a nice, clean, white rope. The first of Pinter's execution scenes serves immediately to contextualize what misbehavior— violation of patriarchal puritan dictates, revolt, claims to freedom—risks; the second, which we see after this love scene in Pinter's structure, builds almost inexorably to Kate's murder of the Commander. In the film version, we cut to the single execution scene following the birthing sequence and Ofglen's request that Kate watch the commander. In the film version, too, remember, Serena Joy's request to use Nick as an in seminator precedes the birthing ceremony; this sequence is less effective, or even logical, in terms of Serena Joy's character, than Pinter's version. In the film, we see Kate in the Commander's study, saying he's a mystery well before the nightclub scene; then we cut to the women's salvaging, which includes the male resistance fighter's execution at the hands of the duped handmaids. Then we get lovemaking with Nick at Serena Joy's request, the nightclub sequence, and so on.

With Pinter's placement, though, the second of these execution scenes— following the horrific scenes at the club, the news that Nick and she are pregnant, and so on—makes for a mounting pattern of motivation that reveals Kate's seemingly sudden action very believable, an act indicative of a willed courage. In the film, partly because of the shift in Pinter's structure, it seems almost a whim, an unthinking spontaneity akin to accident, especially as any understanding of Kate's strength of will is undermined by the film's concluding scenes. In the Pinter script, we see and hear Aunt Lydia's announcement of the condemned prisoner's crime of seduction and fornication with an officer "of our heroic forces," which is followed by Ofglen's whispered question to Kate, asking if she could go to the Commander's room on very short notice. Kate answers, "Yes," to a series of three interrelated questions with this horrific execution as backdrop: the last is, "Would you do anything we asked you to do?" "I would. Yes," says Kate. And Ofglen's response is, "Good. Be ready," as Aunt Lydia goes to the microphone to announce the "male particicution." Offred has already decided that she will risk, that she will support the resistance.

As the guards drag a man into the circle of handmaids, Aunt Lydia announces that he has been convicted of rape at gunpoint, that the handmaid was pregnant, and that the baby died. A horrifying scene of the handmaids beating the man ensues, but in Pinter's script, Ofglen darts through the crowd, reaching him before the others, and kicks his head three times. Genuinely offended, Offred asks why Ofglen did that. Ofglen says he was a political whom she has put out of his misery. In the film, we don't see Ofglen kicking the man, or the victim stuttering out, "I didn't . . . " before the mob descends, as we do in Pinter's script, but we do get Ofglen's information that he wasn't a rapist, that he was a political. Pinter's version is better, truer to the spirit of the novel, for it structurally emphasizes that Ofglen, like Moira, is an example for Kate.

In the Pinter script, immediately after this horrific scene, we see Offred in her room, reading a note which has been in an envelope under a glass; she reads it, then goes to her dresser, opens a drawer, and stares at a knife beneath her petticoats. We finally see the note, which reads, "Top right drawer. Tomorrow. 10 pm" (shots 149–50). The specificity of time is arresting, preparing us for the split-second rescue by the Mayday forces. The next scene shows us Offred meeting Oflgen, whom both members of the audience and Kate expect to be Susan. Chillingly, as Offred tells Ofglen that she's found it, that she's ready, we recognize together that this is a new Ofglen, that Susan as been replaced overnight like a dead dog. Still, despite such a warning scene of what could happen to her, after a series of shots of Kate staring at the clock, receiving Serena Joy who welcomes her potential pregnancy, and worrying that any of the vans on the street might be coming for her, we finally see the Commander coming home with Nick, whose room light swiftly goes out as Kate watches.

Alone, without reinforcements available from her knight, she moves toward the sideboard at 10 P.M. In Pinter's script we don't see her pick up the knife and hide it in her sleeve, but we fill in the missing information ourselves as she moves, unbidden, to the Commander's study (shots 165–66). As she enters, he turns a gun on her, but she stands still, calmly closing the door. In the film, the director "motivates" this scene by having Kate plead for the Commander's help because Serena Joy has found out about the club. In Pinter's script, Serena Joy never discovers the night out; thus, unlike in the film, Kate's fear of Serena Joy reporting her is never a factor; her action is her free choice. In the film, Serena Joy confronts Kate with the cloak prior to the final study scene; in Pinter's script, she's still hopeful that Kate is pregnant so that she may have the joy of raising a child not her own.

In this scene in the film of Kate confronting the Commander in the study, asking for his help with Serena Joy, who may have her killed or sent to the colonies, we have several examples of Duvall's atrocious ad-libbing: "What could I do? She gave me hell. She gave me all kinds of grief. It's unfortunate, the whole thing, it really is." Anyone at all familiar with Pinter's dialogue should recognize that such drivel could never flow from his pen. In the script, Offred knowingly appeals to the Commander's ego: "I just wanted to see you. Sorry. An impulse" (shot 167). As the shot continues, Offred looks at a broadcast about a siege at the Mayday gang's house on Jackson Street. The "news" reveals that the theocracy forces have captured the rebel leader, and as the Commander mouths platitudes of victory on the television broadcast, in the study, grinning with pride, he turns off the TV. This scene continues a musical backdrop of opera, which makes it even more subtly gorgeous, but time prohibits glossing that structural pattern. Offred continues to pry about the Commander's security successes: "But you got the 'big boy'—this week," and she asks what they will do with him. In Pinter's script, the Commander replies: "Do? It's done. You attended a little party for him yesterday afternoon." Offred stares at him, and he reemphasizes that the handmaids have executed, horribly, not a rapist but a "bastard" with no morals. At this news she "acts," again, stroking his neck, yet another motive for something she came into the room to do, and she kisses him gently, getting closer to him. As he proudly tells her of his horrific actions in the Pinter script, as she purposely pretends to sympathize with him, he compliments her, saying that what has kept him going is his thought of her, "coming in here, . . . giving me my drink . . . caring for me . . . being by my side. Do you know that" (shot 167; these ellipses represent Pinter pauses).

At this point in the script, she takes out the knife from her sleeve and slashes his neck. He grabs her, pulling her down to the floor with him, their faces close, but he manages to press an alarm button. She tears herself from him and rushes out. The concluding scene with the fake arrest van follows, and Pinter's three-part coda further emphasizes the strength, the courage, the love, the moral outrage, that has moved Kate to a kind of noble action despite potentially disastrous consequences.

In the film version, Kate comes to the study to plead for the Commander's help against Serena Joy, whom she fears will turn her in after her "betrayal" at the club. He kisses her gently, rather than her kissing him as part of her plan to get close enough to kill him, and tells her to go to her room, that he can do nothing, but he'll always treasure her memory. With his promise never to forget her, the Commander reaches out again to kiss her, and she slashes his neck, not with opera in the background but to a corny drum beat; we have a shot of his face in death, and he does not manage to hit the alarm. So, in the film, Serena Joy, only concerned for the baby, has not turned Kate in, and the whole logic just breaks apart. In short, Pinter's version of the murder scene, springing from his well-structured emphasis on Kate's continuing development of courage, of character, of moral outrage, of a willingness to act despite consequences, results in a much more nuanced understanding of Kate through an interesting "ordering of events," with a wonderful cinematic equivalent of her thoughts about her environment and her past. But it's Kate's actions, Kate's decisions in Pinter's version, well motivated, fully believable, that she takes at great risk to her love for Nick, her daughter, and her unborn child, that finally allow a kind of personal, courageous triumph at the conclusion of Pinter's script, without the knight in shining armor. Most ironically of all, such individual courage may change the destiny of a nation and a world. And just possibly, at that point, Nick and Kate may be reunited in a "balanced" relationship, one of equality where the one does not control the other, or try to make a prisoner of him or her to that ever-so-human desire for power.

Pinter's filmscript adaptation of Margaret Atwood's dystopia is a work about various kinds of prisons, as is hers. But Pinter's Kate strikes a blow against the forces of patriarchal theocracy, which destroys the freedom of all who disagree with its world vision, *and* embodies an emblem of motherhood, and familial and sexual love. She's a variant of the several female characters in Pinter's world who are the rare, but still very human examples of the "courage to be." In a wonderful essay, "Existentialism and Psychology," Paul Tillich writes, "There is no existential description of the negativities of the human predicament without an underlying image of what man essentially is and therefore ought to be. The cutting power of existentialist novels, paintings, even Philosophical analyses of man's predicament, is rooted in the implicit contrast between the negativities they show and the positives they silently presuppose" (6).

In order to artistically deal with the notion of prison, one must view it implicitly or explicitly in comparison with freedom and free will. Pinter's script achieves that contrast with a structural frame of images of freedom, both in real-time and in Kate's memories. But to be truly free, as Peter Weiss suggests through the Marquis de Sade, we must "unlock the cells of the inner self," the thirst for power, fear, the wish to escape responsibility among other things, or else all of our changes in governments or social forms will prove useless. Kate manages to do just that, ironically through the power of love and of moral outrage.

In the interview with Nicholas Hern that is the preface for *One for the Road,* Pinter comments that he had become aware "that the Turkish prisons, in which there are thousands of political prisoners, really are among the worst in the world.... Torture is systematic. People are crippled every day." And then he tells the story of meeting two intelligent young Turkish women, who knew nothing of their prison system's abuses, and, when pushed, said the prisoners probably deserved it. The script for *The Handmaid's Tale,* like Pinter's play *One for the Road,* represents a successful attempt to artistically confront audiences with these unpleasant realities through the narrative of a woman who grows to recognition and to the ability to challenge, to revolt no matter the consequences. It is a much better piece than a work that merely says puritanical, patriarchal theocracies are bad. It's a very great shame that the filmmakers did not use it.

Notes

1. Please see Hudgins, "*Victory*" 23–32.
2. Please see Hudgins, "Harold Pinter's *Lolita*" 123–146.
3. After its success at the Lincoln Center Pinter Festival during summer 2001, *Langrishe, Go Down* finally garnered a theatrical distribution arrangement in the following year. Relegated to television for its 1978 premier, this theatrical release was in part because of the presence of the young Jeremy Irons and Judy Dench, now both hugely respected *and* popular actors.
4. Again, please see Hudgins, "Harold Pinter's *Lolita*."
5. A copy of this script is available in the British Library in the Harold Pinter Archive; boxes 62, 63, and 64 include materials relevant to *The Handmaid's Tale.*
6. Pinter told Steve Gale and me in this 1994 interview, that by the time of his difficulties with *The Remains of the Day,* his contract included a clause allowing him to remove his name from the credits or the project if his script were revised without his approval. When Merchant Ivory bought *Remains,* which was originally to be directed by Mike Nichols, they brought in their scriptwriter, Ruth Prawer Jhabala and wanted to give Pinter joint credit for the screenplay. He refused. At the time of this interview, Pinter still thought that Adrian Lynne would use the script for *Lolita* he had contracted from Pinter.
7. The Margaret Herrick Library at the Academy of Motion Picture Arts and Sciences Center for Motion Picture Study holds a copy of a script for *The Handmaid's Tale.* Its copy is dated 1/17/89, almost two years after Pinter finished his work on the script. I'm reasonably certain that this is a shooting script—that is, a highly revised version of Pinter's final 1987 script—but I haven't examined it since the script I have came into my possession in 1994.
8. Please see Steve Gale's and my article, "The Harold Pinter Archives II: A Description of the Filmscript Materials in the Archive in the British Library." *The Harold Pinter Review: Annual Essays 1995 and 1996.* Ed. Francis Gillen and Steven H. Gale. Tampa, Fla.: University of Tampa, 1997, 101–42.

Works Cited

Anonymous, *Daily Variety,* Oct. 14, 1986, n.p. both of these are clippings from Archives & include no author, N.P.

Anonymous, "The Handmaid's Tale." *Rolling Stone* 22 March 1990: 36.

Atwood, Margaret. *The Handmaid's Tale*. New York: Fawcett, 1986.

Billington, Michael. *The Life and Work of Harold Pinter*. London: Faber and Faber, 1996.

Denicola, David. Interview with Volker Schlondorff in "The Director's Chair" column; an entry from the clippings file, American Film Institute Library, Los Angeles; no source or date listed.

Forsberg, Myra. "Makers of 'Handmaid's Tale' Analyze a Grim Fantasy." *New York Times* 17 May 1989: H-1, 13.

Fowles, John. "Foreword." In Harold Pinter, *The French Lieutenant's Woman*. Boston: Little Brown, 1981, vii–xv.

Gale, Steven H. "Harold Pinter's Screenwriting: The Creative/Collaborative Process." *The Pinter Review: Collected Essays 1999 and 2000*. Tampa, Fla.: University of Tampa Press, 2000. 85–91.

Gale, Steven H., and Christopher C. Hudgins. "The Harold Pinter Archives II: A Description of the Filmscript Materials in the Archive in the British Library." *The Harold Pinter Review: Annual Essays 1995 and 1996*. Ed. Francis Gillen and Steven H. Gale. Tampa, Fla.: University of Tampa Press, 1997. 101–42.

Hudgins, Christopher C. "*Victory:* A Pinter Filmscript Based on the Conrad Novel." *The Pinter Review: Annual Essays 1991*. Tampa, Fla.: University of Tampa Press, 1991. 23–32.

———. "Harold Pinter's *Lolita:* 'My Sin, My Soul.' " *The Films of Harold Pinter.* Ed. Steven H. Gale. Albany: State University of New York Press, 2001. 123–46.

Kauffman, Stanley. "Future Tense." *The New Republic* 19 March 1990: 26–27.

Kroll, Jack. "Brave New World, Feminist Style." *Newsweek* 26 March 1990: 54.

Peary, Gerald. "If Puritans Ruled ... Atwood's Story on Screen." *Los Angeles Times* 4 March 1990: *Calendar* 38, 39, 90.

Pinter, Harold.

Interviews

Billington, Michael. "Harold Pinter and Michael Billington in Conversation at the National Film Theatre, 26 Oct. 1996." Harold Pinter, *Various Voices: Harold Pinter, Prose, Poetry, Politics*. New York: Grove, 1998. 50–57.

Gussow, Mel. *Conversations with Pinter*. New York: Grove, 1994.

Nicholas Hern. "A Play and its Politics." Harold Pinter. *One for the Road*. New York: Grove, 1986. 7–23.

Christopher C. Hudgins, 15 May 1984.

Christopher C. Hudgins and Steven H. Gale, 26 Oct. 1994.

Filmscripts

Collected Screenplays, volumes 1, 2, 3. London: Faber and Faber, 2000.

The Handmaid's Tale, typed draft dated Feb. 1987 on final sheet, 147 pp. ms., Hudgins's Collection, Las Vegas, Nev.

Lolita, typed draft dated Sept. 26, 1994, 136 pp. ms., Hudgins's Collection, Las Vegas, Nev.

Prescott, Peter S. "No Balm in This Gilead. *Newsweek* 17 Feb. 1986: 70.

Tillich, Paul. "Existentialism and Psychotherapy." *Psychoanalysis and Existential Philosophy*. New York: Dutton, 1962.

Tommasini, Anthony. "A Cautionary Tale Taken from Pulpit to Stage." *New York Times* 10 June 2001: sec 2, p. 20.

7
"A World of Bodies":
Performing Flesh in *Marat/Sade*

PAMELA COOPER

> However reasonable we may grow, we may be mastered anew by
> a violence no longer that of nature but that of a rational being
> who tries to obey but who succumbs to stirrings within himself
> which he cannot bring to heel.
>
> —GEORGES BATAILLE, *EROTISM*

In Peter Weiss's famous play, the Marquis de Sade describes the Bastille as the
liberator, rather than the suppressor, of an overwhelming inner criminality:

> In prison I created in my mind
> monstrous representatives of a dying class
> who could only exercise their power
> in spectacularly staged orgies
> I recorded the mechanics of their atrocities
> in the minutest detail
> and brought out everything wicked and brutal
> that lay inside me
> In a criminal society
> I dug the criminal out of myself. (Weiss 53)

This statement is manifestly political and addresses the play's overt philosophical concerns. Weiss uses Sade—the man of isolation and the inner,
imaginative life—as a counter to Jean-Paul Marat—the man of action, social conscience, and reform. The latter represents both the French Revolution
and revolutionary principles in general, while the former embodies the vices
of the ancien regime and the politically narcissistic in general. This binary
thematic is reinforced by the play's setting—Charenton asylum, a kind of jail

for the mad—which stresses the contrast between freedom and confinement, outside and in.

In this context, Sade's perception of the prison as liberating the inner outlaw is a paradox that powerfully ironizes both the play's binaries and the Brechtian aspects of its dramaturgy. The sense of conflicting poles and the counter-rhythms that undermine them is stressed by the play's intellectual action. The anchoring debate between individualism on the one hand and collective responsibility on the other is well known.[1] Weiss generates a protracted dialogue between his two iconic antagonists—a conversation both languid and feverish, reflecting the ennui of the one and the desperation of the other. Swirling around these interchanges, the energies of madness and revolution are embodied in the actor/patients and the audience of the play-within-a-play. In the counterpoint of ceremonious speech and embodied wildness, the play seeks an explosive balance between opposites that are, nevertheless, always already collapsing into each other.

On one level, Sade speaks for the individual and the power of imagination while Marat, with his rhetoric of human rights and embattled faith in social rebellion, speaks for the collective.[2] On another level, this lucid contrast becomes blurred, for both men revel in cruelty, and both shuttle compulsively in their thinking between the private and the public. Each strives to comprehend the relationship of the individual to history and the weaving of personal life into the affective matrix of the political. In fact, as *Marat/Sade* unfolds, cruelty emerges as the bright thread binding together different theories and the men who embody them. Interestingly, the vehicle of this binding is the woman, Charlotte Corday. Stabbing Marat and flogging Sade, Corday brings each to his fearsomely desired climax, wielding the knife and the whip not so much as instruments of repudiation, but of connection and intimacy.

Sade and Marat, furthermore, share a common symbolic destiny. Each represents his own historical moment of ideological bad faith. Marat suggests the perishing of libertarian ideals in the chaos of the Terror; Sade stands for the defunct patrician class while heralding the revived imperialism and totalitarian ambitions of Napoleon Bonaparte. Men of their time, Sade and Marat are also out of their time. The former's combination of nihilism and existentialism gives him an aura of prematurely exhausted modernity. The latter's zeal for social change resonates with the political optimism of the early 1960s, when the play first appeared. Sade is at once a "monstrous" relic "of a dying" aristocracy, and a late-twentieth-century debauchee lost in the political detritus of 1789. Marat embodies both the annihilating extremes of radicalism and a hopefulness echoed in the liberation movements of Weiss's time, such as the civil rights and student protest movements of the 1960s. Marooned in his bath, restless yet supine, Marat implies a modernity vital but thwarted, effectively stillborn.

Not only politically but also psychologically, these men become figures of post-1945 Western humanity.[3] Sade's mood of embittered nostalgia and his

longing for retreat from the incomprehensibility of history, Marat's edgy fervor
and free-floating dread—these traits give to each the broad outlines of contemporary neuroses. At once particular and generic, reachable yet removed,
Sade and Marat clearly recall Brecht's epic and emblematic characters. Like
Mother Courage, they are archetypes in whom history and myth coalesce, and
the old and new meet prismatically.

    This converging of contrasts opens an interpretive perspective on the play
that I want to explore further here. *Marat/Sade* relies upon a constant and irresolute rhythm of opposites simultaneously asserted and denied. In this stylized
interchange between difference and sameness, Weiss's reading of the political,
and his shaping of it in visceral terms, emerges. Embodiment is, as scholars
have noted, a constant concern in Weiss's drama.[4] He seeks to work out per-
formatively, as a kind of three-dimensional conundrum, the imbrication of the
human body in politicohistorical change. Sade's great observation, "This is
a world of bodies" (Weiss 102), captures the tension in Weiss's art between
physicality and mental life, anatomy and ideas. From this tension his dramaturgy of breakdown is produced, as the oscillating terms of body and mind
intertwine with each other, generating violence. In *Marat/Sade,* the promiscuous refusal of polarity among ostensible binaries erodes the rational structures
upon which alienating theatrical effects depend. Reason and unreason perform
themselves as both alienated and overclose, and the legibility—the conventional protocols—of distance and intimacy are rearranged.

    In this way, Weiss draws the *unheimlich* into his play. His portrayal of his-
tory, politics, and the body is shaped by the drastic theatricality with which his
dramatic art invests the term. Specifically, the prismatic meeting of old and new
in the figures of Marat and Sade positions history as a version of the uncanny—
an estranging yet familiar mirror for the present. The dynamic of refraction,
reflection, and focus at work in both Marat and Sade and *Marat/Sade* further
designates history as an affair of projection and transmission: a luminous geometry. Rendered spatial, history—for Weiss as well as for Brecht—embraces
drama as its analogue and in doing so, opens itself inevitably to the fantastic
and hallucinatory. Through drama, fantasy and hallucination infiltrate history,
adjusting its coordinates and remodeling its dimensions. By means of this
exchange, Weiss not only accommodates the political within the historical, he
interrogates history by giving the political both body and voice.

    The reconfiguring of space in *Marat/Sade*—the establishing of drama as
a kind of historical Imaginary—is caught most obviously in the metatheatri-
cal device of the play-within-a-play. Each actor is haunted by doubleness and
performs simultaneously as patient and character. In this way, alienation and
identity unite within the same articulating code; again, boundaries collapse
even as they assert themselves. Within the (doubly) dramatic frame, space
is once more overdetermined through an irresolute counterpoint of distance
and closeness. This counterpoint imparts a stuttering rhythm to the action—a

disrupted enunciation that opens areas of profound ambivalence within the drama: spaces of in-betweenness where repulsion and desire, dread and fascination, converge.

Furthermore, by describing the play's geometry as an indeterminate exchange between aloofness and intimacy, this counterpoint infuses the structure with affect, drenching its spaces in emotion. Given the referent of the Revolution, the guillotine inaugurates most clearly such an affective space of mingled allure and horror, ripped open in a city square in the midst of day-to-day reality. Walking through Paris, Charlotte Corday is stupefied by the acquiescence of civic order to terror: "What are those heaps they fight over / those heaps with eyes and mouths / What kind of town is this / hacked buttocks lying in the street / What are all these faces" (Weiss 25). Suffused with ambivalent feeling, such deranged spaces are the abodes of abjection—of limit, transformation, and dissolution, where subject and object blur together, losing all discretion.

As Corday's words make clear, the play not only spatializes historical events and ideological processes, it consistently uses the language of the violated body to describe them.[5] Later, as Sade discourses on ethics, a patient sings: "A mad animal / Man's a mad animal . . . The earth is spread thick / with squashed human guts / We few survivors / We few survivors / walk over a quaking bog of corpses / always under our feet" (Weiss 37). Such references describe literally the detritus of the Revolution, the waste products of massive social change. They also suggest the underside of intellectual debate and the terrible results of political conviction. In *Marat/Sade,* historical change, progress, and the reforming zeal of nationalism are informed by an anatomy of incoherence: the human body in fragments. The spatial and affective modeling of the political in relation to the human body implicitly shifts the play into a psychological realm, and *abjection* becomes a key interpretive term.

From the standpoint of the early twenty-first century, Brecht and Freud mingle interestingly with Julia Kristeva in casting light on *Marat/Sade.* In the terms invited by my own discussion, one might argue that applying Kristeva's reading of abjection to *Marat/Sade* displaces the historical mirror into a present well beyond the reach of Weiss's play, adjusting its spatial coordinates once again—this time with reference to a posterior space reminiscent of Homi Bhabha's elusive "beyond" and flooded, perhaps, with hallucinatory import.[6]

Moreover, viewing *Marat/Sade* through the lens of Kristeva refracts the play itself through the historically later moment of post-structuralism generally and French feminist theory in particular—intellectual projects that both emerged from and interrogated the liberationist philosophies of the 1960s with which the play is involved. There is something prophetic in Weiss's work which is answered, perhaps, by a retrospective reading of this kind. Specifically, Kristeva's ideas enlarge the scope and effect of *Marat/Sade*'s high theatricality. In *Powers of Horror,* abjection is performative—a drama of unraveling and reshaping, a Theater of Cruelty for the psyche. In extreme theatricality and modes of radical performance, *Marat/Sade* bodies forth the psychic and emotional roots of the political; Kristeva's theory of abjection lends a precise and contemporary taxonomy to our appreciation of this endeavor.

As Kristeva has famously shown, abjection is that physiological state in which we encounter the very limits of our subjectivity: "It is . . . not lack of cleanliness or health that causes abjection but what disturbs identity, system, order. What does not respect borders, positions, rules. The in-between, the ambiguous, the composite" (Kristeva 4). Caught by this anterior modulation of being, we feel, at the parameters of the self, the encroachment of the non human—which nonetheless claims us, for it also installs our humanity: "There, I am at the border of my condition as a living being. . . . How can I be without border? That elsewhere that I imagine beyond the present, or that I hallucinate so that I might, in the present time, speak to you, conceive of you—it is now here, jetted, abjected, into 'my' world" (4–5).

This radically disconcerted subject—the abject—abjuring speech as a function of the Symbolic and thus of agency, utters itself through physicality. The human body in disarray—threatened, splintered, at the boundaries of its coherence—is the realm of abjection: "These body fluids, this defilement, this shit is what life withstands, hardly and with difficulty, on the part of death. . . . Such wastes drop so that I might live, until, from loss to loss nothing remains in me and my entire body falls beyond the limit—*cadere,* cadaver" (Kristeva 3). As her use of the present tense implies, Kristeva emphasizes process and immediacy in her description of the abject, and she links it explicitly to drama: "No, as in true theater, without makeup or masks, refuse and corpses *show me* what I permanently thrust aside in order to live" (3, emphasis in original). In *Marat/Sade,* blood, excrement, and corpses manifest the fleshly debris which we "permanently thrust aside" for our survival. They hail the emergence of the abject into consciousness—an emergence which both undercuts that consciousness and constitutes it. The abjected self violently repudiates, while intertwining with, an other seen as both outside and inside, expelled yet ensconced.

According to Kristeva, the abject is essentially different from the uncanny both in the intensity of its violence and in its forfeiture of maternal recognition (5). The solace of the mother's body and its status as a referent is fiercely rejected by the abject, which experiences itself as disproportionately alone. Such rejection generates shame—through and as a kind of hallucinatory solitude; the abject fails "to recognize its kin; nothing is familiar, not even the shadow of a memory" (5). Spurning the maternal, abjection nonetheless heralds the *unheimlich* as the estranged core of being by positing both lack and longing: abjection is "recognition of the *want* on which any being, meaning, language, or desire is founded" (Kristeva 5, emphasis in original). An accretion of vertiginous isolation and hunger, abjection offers itself to representation as an annunciatory figure; it implies a mode of salutation or ritual induction which invests the uncanny with both an affect and an anatomy. The former is mingled horror and attraction. The latter is broken, illegible, yet—partly through the play of shame, yearning, and deferral—powerfully sensual and erotic.

In *Marat/Sade,* Weiss, prefiguring Kristeva, experiments with a dramatic vocabulary for abjection. If "refuse and corpses" show us what we repudiate "in order to live," their dramatic function is to convene the realm of abjection on stage and to release the energies of shame and longing which attend it. These energies fuel the theatrical extremism of *Marat/Sade,* picking up the registers of madness and illness proclaimed by the setting, and informing not just the play's pantomime elements, but its intellectual debates as well. This is well illustrated in the melodramatic scene where Corday whips Sade as he discourses on ideology. In a speech about imaginary orgies, Sade declares: "And even now I should like to take this beauty here / (Pointing to Corday, who is brought forward) who stands there so expectantly / and let her beat me / while I talk to you about the Revolution" (Weiss 53). As politico-social formations and theories search for the bodies that utter them, pleasure and pain meet; these strange bedfellows at once disclose, and are disclosed as, the physiological matrix of political change.

Weiss's probing of dramatic vocabularies in *Marat/Sade* implicitly stresses style as a crucial component of the play's full range of meaning. I want, at this point, to look more closely at style, especially its relation to the pattern of collapsing binaries in the play, and the mobilizing of abjection as the dramatic inscription of political embodiment. I have said that Weiss politicizes the abject partly through dire theatricality; the properties of that theatricality—the specifics of performance and spectacle—illuminate this process of politicization as a function of both mise-en-scène and language.[7]

Clearly, Weiss draws on both Brecht and Artaud for his dramaturgy in *Marat/Sade.*[8] As Susan Sontag observed in her 1965 essay on Peter Brook's London production of the play: "How *could* one reconcile Brecht's conception of a didactic theater, a theater of intelligence, with Artaud's theater of magic, of gesture, of 'cruelty,' of feeling?" (218, emphasis in original). Such clashing influences—when mixed with a little Marx, Bataille, and Sartre—not only trouble the philosophical clarity of the play, they foreground style as a weighted enterprise for Weiss. In *Marat/Sade,* style functions as a kind of constitutive hyperbole that renders the abject visible. The entire play relies on prodigious spectacle for its effects; it combines the roadshow properties of the carnival, the pantomime, the freak show, and the public execution. Posing and broad dramatic gestures are vital throughout. The most literal pose is setting (both Weiss's and Sade's), and from the play's overdetermined, dizzy theatrical spaces, the language of abjection builds through a choreography of bodies both surreal and wanton.

The play-within-a-play is staged not just in an asylum, a retreat for society's outcasts, but in a bathroom, where the body's animal needs and its boundaries (orifices, membranes) are attended to. Here, on the clearest level of inversion which *Marat/Sade* creates, the borders between private and public are turned inside out. The bathroom becomes a theater, and the body's inscriptive surfaces, as well as its implied interiority, are emphasized. We are inducted directly into the ambiguous spaces of the body, and invited (with Kristevan prescience) to trace its mysterious relation to language and thought.

As I have intimated, the body is enacted—or "styled"—in Weiss's play through a range of performative strategies. For example, *Marat/Sade,* like the works of Brecht and Kurt Weill, has some of the qualities of a musical, where the narrative is periodically frozen and aspects of the themes redramatized through musical performance.[9] This modulation is also found in the novels of the historical Sade (most markedly in *Philosophy of the Bedroom*) where the unbridled action of the orgy is suspended while the libertines discuss political philosophy—usually ethics and issues of human freedom. The relationship between the narrative of sex/violence and its interruption in discourse is complex; in *Marat/Sade* it is difficult to know whether the hieratic exchanges between Sade and Marat constitute the story or its suspension, but they alternate starkly with other kinds of performance. Mime, music, dancing, and singing capture simultaneously the frenzied rhythms of 1793 Paris and the dark energies of 1808 Charenton. Like many features of *Marat/Sade,* these contrasting styles of representation work into the play's binary frame in broadly deconstructive ways.

From one perspective, the difference between dialogue and physical performance stresses the melodramatic swing between stillness and motion that is the basis of the play's temporal power. This difference stands, furthermore, for the basic contrast between reason and instinct, which Weiss carefully builds into a counterpoise of thought and action, order and anarchy, discipline and license.[10] From another perspective, though, such differences dissolve utterly, for the conversations between Marat and Sade are as vividly extreme—as violent, exhilarated, and anarchic—as the bodily enactments of the musical/mimed "numbers." Sade revels, for example, in his story of the execution of Damiens, would-be assassin of Louis XV:

> His chest arms thighs and calves were slit open
> Molten lead was poured into each slit
> boiling oil they poured over him burning tar wax sulphur
> They burnt off his hands
> tied ropes to his arms and legs
> harnessed four horses to them and geed them up
> They pulled at him for an hour but they'd never done it before
> And he wouldn't come apart. (Weiss 29)

Marat experiences his skin disease as a torture and repeatedly laments its afflictions: "Simonne, Simonne / More cold water / Change my bandage / O this itching is unbearable.... This fever beats in my head like a drum / my skin simmers and scorches" (Weiss 19–20; 38). Moreover, the extremity of their words shifts into action when Corday, with knife and whip, ministers to the bodies of both.[11] In *Marat/Sade,* as such careful stylistic strategies show, the forces of reason and unreason express themselves physically; order and disorder take on flesh, as mind and body potently entangle.

The play's imagery of disease and contagion reinforces Weiss's technique: the different dramatic gestures of dialogue and of almost burlesque performance infect rather than interrupt each other. Each vocabulary is equally stylized. As in the writings of the historical marquis, Sade's descriptions of fabulous tortures are rhetorically ordered and calm in tone. Similarly, the mimes and singers are precise about historical detail and often group themselves into stiff tableaus reminiscent of opera. In *Marat/Sade,* such mutual ritualizing of contrasting dramatic elements signals not the triumph of Manichaean logic, but its fatal etiolation. As the syntax of binarism collapses even at a technical level, *Marat/Sade* proclaims the interpenetration of contrasts—the deep imbrication of the other with the self as estranging yet familiar avatars.

The intertwining of opposites in the play opens its spaces to abjection by suggesting an ambivalent intimacy between mind and body, intellect and sense experience. Such entangling of difference with sameness implicates the body in thought—even in the abstract thought of politico-philosophical theorizing—by pitching bodily experience directly into the realm of the political. Marat expresses his own pain as the nation's tumult—"My head's on fire / I can't breathe / There is a rioting mob inside me"—and his physical paroxysm culminates in a cry that is both diagnostic and visionary: "I am the Revolution" (Weiss 21). By framing history and politics in the language of abjected physicality, the play turns inside out its apparently structuring opposites of reason and instinct. Expressed most sharply in the tension between restraint and excess, these opposites effectively become functions of each other. Under the sign of this particular dys- or re-functionality, what we might call the Weissean body becomes fully visible.

Harnessing the abject across a range of dramaturgical aspects, Weiss is able to imagine and dramatize the body of the political. He conjures an anatomy of political process, a physiognomy of both revolution and counterrevolution. Marat proclaims: "The important thing / is to turn yourself inside out / and see the whole world with fresh eyes." Turning themselves inside out—like switching positions—is precisely what the play's protagonist and antagonist, Marat and Sade, have done. Marat's suppurating skin and immersion in bath water suggest a body literally turned inside out; Sade's cruel psychodramas manifest a mind taking on physical expression through pain and erotic excess. The Weissean body is both deranged and libidinous; it is the body turned inside out, and it is recognizable across time, in its early-nineteenth-mid-twentieth-and early twenty-first-century realizations. Such a body—refracted/reflected through history as both prism and mirror—is configured by the Sadean orgy, the Reign of Terror, and their implied representational equivalent, the Peter Weiss text. It is also configured, for Weiss, in the concentration camp, the Vietnam War, and implicitly in all human atrocity. This body reaches beyond those of Marat and Sade as both individuals and emblems: It performs abjection as an historical force and a political category—or rather, as the affective body of these things, their fleshly inscription.

That this body—the physical shape of abstractions and intangibles—is disturbed and dissolute, informed by madness and contradiction, points to a crucial aspect of Weiss's drama and a striking overlap between his work and Sade's. For both writers, energy is a primal force; it is the raw stuff of action and thus of change or creativity of any kind. Energy becomes a species of wealth, even the "true" protagonist of their texts, which elaborate morality tales about the getting, spending, and storing of energy. The Sadean orgy, like the Weissean play (with the Reign of Terror as an historical analogue), crucially describes an economy. In the boundless switching of bodies and its periodic lugubrious suspension, energy organizes itself as a kind of stock exchange, playing rhythmically between consumption and retention.

As wealth or currency, energy within such an economy is to be lavishly expended and hoarded at the same time. Drawing on Bataille, we may argue that the erotic extremism favored by both writers is based on this exchange between extravagance and thrift. Even at the literal level—Sade's overly detailed plots, Weiss's tumultuous stage action—both writers' texts move inexhaustibly between the wasting and stockpiling of energy—the former manifests as profligate sexuality, the latter as the severe rituals and disciplines which attend its expression.

As it is for Weiss, so is waste an obsession for Sade. Coprophagia is a perfect example of the deployment of energy in his works: It is not only an erotic practice but is also, like sodomy, a kind of wisdom or good economic judgment. Coprophagia in Sade's formulation requires great discipline on the part of the libertine. It is an act of counterintuitive husbandry which reclaims and recycles the profuse energies to which, as remnant, fecal matter refers. Coprophagia is a way of taking an economy of circulation beyond its endpoint—of husbanding energy beyond death. Reincorporating waste and debris into the body, it also implodes the abject, collapsing even the (non)logic of the latter's anteriority and challenging the boundaries of boundaryless-ness. There are suggestions of coprophagia (as well as cannibalism and sodomy) in Corday's references to citizens fighting over "heaps with eyes and mouths," and to "hacked buttocks lying in the streets." The passionate excesses of insurgency and the fight to conserve the work of the Revolution as a national program—with Marat and Sade standing, at different phases of the action, for one or both of these movements—imply an economy of energy exchange operating in the play. In his next drama, *The Investigation,* Weiss's preoccupation with waste, circulation, efficiency, and conservation finds its contemporary thematic home: Auschwitz.

The concentration camp is, in Weiss's depiction, an economic system—an order of waste production and recycling underpinning political formations like fascism and the resistance movements they inspire. Moving between excess and frugality—the spending and hoarding of bodies, as humans are killed and their body parts recycled into textiles or consumer objects like soap—the camp produces the debased body of war, and a space "spread thick with squashed human guts . . . / rotted bones ashes matted hair / under our feet." In its swing between fleshly prodigality and the authoritarian strictures that contain it, the concentration camp savagely forgoes all decorum. Abandoning the politesse of contraries—particularly the spatial opposites of distance and closeness and the civil opposites of private and public—such a system, seething with shame and desire, collapses in brutal indecency. In this way, Auschwitz acquires an obscenity comparable to that of the Sadean orgy. The pornography of atrocity, which both Sade and Weiss strive to represent, is based essentially on this tension between—an economy of—profligacy and parsimony. On both the most literal and most theoretical levels, their texts enact the incivility of nihilistic promiscuity in savage play with perverse retention.

The ambivalent register of stricture and discipline, which I have noted in the play, returns us, in conclusion, to the prison. Sade captures its paradoxically confining and liberating effect when he describes it as a "stone sea," both solid and liquid.[12] Marooned in the Bastille, he "heard lips whispering continually / and felt all the time / in the palms of my hands and in my skin / touching and stroking" (Weiss 103). Inflamed by "the cruellest imagining," he "dreamed only / of the orifices of the body / put there / so one may hook and twine oneself in them" (Weiss 103). In confinement, banned sensuality flowers, manifesting those "cells of the inner self," which, for Sade, "are worse than the deepest stone dungeon" (Weiss 103). Such forced introspection conjures a body broken and violated; disavowed, it nonetheless announces itself figurally as the abject, the outlaw: "In a criminal society / I dug the criminal out of myself." This inner criminal bodies forth the irrationality and chaos that haunt rationality and order: a foreshortened manifestation of the body politic. Sade describes the broader function of the disemboweling of self he undertook in prison, digging out the criminal "so I could understand him and so understand / the times we live in" (Weiss 53). Emerging under the discipline of the lash from the "stone sea" of the prison, the estranged flesh of political philosophy literally oozes from Sade's pores: "When I lay in the Bastille / my ideas were already formed / I sweated them out / under the blows of my own whip" (Weiss 53). This body—the torn viscera and festering skin of thought—claims dramatic space in *Marat/Sade;* it fiercely slits open the familiar classifications of history, language, and representation.

Notes

1. For recent critical commentary on this debate, see Cohen (1993, 2000), and Garner.

2. In a 1965 interview with Michael Roloff, Weiss commented: "For a playwright, naturally, it is most important that a production should express a play's dualism, the ambivalence of its situation—in *Marat/Sade,* the confrontation of individualism and Socialism/Collectivism" (231).

3. Weiss's writings on World War II and the Vietnam War suggest his deep concern with late-twentieth-century malaise and catastrophe. The French Revolution functions in some ways as a parallel. Weiss told Roloff: "At the end of [*Marat/Sade*] the question is: Why did the Revolution fail? Why did Napoleon come? One can then take this question and apply it to any number of historical situations, right up to the present" (232).

4. See Cohen (1993), Garner, Sontag.

5. Garner's reading of the play centralizes pain and its relation to political upheaval. He comments: "The Revolution constituted a spectacle of bodily exigency: the desiring body seeking to redress the poverty that afflicts it, and the body punished within a historical theater of pain" (154).

6. For Bhabha's formulation of the "beyond," in explicitly postcolonial terms, as an interstitial space heralding the future, see the first chapter of *The Location of Culture.*

7. Sontag, whose reading emphasizes Weiss's style, observes the dazzling play of word and deed in *Marat/Sade:* "The verbal action, conducted by Sade, is repeatedly interrupted by brilliant bits of acting-out performed by the lunatics.... The Charenton setting insures that [the intellectual debate] takes place in a constant atmosphere of barely suppressed violence: all ideas are volatile at this temperature" (211–12).

8. Artaud's drama sought "true action," but without social application or "moral and psychological levels" of meaning. Clearly Weiss is drawn to this idea of dramatic tumult and is in some ways impatient with words, although he also relies on them—as did Artaud and Sade. The former railed against the "obstinacy" that he saw "in making characters talk about feelings, passions, desires, and impulses of a strictly psychological order, in which a single word is to compensate for innumerable gestures" (quoted in Sontag 214).

9. Linda Williams discusses the structure of the musical (in its cinematic form) in chapter 5 of her study of video pornography, *Hard Core: Power, Pleasure, and the "Frenzy of the Visible."* Williams compares the musical to the hard-core feature film in its alternating of narrative with sexual displays or "numbers." This link between the musical form and pornography obliquely illuminates *Marat/Sade,* which casts obscene violence and obscene sexuality in the ostensibly benign light of musical theater.

10. These contrasting terms could be assimilated into the basic difference that Bataille identifies in the erotic life between excess and work, transgression and taboo. Bataille links these two modes to, respectively, a concern for and a disregard of the social collective. We might, up to a point, apply these categories to the figures of Marat and Sade in the play, with the former suggesting the imperatives of work and taboo, the latter the impulses of excess and transgression.

11. In both his stage production and film of *Marat/Sade,* Peter Brook had Corday beat Sade not with a whip but with her own hair. This gesture both intensifies the eroticism of Corday's action and imparts to the body itself (significantly, the female body) the properties of a weapon. The gender issues in the play are troubling, but beyond the scope of my inquiry here.

12. In his discussion of Sade in *Erotism,* Bataille uses the metaphor of the desert to describe the Bastille. Such desolation, together with Sade's sense of being unjustly punished, produced in his work (Bataille avers) an overwhelming sense of moral isolation: "These books distilled in prison have given us a true picture of a man for whom other people did not count at all" (167).

Works Cited

Bataille, Georges. *Erotism: Death and Sensuality.* Trans. Mary Dalwood. San Francisco: City Lights Books, 1962.

Bhabha, Homi. *The Location of Culture.* New York: Routledge, 1994.

Cohen, Robert. "A Dream of Dada and Lenin: Peter Weiss's *Trotsky in Exile.*" *Rethinking Peter Weiss.* Ed. Jost Hernand and Marc Silberman, Washington, D.C., Baltimore: Peter Lang, 2000.

———. *Understanding Peter Weiss.* Columbia: University of South Carolina Press, 1993.

Garner, Stanton B., Jr. "Post-Brechtian Anatomies: Weiss, Bond, and the Politics of Embodiment." *Theatre Journal* 42.2 (1990): 145–64.

Kristeva, Julia. *Powers of Horror: An Essay on Abjection.* Trans. Leon S. Roudiez. New York: Columbia University Press, 1982.

Roloff, Michael. "An Interview with Peter Weiss." *Partisan Review* 2 (1965): 220–32.

Sontag, Susan. "Marat/Sade/Artaud." *Partisan Review* 2 (1965): 210–19.

Weiss, Peter. *The Persecution and Assassination of Jean-Paul Marat as Performed by the Inmates of the Asylum of Charenton under the Direction of the Marquis De Sade.* Trans. Geoffrey Skelton. Woodstock, Ill. Dramatic Publishing, 1964.

Williams, Linda. *Hard Core: Power, Pleasure, and the "Frenzy of the Visible."* Los Angeles: University of California Press, 1989.

8

The Disposal: William Inge's Abject Drama

ROBERT F. GROSS

This is not a paper about the reality of prison and its reflection, subversion, or critique in American and British drama. This is about the fantasies of male incarceration as a byway of the American imagination. Its focus will be an almost forgotten—or to put it more accurately, almost unnoticed—play by a canonical American playwright, and it will investigate some of the implications of acquiescence to, and subversion of, fantasies of male criminality, sexuality, and anality.

Neither critics nor audiences have found much reason to rediscover William Inge's *The Disposal.* The play (which premiered in an earlier version under the title, *The Last Pad*) has, from its premiere, been treated as a major embarrassment and has garnered negative reviews on the few occasions that it has been staged. Once slated for an Off-Broadway premiere, which never materialized, *The Disposal* eventually opened at the Off-Off 13th Street Theatre in December 1970. Usually a production in such a venue would gain little attention, but major newspaper reviewers flocked downtown to see it, with a seeming eagerness to draw public attention to the latest stage of Inge's much-heralded artistic decline. Edward Sothern Hipp expressed the commonly held view that the play was easily Inge's "worst play to be exhibited in Manhattan" (26) and suggested that it was a pathetic imitation of John Wexley's 1930 prison melodrama, *The Last Mile.* Two years later, it was performed in a revised version even farther from Broadway, at the Southwest Theatre Ensemble of Phoenix, Arizona—far enough from Times Square to discourage even the most rabid New York reviewer. Outside of an unsuccessful revival as an Equity Showcase in New York in the summer of 1992—which boasted better performances and direction than the New York premiere and elicited an unusually compassionate, if not enthusiastic, review from Joan Ungarno— *The Disposal* has remained locked in an obscurity that, reviewers agree, is well merited. It has been described as stereotyped (Washburn, Feld), dated

(Gottfried, Mishkin), padded (Hipp), and a "goulash of 1950s existential despair and pat psychology" (McNulty). R. Baird Shuman concludes that the play "seems to be proof that during his last years, Inge no longer knew what good drama was" (247). Inge's advocates have reacted to this widespread negativity, not by mounting a defense, but by trying to erase all memory of the play. Richard M. Leeson's useful bibliographical volume on Inge contains a summary of the play's action but omits any references to productions or reviews, while Ralph F. Voss's otherwise thorough thirteen-page entry for the *Dictionary of Literary Bibliography* lists *The Disposal* in the bibliographical section but otherwise passes over the play in silence. For the most part, *The Disposal* has been disposed of, and I am momentarily reversing its critically induced flow toward literary and theatrical oblivion by retrieving it here. No one has, to the best of my knowledge, argued in print for an aesthetic reevaluation of *The Disposal,* and I am not about to attempt one here. Nor am I interested in how this play sheds light on Inge as the author of those canonical works of American drama, *Bus Stop, Picnic,* and *Come Back, Little Sheba.* Rather, in the context of this volume of essays on prisons in British and American drama, I want to put all evaluative and biographical considerations aside and concentrate on a question of interpretation: How does *The Disposal* construct an imaginary of prison life that participates within a larger American imaginary of masculinity, homosexuality, anality, and criminality?

The Disposal is set on death row in a prison in the Midwest. There are three prisoners: Luke, a middle-aged man who killed someone in the course of a robbery; Archie, an aggressively campy "queen," a devotee of Nietzsche and existentialist thought, who murdered his mother and grandmother; and Jess, a young man who murdered his wife and infant son without giving any explanation for it. The play takes place on the day of Jess's execution, and the condemned man rages desperately against his fate, refuses the consolations of the prison chaplain, orders a last meal, which he does not have the stomach to eat, and waits for a visit from his father. The long-awaited visit turns out to be a devastating encounter, since the father only continues to insist on Jess's innocence, robbing the young man of any help in dealing with his guilt. Finally, Jess is taken off and executed, and a new condemned man, a serial rapist and murderer, is brought in to take his place in what only recently had been Jess's cell.

The focus of *The Disposal* is abjection. Abjection, according to Julia Kristeva, whose *Powers of Horror: An Essay on Abjection* has become the central text for the discussion of this concept, marks the place where meaning breaks down, presenting a threat to the integrity of the ego or group.[1] It is grounded in a fundamental sense of acute physical disgust:

> Loathing an item of food, a piece of filth, waste, or dung. The spasms and vomiting that protect me. The retching that thrusts me to the side and turns me away from defilement, sewage, and muck. The shame of compromise of

being in the middle of treachery. The fascinated start that leads me toward
and separates me from them. (Kristeva 2)

The abject violates the order between the outside and the inside of the body
(Kristeva 53) through objects that are either excremental or menstrual (71). The
very title of Inge's play—*The Disposal*—provides the play's major metaphor:
the elimination of abject entities, whether from the human body or the body
politic. The play coalesces around images of the abject. The prisoners are
fascinated as to whether Jess will lose control over his bowels as he is led
to execution, as all the others have before him. Though Luke is kind enough
to bet that Jess will not suffer this final indignity, Jess suffers this physical
abjection at the play's climax. Abjection turns out to be the only inevitable
force here. "One thing you can allus depend on in this life. The crap allus
comes through" (Inge 133).

For Kristeva, the female body is presented in culture as the abject sex
because of its role in maternity. A body of excrement, milk, menstrual blood,
and childbearing, it is also the body that imposes the authority to both separate
the child from the breast and teach it to control its sphincter muscles (Kristeva
70–72).

By contrast the idealized male (read "heterosexual") body is one that
maintains successful patrol over its own boundaries, keeping abjection under
control. The incontinent male and the homosexual male are both identified as
men who cannot control the major gateway of abjection in the male body, the
sphincters. A male who cannot control abjection is, by metonymic extension,
himself abject and feminized. The fantasmatic image of the male homosexual
in American culture is "the seductive and intolerable image of a grown man,
legs high in the air, unable to refuse the suicidal ecstasy of being a woman"
(Bersani 212). The ecstatic opening of the male body to penetration, most
particularly anal penetration, threatens to undo the entire project of modern
American masculinity.

In late-twentieth-century American culture, the prison is imagined as the
place for abject males; the idea of a prison as disposal is not unique to William
Inge. Here are two examples: one from the sexual margins, the other from the
Hollywood mainstream.

(1) The web page for the Rochester Rams, a gay leather club (at
http://uglybear.com/rams/run2001/index.shtml) announces the 2001 theme
for its annual summer outing: *Jailbreak*. Attendees are invited to participate
as prisoners, guards, or observers. The roles are described:

> The inmates are treated like the human refuse they know they are; they
> get deloused, shorn, put into prison uniforms (which you keep!) and walk
> around in a chain gang. They may even have separate housing and face extra,
> mandatory time in Cabin 4 as hapless victims of the guards.

> [. . .] The Guards are in charge of the Inmates, and get to subject them to whatever abuse and humiliation they please (within limits—go outside the limits and you might wind up an Inmate yourself). You get a badge (yours for life!) and the authority that goes with it.
> [. . .] Everyone else is Just Visiting.

This mimicry has nothing subversive in it. The power relationship between guard and convict is eroticized in terms that are utterly unproblematized. The subjectivity of the prisoners is completely determined by the judgment of the outside world—"the human refuse they know they are"—and this realization and enactment of their own abjectness is held out as a source of pleasure. It effortlessly maps the social abjection of the gay man onto the abjection of the prisoner. Such a mimesis certainly strains the limits of Judith Butler's celebrations of the liberating dynamics of performing gender. Rather, it brings to mind Leo Bersani's clear-sighted observation: "If licking someone's leather boots turns you (and him) on, neither of you is making a statement subversive of macho masculinity" (Bersani 208).

(2) *Mallrats.* Kevin Smith's 1995 teen comedy, which pretends to be iconoclastic while being firmly rooted in American middle-class, heterosexist attitudes, shows how the brutal and sexually exploitative young proprietor of Fashionable Male, Shannon Hamilton (played by Ben Affleck), gets his comeuppance. An arrogant seducer who prefers anal intercourse, he boasts that he uses his manipulative skills on young women in order to "fuck 'em someplace rather uncomfortable [. . .] someplace girls dread". When the plot's intrigues finally land him in prison for the statutory rape of a sexually precocious fifteen-year-old, the film delights in a reversal of sexual roles. As we see a male's hand in close-up, clutching the bar of a cell, a title underneath the shot tells us "Shannon made a lot of new friends in Rahway State Correctional Facility," and another hand, this one with "love" crudely tattooed on it, places itself over the first. Shannon, we are coyly led to infer, is being taken "someplace rather uncomfortable," a place that not only *girls* dread. Indeed, while the movie can include talk and visual representations of females being anally penetrated by males, the film can only imply the anal penetration of males by males through visual and verbal indirection. In a movie that prides itself on its bawdiness and gross-out humor, its timidity around the subject of male homosexuality is a sign of its ultimate conservatism. The culture of male rape in prison is trivialized to give a sniggering, comic poetic justice to the sodomite and his "filthy" desire.[2]

The incarceration of Shannon, ostensibly for sexual relations with a minor (though teen sexuality is so taken for granted in the movie that the offense seems pointless), adumbrates that laws against anal intercourse, even between consenting adults, have been a major weapon in the oppression of gay men, and, although such laws have diminished both in number and in frequency of application, the Supreme Court of the United States still upholds the right of the states to enact and enforce such laws. Shannon's putative offense, sexual relations with a minor, stands in for a second offense, anal intercourse with a woman, which in turn stands in for the barely mentionable "real" offense, which is sexual relations with a *man*. Shannon, for all his macho preening, is ultimately coded as a queer—a sodomite with an unseemly interest in the men's fashions that he sells at the mall. Best to send him off to prison, the film suggests, and rape him. For, at base, in the social imaginary of *Mallrats* every gay man is a criminal deviant.

A similar dynamic is at work in *Jailbreak,* in which the one quality all prisoners share in their abjection is a common gay desire. The fact that very desire could easily have landed them in prison in many states, and still leaves them vulnerable to harassment and the threat of violence, is obscured by the presentation on the website; but, in fact, one of the things that *Jailbreak* reenacts is the abjection of gay men.

The Disposal. Jailbreak. Mallrats. Through American theater, fantasy enactment, and Hollywood cinema, over three decades, the terms circulate with disturbing tenacity: Criminality = Abjection = Anality = Male Homosexuality.

Given this discursive dynamic of abjection and male homosexuality, one would expect Archie, the *"screechingly effeminate"* (Inge 125) homosexual on death row to be the most abject character in *The Disposal,* and in certain respects he is. Sarcastic, cruel, and altogether lacking in compassion, he verbally castrates his fellow inmates by referring to them as if they were women. He perversely refers to his sexual molestation at age eight as "undoubtedly the happiest day of my life" (131). He pretentiously orders a *haute cuisine* last meal for Jess, which the condemned man is unable to enjoy; he therefore winds up consuming it himself. He is seen by the others as a monstrosity; Luke refers to him as a hermaphrodite with a vagina in his esophagus (141). A strident mixture of masculine aggressivity and feminine affectation, he seems at first to be an improbable killer. Yet, in other respects, Archie is the strongest of the prisoners. Rather than internalizing the negative image others have of him, he asserts it. Resolutely unsentimental, unrepentant, atheistic, and unapologetically "out," he provides a stance of opposition to the ideology of the prison. Relishing the prospect of a last meal of Sénégalese soup, salade mimosa, and chicken paprikash, he works to shape the minuscule areas of freedom available to him as a prisoner to assert both his sensibility and his desire. Similarly, he can create an atmosphere of flirtatious play between himself and one of the guards:

ARCHIE: [. . .] I always have *you* dear to greet me every morning in those crazy boots.
GUARD: You *like* these boots, huh?

ARCHIE: Mad for them.
GUARD: If you're a good boy, I'll come along some time and let ya lick
'em.
ARCHIE: Promise?
(*The* GUARD *laughs*) (127)

There are shades of *Jailbreak* here, and certainly Archie is not subversive of
macho masculinity. He later brings his admiration for masculine violence to
an appalling extreme as he professes his attraction to rapist-murderer Joe. But
in his exchange with the guard, it is never clear whether either of them is at all
serious about the sexual exchange or merely playing at the cliché for its comic
effect. Certainly the effect of the exchange, climaxing in laughter, is one of the
more relaxed moments of interchange in an otherwise intensely grim play. At
the same time, Archie is a realist who harbors no illusions about his impending
execution and relies on no sentimental beliefs to soften the harshness of his
situation. He has nothing but his abject self, which he asserts nakedly.

Inge also renders Archie more complex by making him the play's most intelligent and well-read character. Although he could have identified the play's
existentialist thought with Luke, the mature and restrained heterosexual, thus
casting him in the character type of the reflective prison intellectual, Inge
makes the interesting choice of linking abjection with intellectual sophistication. Archie cites Nietzsche, Kierkegaard, Proust, Wilde, and Edna St. Vincent
Millay. His ultimate model might be Jean Genet, with his idiosyncratic mixture of existentialist themes, unmotivated crimes, unrepentant tough guys, and
queer sexuality. Turning his abjection into a sign of provocation, Archie works
a queer Nietzschean recalibration of values, becoming a prison *übermensch,* or
as Archie might prefer to put it, *übermädchen.* European existentialism finds
its proponent in the phallic mother of camp entertainment (Gross 15–16).

In its idiosyncratic mixture of camp, European existentialism, and realistic
prison melodrama, *The Disposal* is more quirky and complex than its reviewers
acknowledged. For example, in his attempt to dismiss it as a piece of outmoded
melodrama, Edward Sothern Hipp charged that Inge's prison play was little
more than a pallid imitation of John Wexley's prison melodrama, *The Last
Mile,* which had enjoyed a critically successful run on Broadway in 1930. Even
Inge's title for this early version of "The Disposal" that Hipp reviewed—"The
Last Pad," echoed Wexley's title, but with a touch of Beat "cool" in the idea
of a prison cell as a "pad." Given the similarity of setting and title, Hipp's
intertextual connection seems valid at first. On closer examination, however,
the assertion is misleading. Actually, the differences between Wexley's play
and Inge's are more illuminating than the similarities. *The Last Mile* is a
realistic prison melodrama that depicts an unsuccessful uprising on death row
in a state penitentiary. In the first act, we see the preparations for Richard
Walters's execution in the electric chair and the effects it has on him and

the six other prisoners. The characters are quickly identifiable types whose crimes are unambiguous and easily explained. D'Amoro, for example, shot a policeman in self-defense, while Walters accidentally killed his sweetheart in an outburst of jealous rage. There is the placid African American who sings spirituals, the eccentric intellectual who quotes Tennyson, and the volatile and dangerous John "Killer" Mears. The act builds as Walters's walk of "the last mile" (from the convict's cell to the electric chair) nears. We learn that the governor has refused to stay the execution. Walters's hair is cut, he makes a confession to the chaplain, and he is led offstage. As the curtain is about to fall, the lights in the cellblock rise, dip, and rise again, as the electric chair drains power from the cellblock with each surge. Mears yells in agony, "They're givin' him the juice again (*shouts in terrible rage*). What the hell are they tryin' to do? Cook him?" (1:41).

In the second act, another man is about to be executed when Mears rebels, taking the chaplain, the principal keeper, and guards hostage. "Better to go down fighting" he asserts (2:14). Taking matters into his own hands, he repudiates the entire system that has condemned and imprisoned him. "I'm sick of you and your talk of God," he tells the chaplain. "I'm the law now" (2:17). Demanding freedom for himself and his fellow inmates, he threatens to begin killing the hostages if his demand is not met. The terms of the first act are neatly reversed; now it is the prison staff that is powerless and terrified in the face of death, while the prisoners become guards and executioners.

In the final act, the revolt has elicited the full power of the state: Five hundred soldiers with machine guns and a thousand armed civilians stand outside the prison walls, while Mears holds fast to his threat, killing the first of the hostages, even though he knows he has only six bullets left. He realizes that he has no chance of winning freedom for himself and the others, but he is determined to make the people realize what it means to be forced to sit and count down the moments until one's death. If he must die in the uprising, it is better to die this way, "like men, not rats in a trap" (3:16). Suddenly, however, one of the prisoners is seriously wounded by a shot through the cell window, and Mears calls an end to the uprising so the wounded man can be taken to the hospital and cared for. Mears goes out shooting, the intellectual prisoner intones lines from Tennyson's "The Charge of the Light Brigade," and the curtain falls on a scene of heroic nobility.

The Last Mile and *The Disposal* ultimately have little in common but setting. Wexley's play accentuates a hierarchy of power in the prison. It is a suspensefully plotted melodrama with two major reversals. In the first, the prisoners take control of the cellblock; in the second, they relinquish it. The reversals are key moments in a carefully wrought succession of causally bound events. The play is overtly political insofar as it uses its melodramatic devices to foreground inequalities of power in a social institution and to critique it. Inge, however, shows little interest in any political dimension of his setting, but he uses it metaphorically. In Inge's play, the prisoners remain subordinated from beginning to end, without even a fantasy of rebellion or escape, but the workers in the prison are reduced to ciphers. In *The Disposal,* the prison becomes a site of anxiety, abjection, and Being-toward-death. Inge's inspiration seems more drawn from Archie's existentialist reading list than from documentary or political writings on prison. He links the dramatic episodes loosely, filling in the time from the rise of the curtain to Jess's inevitable death. Since the prisoners are put in a situation where their actions can have no effect, the play generates no suspense. The mechanism of disposal works impersonally, apart from any individualized agent.

Wexley shows the inmates as bound together by a common sympathy, which guides them in their conduct toward each other. When Tom D'Amoro is introduced into the cellblock, Major observes, "D'Amoro sounds like a French word I know. Amour. It means ... love," to which Tom replies, "Say, ain't that a funny word to say at this place and at this time" (1:29). But there is love in the cellblock, a presence that is made clearly manifest when Mears agrees to surrender in hopes of saving Major's life. The prisoners in *The Last Mile* gain dramatic stature and dignity in potentially dehumanizing circumstances; the final evocation of Tennyson's Light Brigade is apt.

While eros in *The Last Mile* is sublimated into Tennysonian idealism, it is perverted into aggressivity in *The Disposal.* Inge's prisoners share no common bond, not even the threat of capital punishment, and they lash out at each other in their desperation. Archie baits the other men endlessly, and they repudiate him in turn as a "faggot" and "commie." The convicts take bets as to whether the condemned man will lose control of his bowels as he goes to his death. Unlike Wexley's convicts, whose crimes are described as acts of self-defense, jealousy, or accident, only Inge's Luke, who shot a man during a robbery, is free of any tinge of psychosis. Luke alone hearkens back to Wexley's play, as if he is a remnant of an earlier form of prison drama. All the others have murdered women out of motives that remain obscure. Archie murdered his mother and grandmother. Joe "entered a sorority house and raped three girls and killed almost a dozen" (145). Jess explains that he murdered his unborn child because he found the idea of his offspring abject; he views his wife as nothing more than a vessel for the child's gestation. The play is permeated with a violent misogyny. Luke's mother was a sexually voracious woman who had sex "with the plumber, the ice man, the electrician" (131), Jess's sister is a prostitute, and Jess's father insists that his son's wife was promiscuous as well. But religiosity, which is presented as the alternative to promiscuity, is presented as equally dangerous. "I dunno which is worse," reflects Jess, "to have a mother that's a whore or one that is crazy religious" (131). Luke's wife, Mona, is an upright Christian woman who reduces her usually stoic husband to tears, because, as Luke explains, "She talks to me . . . like I was already dead" (139). Both the pious and the promiscuous woman alike reduce their men to a state of nonexistence. Mothers, and by extension all women, are repeatedly figures of abjection.

The play's three fathers—the state, the divinity, and the domestic patriarch—are no better than the women at helping the men come to terms with their abjectness. The state and the godhead are remote and unknowable. Jess's father (who is given no proper name but is presented as a type) refuses to work as an embodiment of law, but surprisingly insists on his son's innocence, and refuses to even consider the possibility of his guilt even when his son admits it. While Mona reduces Luke with her pious distance, the father hurls Jess into an abyss of despair by refusing to engage his guilt. In *The Disposal,* the prisoners are surrounded by figures—spouses, parents, offspring and chaplains—who deny them by refusing to engage them on the level of their abjection.

After he leaves, Jess, whose clean-cut and boyish qualities seem completely at odds with his status as murderer of wife and unborn child, breaks loose in a torrent of self-excoriation, "I've robbed. I've lied. I've stolen. I've pushed dope. I've committed *every* sin in the book!" (144). This admission seems abrupt and unjustified in this character who was first introduced by Inge in a stage direction as "*a young man of about thirty who, despite his mature years, still acts like a boy, still seems to us like a boy*" (125). It is possible to tease out a somewhat tortured line of reasoning for the construction of this oddly incoherent character: Jess, the argument would run, is one of life's innocents, who has not been hardened by his offenses but disgusted by them, so much so that his disgust and self-hatred found its object in his unborn child. He finally admits that he killed the child because "I didn't have the guts to look at any life that came from *me*" (144). It is ultimately the boyish Jess, rather than the overtly homosexual Archie, who is tormented by abjection. But the combination of abject horror and boyishness is contrived. It makes it necessary for Jess to remain boyish, innocent, despite the life he has lived. Inge keeps us ignorant of Jess's moral abjection through most of the play so that it can spill out, incontinently, after the patriarch appears and refuses to act as a carrier of law. Jess is a fractured figure who is unconvincing as a realistic character and whose movement from innocence to abjection owes less to verisimilitude than to allegory. It is not worth the effort trying to justify Jess as a psychologically coherent character, which would lead to nothing more than a psychoanalytically based sophistry imposed on a fictional construct. Far better to interrogate the highly charged and contradictory associations that cluster around Jess, to consider him, in Deleuzean terms, as an "assemblage."[3]

While Luke is presented as a mature heterosexual man whose masculinity is never questioned and who seems not to be threatened by Archie's references to him as "Princess Lukemia" (126), and Archie is an aggressively energetic performance of a monstrous aberration of gender, Jess's position is anxious. The boyishness that Inge is at pains to emphasize from the start may be on the road to masculinity but has not yet arrived there. Both Jess and Archie are seen as less manly than Luke is, but while Archie repudiates the traditional masculine role, Jess is tormented by his relationship to it. Jess, unlike Luke, feels threatened by Archie's camp feminizing of everyone: "Don't call me a bitch, you faggot. A bitch is what you call a woman. You talk like everyone in the whole goddamn world was a woman. But *I'm* no woman, see" (123). Here Jess positions women as the abject. After all, a "bitch" is not what you call a woman; it's what you call a female dog. Jess feels the need to distance himself from a language that feminizes him, in part because his masculinity is insecure. He needs his father to come and help him deal with his crime, needing a personalized and yet idealized figure to compensate for his own abjection.

How does Jess's admission that he has committed *every* sin in the book resonate in a play so involved with issues of queer male sexuality? The word *every* includes homosexual sex acts, but it moves by quickly enough to blur the significance of this admission. To what extent is Inge summoning up Bersani's "seductive and intolerable image of a grown man, legs high in the air, unable to refuse the suicidal ecstasy of being a woman," in that *every,* and to what extent does it make even the playwright nervous, anxious to move on from a spectacle both attractive and abject?

It is only when the guards come to take Jess to the electric chair, however, that we are faced with the full extent of Jess's abjection. He not only loses control of his bowels, but he also loses control of his temper, and, for the first time, challenges the forces that have judged him and condemned him to death:

> Git away from me you sons a bitches! Get away! Ya got no right to make me die! *You* ain't no rightful judge a anything I done. Take your hands off me, ya dirty mother-fuckers! I hate your goddamn guts! I hate all of you! I got enough hate inside me now to rile up heaven forever! I got hate enough now to turn heaven into hell! (144)

Hatred and fecal matter are released simultaneously. From the release of guilt in his confession to his final release of hatred as he struggles for his life, Jess's precarious masculinity is increasingly unable to contain his powerful abjectness. Yet only at the last moment does that abjection begin to take on some of the oppositional power and rage of Archie's speech.

The play's ending returns to the chaplain's point of view, one that has been changed by Jess's abjection. He has been convinced by the experience that we need to look at "man" not from any idealizing or judgmental perspective, but to find humanity in the abjectness of fear, horror, and incontinence. "Let us love man as he is, with his weakness and fears," he urges (146). He rejects a notion of heroic masculinity, as found in *The Last Mile,* and replaces it with an acceptance of abjection. Inge argues for a Christianity and a dramaturgy that can embrace abjection rather than treat it with loathing and exclusion.

Inge begins his play with a prayer and ends it with a homily, as if to contain the play's abjection within the most edifying and idealized genres. This framing, however, is insufficient to contain the forces released by the play. The chaplain's speech monologically imposes a conclusion on the play. It does not engage any of the other viewpoints that have been voiced. Most importantly, it ignores Jess's anger, which becomes rescripted as "weakness and fears" (significantly, while Jess exploded in rage, the chaplain intoned a prayer for the dying, whether to comfort him or drown out his challenge to the system, is far from clear), and it is blind to Luke's stoicism and Archie's contemptuous nihilism. Jess's final moments become paradigmatic of every man's; "Jess took his destruction as any man might" (146). The chaplain forecloses the question of how Luke, Archie, and Joe will meet their executions by imposing the figure of Jess as Everyman, just as Inge does by bringing the curtain down so soon after Jess's death. These techniques of closure provoke no questioning, only a somewhat complacent acquiescence to the status quo: "I am proud that men are as good as they *are,* and have come as far as they have from their humble origins" (146). The chaplain's rapid and easy intellectual distancing from the horrors of the execution makes his conclusions seem facile; his self-aggrandizing gesture of referring to men in the third-person plural, as if they are a group he can stand apart from and judge compassionately, makes his speech ring disingenuously; and his rapid exit cuts off any possible challenge to his words. The *agon* between Archie and the chaplain, outsider and insider, existentialist and Christian, pervert and idealist, is never allowed to take place. Works that release the abject run the risk of being seen as abject themselves, and such is the case with *The Disposal.* Masterpieces are rare; good plays are unusual enough to merit heartfelt thanks; and the overwhelming majority of dramatic literature is boring and inept. Dedicated theatergoers learn to endure this reality stoically, looking for the silver lining of every theatrical cloud that passes their way, while at the same time trying to protect themselves from the next fiasco. But the avidity with which reviewers ran down to the Thirteenth Street Theatre to document what seemed to be the next stage in Inge's professional decline, and the scorn with which they met it, suggests that more was at stake here than a mere concern with maintaining theatrical standards. When some of them take pains to point out that this is a homosexual play by a homosexual author, they betray a bias of their own. Martin Gottfried takes this the furthest, using the occasion to link Inge with Edward Albee and Tennessee Williams, citing *Tiny Alice* and *The Milk Train Doesn't Stop Here Any More* as plays flawed by virtue of a similar "obsession" with homosexuality (Gottfried 15–17). Gottfried's summary disposal of these gay playwrights makes the act of reviewing itself a ritual of abjection. The silence that has grown up in the wake of that ritual is revealing as well, as if the best way to protect Inge's maligned reputation is to dispose of *The Disposal* as efficiently as possible. In light of these strategies of reception, I would suggest that *The Disposal* is not merely a drama about abjection, but it is itself an abject drama.

Kristeva writes about a strain of abject writing in modern literature: Dostoevski, Lautréamont, Artaud, Proust, Borges, and, above all, Céline. One could easily add to her list: Alan Ginsberg, William Burroughs, Jean Genet, Sarah Kane, Karen Finley, and Dennis Cooper. Kristeva finds the writing of the abject a perverse writing, one that registers the oppressiveness of religion, morality, and law, that requires a softening of the superego and a projection into the abject itself. By doing so, this writing is often judged as abject itself. It is often rejected during the author's lifetime, usually lapsing into oblivion. Only in some cases is it rediscovered posthumously and reevaluated, allowing the "writer of abjection to escape his condition of waste, reject, abject" as it is claimed for "literature" (Kristeva 16). The scandal of *The Disposal,* particularly as the product of an author known for such canonical texts of American Cold War heteronormative romance as *Bus Stop, Picnic,* and *Splendor in the Grass,* has led to the oblivion that Kristeva finds is so often the fate of abject literature.

The Disposal seems ill at ease with its own abject status. The reintroduction of the chaplain as an idealizing figure seems a desperate attempt to fashion a kinder, gentler superego that can embrace the abject and reward it for having come as far as it has. But the attempt is brisk, awkward, and truncated, making no attempt to engage abjection on stage as it manifests itself in the three condemned men who are still alive. One almost wishes that Wexley's "Killer" Mears was onstage to respond, "I'm sick of you and your talk of God" (2:17). Abjection, once released in a work of art, is impossible to safely contain.

The most important abject drama to appear in the American theater in recent decades is David Greenspan's 1991 *Dead Mother, or Shirley Not All in Vain.* It elicited much the same savage attack that *The Disposal* suffered and that Kristeva noted is often the fate of abject writing. Frank Rich considered it a slight domestic drama tricked out with hours of pretentious filler, remarking that "the playwright's ego knows no limits" and that he is a person of "apparently boundless pretension and self-indulgence" (3). John Simon left after the first act, fumed over watching the work of a "profoundly untalented and deeply incoherent" playwright "fond of bathroom scenes" (64), and indignantly asked how producer Joseph Papp could use taxpayer dollars to underwrite such work (65).

Dead Mother revisits the notion of embracing anal abjection as a source for opposition to an unjust social order. Here it is the closeted Harold who, following a farcical premise reminiscent of *Charley's Aunt* (Feingold in Greenspan 299), begins to channel the impulses of his dead mother, Shirley, as he impersonates her. Shirley was committed to a mental institution and killed herself years before. Her speeches are abject streams of scatology and bigotry, and her anger is as great as Archie's, or even Jess's at the full flood of his abjection. Appalled by his mother's tirades and homophobic prejudices, he nonetheless finds himself descending into the underworld to get information about the past from her. Led through a queer version of Dante's *Inferno* (perhaps Western literature's most famous journey of abjection) with Alice B. Toklas as his Virgil, Harold sees the myriad forms of homophobia at work in his culture. Finally Harold finds Shirley in the underworld, where she is watching *Hollywood Squares* on television, and gains the information and magic talismans he needs. As he does so:

> a contestant on the game show says "I'll take Paul Lynde to win." Then Peter Marshall asks Paul Lynde, "Paul—what does it mean if you are anally retentive?" Paul Lynde responds "It means you're full of shit." Shirley smiles; at that, Harold bursts into flame, and flaming surges toward the surface. (367)

The elements are familiar: the abject mother, the abject gay hero, the campy gay celebrity, the linkage of anality with the gay man, and the comic knowledge that being "anally retentive"—holding one's sphincters tight—only means that one is "full of shit." The knowledge is liberating for Harold, who is transformed from his closeted self to a "flaming" self. Once back on the surface, he uses the persona of his dead mother to confront his father, accusing him of making his life miserable, of exploiting undocumented alien labor, and of falsifying his own family history. Shirley's accusations and rage are no longer mere scatological rantings. Fused with Harold's growing queer understanding, they provide a powerful moral critique of white, patriarchal, middle-class mendacity and corruption. Harold's embrace of the abject provides him a way to move forward, revealing family secrets, settling scores, and moving out, not only out of the confinement of his closeted existence and marriage, but out of the play itself. In the last scene, Harold has disappeared altogether.

Twenty-one years after *The Disposal,* Greenspan is able to rework the tropes of abjectness, homosexuality, and incarceration, finding a way to use the politically committed critique of *The Last Mile* without its stoic idealization, and the abject energies of *The Disposal* without the despairing tone and compromised ending. By breaking the linkage between anality and criminality, Greenspan is able to imagine emancipatory possibilities completely undreamed of in *Jailbreak* and *Mallrats,* possibilities approached bravely but with deep conflicts in *The Disposal.*

Notes

1. For an insightful explanation and critique of Kristeva's complex and often elliptical work, see Bruneau. For a fascinating application of Kristeva's insights to a dramatic text—in this case, Friedrich Schiller's *The Robbers*—see Hammer, 27–49.

2. For the use of the term *male rape* as preferable to the more common term *homosexual rape,* see Sedgwick 225.
3. For a discussion of Deleuze's notion of assemblages in relation to fictional characters, see Colebrook 81–87.

Works Cited

Bersani, Leo. "Is the Rectum a Grave?" *AIDS: Cultural Analysis, Cultural Activism.* Edited by Douglas Crimp. Cambridge, Mass.: MIT Press, 1988. 197–222.

Bruneau, Marie-Florine. "Psychoanalysis and Its Abject: What Lurks behind the Fear of the 'Mother.'" *Studies in Psychoanalytic Theory* 1 (Fall 1992): 24–38.

Colebrook, Claire. *Gilles Deleuze.* New York: Routledge, 2002.

Feld, Bruce. "*The Disposal.*" *Drama-Logue* 9 (August 1990) 9.

Gottfried, Martin. "*The Last Pad.*" *Women's Wear Daily* 8 December 1970.

Greenspan, David. *Dead Mother, or Shirley Not All in Vain.* In *Grove New American Theater.* Ed. Michael Feingold. New York: Grove Press, 1993. 297–386.

Gross, Robert F. "O'Neill's Queer *Interlude:* Epicene Excess and Camp Pleasures." *Journal of Dramatic Theory and Criticism* 12.1 (Fall 1997): 3–22.

Hammer, Stephanie. *Schiller's Wound: The Theater of Trauma from Crisis to Community.* Detroit: Wayne State University Press, 2001.

Hipp, Edward Sothern. "New Drama by Inge." *Newark Evening News* 7 December 1970: 26.

Inge, William. *The Disposal.* In *Best Short Plays of the World Theatre, 1958–1967.* Ed. Stanley Richards. New York: Crown, 1986: 125–146.

Kristeva, Julia. *Powers of Horror: An Essay on Abjection.* Trans. Leon S. Roudiez. New York: Columbia University Press, 1982.

Leeson, Richard M. *William Inge: A Research and Production Sourcebook.* New York: Greenwood Press, 1994.

McNulty, Charles. "Cameos." *Village Voice* 11 August 1992: 100.

Mishkin, Leo. "Inge's 'The Last Pad' an Amateurish Job." *New York Morning-Telegraph* 8 December 1970: 3.

Rich, Frank. "A Dead Jewish Mother and Layers of Guilt." *The New York Times* 1 February 1991: C, 3.

Sedgwick, Eve Kosofsky. *Between Men: English Literature and Male Homosocial Desire.* New York: Columbia University Press, 1985.

Shuman, R. Baird. *William Inge.* Rev ed. Boston: Twayne, 1989.

Simon, John. "Near-Myth." *New York* 24.6 (February 11, 1991): 64–65.

Smith, Kevin, dir. *Mallrats.* Video cassette, 1995.

Ungarno, "Beyond Broadway." *Theatre Week* 24 August 1992: 41.

Voss, Ralph F. "William Inge." *Twentieth-Century American Dramatists.* 3rd ser. Ed. Christopher Wheatley. Vol. 249 *of Dictionary of Literary Biography.* Boston: Bruccoli Clark Layman, 2002: 167–179.

Washburn, Martin. "Concept of Betrayals." *Village Voice* 10 December 1970: 60.

Wexley, John. *The Last Mile.* Typescript. 13 February 1930. Theater Collection, New York Public Library.

9

"In Dark Corners": Masculinity and Art in Tennessee Williams's *Not about Nightingales*

THOMAS FAHY

Locked away and forgotten for more than fifty years in the archives of the Harry Ransom Humanities Research Center at the University of Texas at Austin, *Not about Nightingales* (1938) has a history of neglect and obscurity that seems fitting for its subject matter: prison.[1] Tennessee Williams wrote this play, which remained unperformed until its 1998 London premiere, as an impassioned response to the 1938 "Klondike" massacre at the Philadelphia County Prison in Holmesburg, Pennsylvania. According to *Newsweek* in September of that year, twenty-five prisoners were locked into small cells "equipped with a bank of steam radiators nearly sufficient to heat a baby skyscraper" and "given the heat" for instigating a hunger strike that involved 650 of the 1,481 prisoners ("Prison Scandal" 10). Four men (Henry Osborn, Frank Comodeca, John Walters, and James McQuade) "had been baked to death. Their hearts had been shrunk to half normal size by the process of dehydration" (10). With this horrific event as subject matter, Williams clearly places *Not about Nightingales* in the tradition of both 1930s proletarian drama, such as Clifford Odets's *Waiting for Lefty* (1935) and Lillian Hellman's *The Little Foxes* (1939), and the work of the Federal Theater Project.[2] Yet Williams's play is not merely theater of social protest; it also uses captivity to dramatize a tension between masculinity and art as the protagonist struggles for both literal and creative freedom.

It is not surprising that *Nightingales,* the first play Thomas Lanier Williams signed as "Tennessee,"[3] makes a statement about artistic identity as well as social injustice. Still a struggling playwright in 1938, Williams sent the manuscript and several one-act plays to a literary contest in New York. The result would galvanize his career, but not because of *Nightingales.* As Allean Hale explains in "*Not about Nightingales:* Tennessee Williams as Social Activist," "The reader [for the contest] (Mrs. Elia Kazan) wrote that *Nightingales* had 'interesting elements' but was not as completely realized as were the one-acts. The short plays won an award of $100, which drew the attention of agent Audrey Wood, who started Tom's Broadway career" (348). This critique may have contributed to Williams's decision to shelve the play, but its subsequent neglect does not mitigate the importance of *Nightingales* as a statement about artistic identity. Williams tells the story of a hunger strike and prison revolt primarily through the eyes of "Canary" Jim, a prison snitch who writes propaganda for the warden in order to expedite his parole. Scorned by fellow inmates and stifled by the newsletter he is forced to write, Jim feels emasculated by his choices not to act against or write in protest of the abusive conditions at the prison. Only participating in the revolt *and* jumping to literal (and artistic) freedom at the end of the play restore his manhood. At this moment, Jim not only moves from captivity (a space where art, like love, occurs "in dark corners") to freedom (where art and expression are openly possible), but he also forges an artistic identity that is compatible with his definition of masculinity.

In some ways, the masculine-centered world of *Nightingales* may seem strange, considering that Williams's later career would be defined, in part, by his exceptional female characters. As critic C. J. Gianakaris notes, "During his banner years on Broadway, women characters formed the core of his stories. Women dominated the action, and women's names—such as Laura, Blanche, and Maggie—have since become synonymous with Williams's dramas" (71–72). Yet the women in *Nightingales* are either weak, ineffectual, or victimized. In a sense, they are held captive by men—unable to take the kind of social action validated in the play—and Williams contrasts this inertia with male action. Williams limits the agency and complexity of these women characters, in part, to make this play about the solidarity and art of men. When Jim decides to act for both his own writing as well as the other inmates, he achieves heroic stature. Art becomes more powerful than violence. And Williams uses this moment to suggest that art can inspire social change/action and, in doing so, redefine conventional notions of manhood.

"Zero Hour!": Acting Like a Man

By making prisoners visible on stage, the theater of imprisonment challenges audiences to "see" the humanity of these figures and in turn recognize some of the social injustices of incarceration. Prisons are designed, in part, to make criminals invisible, hiding them behind stone walls and steel bars to make mainstream society feel physically and ideologically secure. As Elliot Currie explains in *Crime and Punishment in America:*

> Our growing reliance on incarceration helps us avoid confronting a host of deep and stubborn social problems: continuing joblessness in inner cities, persistent child poverty, and the virtual collapse of preventive public-health

and mental-health care, the paucity of effective drug treatment and adequate schooling for children of the poor, the absence of the kind of supportive family policies that virtually every other advanced nation maintains. A swollen correctional system allows us to sweep these problems under the rug, but it does not make them go away, and, indeed makes them worse. (191)[4]

Our reliance on the penal system not only fails to address these social problems, but, as Currie suggests, it also contributes to the popular and political indifference about those behind bars. Once an individual has been convicted and imprisoned, what happens to him or her no longer matters in the public imagination. As Butch, one of the central characters in *Not about Nightingales,* explains to a new arrival: "A con ain't a human being. [. . .] He's stuck in here and the world's forgot him. As far as the world is concerned he don't exist anymore. What happens to him in here—them people outside don't know, they don't care" (53). The theater of imprisonment tries to rectify this indifference through visibility—putting the prison experience into a palpable and confined space (on stage) with real people (actors). The subsequent intimacy between audience and actor forges a personal investment in the topic that can become the starting point for social change. In *Not about Nightingales,* for example, Tennessee Williams attempts to break the "conspiracy of silence"[5] surrounding the "Klondike" massacre by making his audience care about Butch's and Jim's outcomes. A true investment in their story, therefore, demands some kind of commitment to their cry for justice.

To encourage this, Williams retells the Holmesburg incident in a way that emphasizes solidarity as essential for fighting injustice. The central story of *Nightingales* involves the struggle between Butch, a tough, petulant inmate who threatens to organize a hunger strike in protest of the sickening food, and "Boss" Warden, the man who runs the prison with sadistic fury. The monotonous servings of beans, hamburger, and spaghetti continue, however, and Butch (along with the men of hall C) refuses to eat. The Warden, hoping to avoid the public attention of a prolonged strike, decides to torture the men, sending twenty-five strikers to the "Klondike." Every few hours, the temperature is raised another five degrees (ten for Butch's cell), and ultimately, the four men with Butch are scalded to death. At the end of the play, Butch escapes the cell with the help of Jim and leads a revolt against the Warden. Both Butch and the Warden are presented as strong, unrelenting men, and their mutual animosity is expressed through displays of power—such as Butch's threats ("Tell him some day we're going to appoint a special committee of one to come down there an' settle up the score" [22]) and the Warden's vindictive response to defiance ("Git it up to 145 in Butch's compartment" [142]). Yet *Nightingales* is not merely a story about the power struggle between two strong men. It is about pervasive problems in the American penal system. Williams makes this clear in his opening stage directions: "The action takes place in a large American prison during the summer of 1938. The conditions which the play presents are those of no particular prison but a composite picture of many" (1). This composite shows prison to be an abusive space where questions of justice and humanity are irrelevant. It is also a space where the individual cannot survive alone. The men who spend too much time in the "hole," for example, are physically and psychologically destroyed. Jim is ostracized for working independently with the Warden. It is only collective action, therefore, that has the power to make meaningful changes.

For Williams, Butch and Jim—who embody masculinity and art respectively—establish the most important dichotomy of the play. With his generic name and physical prowess, Butch begins the play as a stereotypical embodiment of manhood, but his reliance on others ultimately modifies this image, reinforcing Williams's message about communal power. His name, like that of "Mex" (for the Hispanic), "Queen" (for the homosexual), and "Swifty" (for the runner), functions metaphorically. They are all appropriately nondescript, capturing the anonymity of inmates—people who are locked behind bars so society can forget about them. Though Butch has a last name (O'Fallon), unlike Mex or Queen, his first name clearly defines his character—tough, strong, blunt, and working class. Butch is so quintessentially masculine that his physical power instills fear and admiration in the other men:

> BUTCH: Lissen here now!—Anybody in Hall C that eats is gonna pay for his supper in Kangaroo Court. I'll assess the maximum fine, you know what!— You're scared of Klondike? I say let 'em throw us in Klondike!—Maybe some of you weak sisters will be melted down to grease-chunks. But not all twenty-five of us! Some of us are gonna beat Klondike! And Klondike's dere las' trump card, when you got that licked, you've licked everything they've got to offer in here! [. . .]
> VOICE: Okay, Butch.
> ANOTHER: We're witcha! (122–23)

Butch presents weakness, inaction, and capitulation as feminine traits ("you weak sisters"), in part, to persuade his fellow inmates to be men—to take action by refusing to eat. This implied comparison also reflects an important distinction in the play between being a man and acting like one. As suggested earlier, a true man needs both physical strength and communal solidarity to survive, and Butch continually persuades/threatens the men to strike because he realizes that his strength alone is not enough. In the end, he survives the "Klondike" and, as promised, enacts revenge on the Warden in the final episode: "(*Butch strikes him with the hose.* [. . .] *The* [Warden's] *final word turns into a scream of anguish as Butch crouches over him with the whip beating him with demoniacal fury till he is senseless*)" (158). Yet this individual act of retribution is only possible because of Jim, who unlocks Butch's cell and steals a gun from one of the guards. Together, they free each other and the other men (if only temporarily); they become heroic by working together to destroy the warden's regime of abuse and terror. At this moment, Williams is clearly manipulating the trope that equates passivity (and femininity) with art and masculinity with action. If Jim takes action, then the artist is masculine. (Without Jim, Butch cannot survive.) Therefore, it is art—like the play Williams writes—that has the real power to fight injustice.

Through Jim, the play also suggests that every man is faced with a "Zero Hour"—a choice between selfishness and social sacrifice, waiting and action—and as with Butch, Williams presents this moment in gendered terms. For ten years, Jim has worked for the Warden, compromising his integrity and sense of self-worth for the prospect of an early release. As editor and writer for the monthly prison newspaper, *The Archaeopteryx,* he has discovered the power of language to influence the way people see the world and plans to write about the atrocities at the prison after his release. He even tries to convince Butch to put off the strike for another month:

> JIM: And if I do [get parole next month] I'm going to justify my reputation as a brilliant vocalist, Butch. I'm going to sing so loud and so high that the echo will knock these walls down! I know plenty from working in the office. I know all the pet grafts. I know about the intimidation of employees and torture of convicts, I know about the hole, about the water-cure, about the over-coat—about Klondike! You wait a month! That's all! [. . .] And I promise you things will change in here—look—here's an article about the Industrial Reformatory in Chillicothe!—that's the kind of place this'll be.
> BUTCH: I don't want no articles! [. . .]
> JIM: [. . .] Do yourself a favor. Work with me. We can case this jug. But not if we keep going opposite ways—Give me your hand on it, Butch. (69–70)

Butch's furious rejection of this proposal is both a condemnation of Jim and, more importantly, of passivity. In this setting, art is not enough. Butch may not recognize the power of art/writing to bring about lasting social change, but his unquenchable desire to act eventually helps Jim realize the need for action to accompany words.

The tenuous promise of freedom (an early parole) prevents Jim from resisting like Butch does, as a stereotypical man. At one point, he sheepishly admits his own selfish motives to Eva: "Well—I ought to spill it myself—but if I did it would cost my ticket-of-leave!—It's funny. [. . .] Nothing has quite so much value as the skin our own guts are wrapped in" (98). Instead of acting, Jim turns to writing, but Williams cautions against art that is apolitical, or as George Orwell once remarked, "inside the whale"—insulated from the social and political concerns of the day. Early in the play, Jim views the imagination as essential for defining freedom: "A guy can use his brain two ways. He can make it a wall to shut him in from the world or a great big door to let him out. Intellectual emancipation !" (38). Convinced that all men are trapped by loneliness and isolation, he has turned to his imagination as a refuge: "Ev'ry man living is walking around in a cage. He carries it with him wherever he goes and don't let it go till he's dead. Then the walls come to pieces and he stops being lonesome—" (37). Thinking, writing editorials, and reading the dictionary are Jim's responses to both the isolation of his captivity and his estrangement from other inmates. These things give him a way to feel free despite the circumstances: "But they can't tell us what to *think*! And as long as a man can think as he pleases he's never exactly locked up anywhere. He can think himself outside of all their walls and boundaries and make the world his place to live in" (38). Though Jim feels liberated by his imagination, he remains unsure about his ability to use writing as a tool for change, in part, because he is still writing prison propaganda. When the Warden decides to torture the strikers in the "Klondike" and intimates that Jim might not get his recommendation for early release, however, Jim tears up a copy of Keats's "Ode to a Nightingale." This act is a clear rejection of art for art's sake: "Don't those literary punks know there's something more important to write about than that ?" (98). At this moment, Jim realizes that art needs to act—to have the potential to precipitate social change—and as a result, he must also participate in the uprising.

Through Jim's move from waiting to action, Williams aligns art with masculinity as a force for social agency. The art of *Not about Nightingales,* like the work that Jim imagines writing, is not only politically and socially directed, but it also occurs in the realm of men. In this way, Jim's heroism and introspection call into question stereotypical notions of masculinity. Jim has the power as a writer to impact social injustices in more lasting ways than Butch's truculent solutions. He—the writer—literally makes escape possible. As Eva suggests:

EVA: "Explosions are such a—waste—of power."
JIM: "Yeah. But what's the alternative here?"
EVA: "Your writing!" (86)

In her love for Jim, Eva validates his desire to write as powerful, important, and masculine. Only when Jim sees writing as a masculine virtue can he recognize his own power as an artist—shedding his selfish concerns, saving Butch from the "Klondike," and jumping from the Warden's window to literal and artistic freedom. In other words, this redefinition of masculinity—one that sees masculinity as something more than physical power—frees Jim to act.

Keeping Still: Captive Women in *Not about Nightingales*

In act 2 of the play, Jim, rather hypocritically, accuses Eva of being ethically and socially irresponsible:

> JIM: How do you sleep at all knowing what you know and keeping still?
> EVA: What else can I do but keep still? (112)

While Jim primarily criticizes her inaction as a way of mitigating his own guilt, her response says a great deal about the social restrictions placed on women. The male-centered world of the play demands stillness of women. They wait for men. In fact, they seem less capable of action than the inmates, suggesting the extent to which women are held captive by patriarchal mores. Unlike some of Williams's later plays, which explore the psychology of women who feel trapped, his female characters in *Not about Nightingales* seem to exist in a perpetual state of waiting. He uses them primarily as foils, juxtaposing their stasis with the action of men to reinforce what critic C. J. Gianakaris calls the "masculine ethos" (86) of the play. By creating superficial and mostly ineffective women, Williams emphasizes the importance of collective male action (regardless of sexuality, ethnicity, or avocation) and further undermines assumptions about the artist as effeminate.

The two minor female characters of *Nightingales*, Mrs. Bristol and Goldie, are explicitly defined by inaction. Like many of the inmates, they are character types (mother and sexually liberated woman) who lack individuality and agency. In the opening scene of the play, Mrs. Bristol, Sailor Jack's mother, waits passively for days to speak with the Warden about her son, and it becomes clear that she too is held captive by Jack's prison term:

> EVA: How long does he have to stay here?
> MRS. B: Five years!
> EVA: Oh, that's not so long.
> MRS. B: It seems like forever to me. [...] I know one thing—whatever happened it wasn't my boy's fault!—And that's what I'm going to say to the Warden soon as I get in to see him—I've been waiting here two days—he never has time! (6–7)

Mrs. Bristol's life is defined by various types of waiting—for her son's letters, for his return from the Navy, for his freedom, for the Warden. Just as this waiting helps her deny certain truths about her son, it is also physically and psychologically self-destructive: "I've got the most awful palpitations! [...] I'll just take one of my Phenobarbital tablets, and I'll be all right in a jiffy. I've been under such a strain lately with Jack on my mind all the time" (5–6). Unlike Jim, who can imagine using writing as a productive outlet for his anger and frustration, Mrs. Bristol can only worry "all the time"; she hopes that talking with the Warden and taking blame for her son's failings will help: "I regret *myself* when I look back at things—Mistakes that I made" (30). Yet ultimately she is powerless to help Jack and, as the Warden explains, powerless to fight the institution that imprisons and kills him: "I got all the sympathy in the world for you women that come in here, but this is a penal institution and we simply can't be taking time out from our routine business for things like this" (32). Of course, incarceration is about *time* and *waiting*. For Mrs. Bristol, however, the waiting is over. Once she admits the truth, she can no longer deny what is happening at the prison: "I know—You tortured him there, that's what you did [. . .] [*She breaks down, sobbing wildly.*]" (32–33). This realization doesn't inspire to fight back or seek justice. Instead, she collapses, disappearing ineffectually from the play.

Unlike the other women of the play, Goldie, a dancer and self-proclaimed bimbo, only exists in Butch's dreams, and his idealized image of her as both sexually pure and in waiting suggests what characteristics he (and arguably the play) values in women. In an attempt to assuage his anxieties about her job as a dancer, Butch reflects on the times when he watched her sleep: "I lay and watched you sleeping. Your face was like the face of a little girl then. A girl no man ever touched" (57). Imagining her as sexually pure (except with him) is a way for Butch to possess her and to deny the sexual implications of her job. By associating her with a little girl, he also makes her ageless or, at least, timeless, and in this way, he can imagine their love as unchanged by his prison sentence:

> GOLDIE: Some girls say one man's as good as another. They're all the same. But I'm not made like that. I give myself, I give myself for *keeps*. And time doesn't change me none. I'm still the same. [. . .] Running my dancing slippers down at the heels. But not forgetting your love. And going home nights alone. Sleeping alone in a big brass bed. Half of it empty, Butch. And waiting for you.
> BUTCH: Waiting for me!
> GOLDIE: Yes! Waiting for you! (58)

The male fantasy here is about unchanged desire and purity. Butch envisions her as both waiting for him (alone) and having no concern about lost time. He may not be able to escape (he can't swim), but he can hold Goldie captive in his imagination. And while Goldie waits, he acts—against the abuses of the prison and those who oppose him. Once again, Williams makes an important distinction between men and women through this pairing. Butch's waiting is imposed; whereas, Goldie, like the other women in the play, waits willingly.

Unlike Mrs. Bristol and Goldie who are imagined as perpetually waiting for a man to return, Eva Crane, the primary female character, does act for herself. She goes to the prison for a job. She pushes her way into the Warden's

office. She instigates a romantic relationship with Jim. She convinces the
Warden to send his letter approving Jim's early parole. Yet these moments
are fundamentally selfish, stemming from personal and economic need. This
is not necessarily a condemnation of Eva. Most people need to work and
experience love. But in the context of this play, Williams validates action that
is socially motivated. Jim's selfishness, in other words, is a problem that he
must overcome. He must work with the other men *and* free himself to create
socially conscious art. Eva's character, however, is not able to achieve this
type of consciousness, and in this way, she becomes another foil for Jim. At
the outset of the play, she completely subscribes to contemporary propaganda
about prison and rehabilitation: "The old idea used to be punishment of crime
but nowadays it's—social rehabilitation. [. . .] I read all about it in the *Sunday
Supplement*! [. . .] He [Sailor Jack] will probably come out a better and stronger
boy than before he went in" (4, 5, 7). Her naive belief in this institution is
immediately juxtaposed with Mrs. Bristol's anxiety, the torture of her son, and
Jim's admission that his editorials, such as "Prison: the door to Opportunity!"
(11), are merely designed to mask the abusive treatment of inmates. Eva—
through her beliefs and passivity—represents a society that wants to believe
these things about prison in order to avoid confronting the failings of the
system.

Williams also uses Eva's inaction to enhance Jim's status as an artist-hero.
Eva wants to believe that prison is an effective means for rehabilitation, in
part, to assuage her ethical concerns about working for the Warden. Even as
Jim challenges her to do something, she chooses denial ("I don't believe it!"
[98]) and silence:

> JIM: You could talk. You could tell the Humane Society that thirty-five
> hundred animals are being starved to death and threatened with torture.
> EVA: And lose my job? [. . .] You don't understand. I was out of work six
> months before I got this job. [. . .] I got down to my last dime. Once a man
> followed along the street and I stood still, waiting for him to catch up with
> me. Yes, I'd gotten down that low, I was going to ask him for money—
> [. . .] At the last moment, I couldn't. I went hungry instead. Now you want
> me to go back to that? Times haven't improved. Now maybe I'd have more
> courage, or less decency, or maybe I'd be hungrier than I was before.
> JIM: You'd better hold on to your job, Miss Crane—even if it does mean
> participating in a massacre! (112–13)

Eva's fears are understandable in 1930s America, but Williams uses Jim's
outrage as a way to address the complacency of such attitudes. Williams
suggests that taking a stand against injustice involves sacrifice, and Eva's flaw
is her unwillingness to make any personal sacrifice for a larger cause. In fact,
Eva only agrees to "go public" with the truth about the prison to protect Jim

(so he doesn't jeopardize his early parole). This promise also comes with the understanding that Jim will subsequently take care of her:

> EVA: I'll be in the newspaper offices. And at City Hall. Any place where people will listen!
> [...]
> JIM: And afterwards what will you do? With no job?
> EVA: I'll only have to wait three weeks. And then I'll be your responsibility, Jim!
> JIM: I hope to God you're right. (129)

Even though Eva is responsible for giving Jim the encouragement he needs to view writing as power—enabling his transformation and giving him the confidence he needs to act—she, like the other women in the play, is ready to go into waiting. She acts out of love and ultimately a desire for dependency, not social consciousness.

Not about Nightingales ultimately calls audiences and artists to act. As Jim asks Eva in Act II: "You know a lot you could tell. [...] Why don't you then?" (97). This question goes out to the theatergoers who watch the captivity and torture of these men from the safety of darkened seats. The juxtaposition of action and passivity, justice and cruelty, and masculinity and femininity implicitly criticizes the passive observer, and in this way, *Not about Nightingales* embodies the most important qualities of proletaria drama. Likewise, through Jim's quest for artistic freedom, the play challenges other artists to produce socially conscious art. The days of Keats's romanticism are over, for the hardships and injustices of 1930s America demand art that speaks to these issues. Early in the play, Jim's decision not to act or write truthfully about the abusive treatment of convicts until his own freedom is secured is juxtaposed with Butch's physical strength and leadership. Jim learns, however, that art is a form of action that is compatible with manhood. It even has the potential to be more powerful than explosions and destruction. And Williams ultimately uses this revelation to align art with masculinity and the power to incite change.

Notes

1. With the help of Maria St. Just, executrix of the Williams estate, Vanessa Redgrave "discovered" the manuscript for *Not about Nightingales* and "arranged for its 1998 world premiere at the Royal National Theatre in London" (Hale xiii). See Vanessa Redgrave's "Foreword" and Allean Hale's "Introduction: A Call for Justice" to *Not about Nightingales*.
2. For more information on the Works Progress Administration's Federal Theater Project, see Kazacoff. In *Not about Nightingales,* Williams specifically uses "The Living Newspaper" technique common in WPA theatrical productions of the time. Much like John Dos Passos's use of "newsreels" in the *U.S.A.* trilogy a few years

earlier, this form "enacted contemporary social problems in fast-moving scenes introduced by an 'Announcer' or projected headlines" (Hale, *"Not about Nightingales"* 358).

3. See Leverich *Tom: The Unknown Tennessee Williams* (274–75).

4. For more information about the myths and problems surrounding the penal system in the United States, see Simon, *Poor Discipline,* and the collection *The Dilemmas of Corrections.*

5. See "Prison Scandal" in *Newsweek* 5 Sept. 1938: 11.

Works Cited

Currie, Elliot. *Crime and Punishment in America.* New York: Metropolitan Books, 1998.

Gianakaris, C. J. "Tennessee Williams and *Not about Nightingales:* The Path Not Taken." *American Drama* 9.1 (Fall 1999): 69–91.

Haas, Kenneth C., and Geoffrey, P. Alpert, eds. *The Dilemmas of Corrections* 4th ed. Prospect Heights: Waveland Press, 1999.

Hale, Allean. *"Not about Nightingales:* Tennessee Williams as Social Activist." *Modern Drama* 42 (Fall 1999): 346–62.

———. "Introduction: A Call for Justice." *Not about Nightingales,* by Tennessee Williams. New York: New Directions, 1998.

Kazacoff, George. *Dangerous Theater: The Federal Theater Project as a Forum for New Ployz.* New York: Peter Lang, 1989.

Leverichy Lyle. *Tom: The Unknown Tennessee Williams.* New York: W. W. Norton and Company, 1997.

Orwell, George. *Inside the Whale and Other Essays by George Orwell.* London: Victor Gollancz, 1940.

"Prison Scandal." *Newsweek* 5 Sept. 1938: 10–11.

Simon, Jonathan. *Poor Discipline: Parole and the Social Control of the Underclass, 1890–1990.* Chicago: The University of Chicago Press, 1994.

Williams, Tennessee. *Not about Nightingales.* New York: New Directions, 1998.

10

Physical Prisons: Naomi Wallace's Drama of Captivity

CLAUDIA BARNETT

In his poem "The Flea," John Donne's speaker revels in his realization that the flea that has bitten him has also bitten his beloved, thereby establishing an intimate bond between them: "It suck'd me first, and now sucks thee, / And in this flea our two bloods mingled be" (3–4). As he tries to convince her not to leave, he romanticizes the insect:

> O stay, three lives in one flea spare,
> Where we almost, yea, more than married are.
> This flea is you and I, and this
> Our marriage bed, and marriage temple is. (10–13)

Within the flea, the speaker's blood has mixed with that of his beloved, thereby making them, in his mind, "more than married," the flea itself hallowed ground. His interpretation of the events, at once sensual and grotesque, reeks with irony but has its serious side—and that is what appeals to Naomi Wallace, a political American playwright who named her best-known drama after Donne's poem. *One Flea Spare*, a play about four characters quarantined together during the London plague, likewise combines beauty and horror, gravity and wit, to explore issues of power and chance. Perhaps the most shocking quality of the play is the physicality of its prison and the sexuality which necessarily ensues, with Wallace's staged setting itself a manifestation of Donne's flea. Confined to two rooms of William and Darcy Snelgrave's mansion, the Snelgraves and their accidental guests, a sailor named Bunce and a twelve-year-old girl named Morse, embark on a metaphorical but life-altering journey. One critic summarizes the action with a question: "What happens [. . .] when members of different economic groups are thrown together in a claustrophobic space? What power struggles occur when they are all prisoners in the same cell?" The answer: "Strange things happen in isolation" (Hartigan C9). And stranger things happen in the belly of the flea. These four characters may have been spared the bite that spreads the plague, but they have been stung by something more dangerous and more symbolic—something that overturns their world in much the same way that Donne's language overturns romance.

While Wallace works within such metaphors, she also literalizes them, creating physical prisons on stage: The Snelgrave home, for instance, has been boarded up and is guarded by a watchman; *The Trestle at Pope Lick Creek* takes place within a jail cell; and the set of *Birdy* is a mental institution where a young soldier is confined. Paul Taylor sees a practical component in Wallace's choice: "The abiding problem for the stage dramatist—how to get people on and off plausibly—is mightily reduced in situations where the characters' own freedom of choice in these matters is minimal. Hence the convenience of hostage/prison dramas." The prison-drama tradition may have developed as a convenience, but it is also theoretically compelling. Michel Foucault writes in *Discipline and Punish* of the architecture of the modern prison. Standing at the center of Bentham's Panopticon, the spectator can see every inmate, as Foucault explains: "By effect of backlighting, one can observe from the tower, standing out precisely against the light, the small captive shadows in the periphery. They are like so many cages, so many small theatres, in which each actor is alone, perfectly individualized and constantly visible" (200). Foucault employs the theater as a metaphor for the prison; the prison can likewise serve as a metaphor for the theater. The audience, like the spectator in the Panopticon's tower, witnesses the action on stage (unknown to the characters, as the spectator is unknown to the prisoners). The audience may leave; the actors/characters may not. Yet while the audience may align itself with Foucault's warden-like spectator, it also identifies with the prisoner—often feeling trapped in its seats. While no one is physically trapped in the theater—except arguably the fictional characters who exist only on its stage—the feeling of captivity may extend to everyone involved, in a variety of seemingly contradictory ways. In many modern dramas, the characters seem trapped by their settings, making the prison metaphor even more fitting.

Women playwrights of this century have worked diligently to subvert terms such as *crime* and *punishment, freedom* and *imprisonment.* Throughout Susan Glaspell's *Trifles,* Mrs. Wright waits in jail as neighbors search her home for signs of her guilt. Mrs. Wright has likely killed her husband, but two fellow farmwives deem her not guilty and hide the evidence from their law-enforcing husbands who would never understand: Mrs. Wright was driven to desperate means when Mr. Wright strangled her bird, a sign of his emotional cruelty and her solitary confinement. Despite having committed a cold-blooded murder, Mrs. Wright is cast as the injured party in this play. Furthermore, imprisoned offstage, Mrs. Wright is now *free* of her husband's abuse. With this simple division between the sexes in *Trifles,* Glaspell creates a model for twentieth-century drama by women: The men represent the dominant and frequently corrupt society, while the women must behave subversively, often criminally, in order to do what is right. As a result, the women in these plays tend to land in prison, through no fault of their own, and often through the fault of men. Liz, a convict in an Australian penal colony in Timberlake Wertenbaker's *Our Country's Good,* tells how her troubles began with her father (whom she tried to kill when he beat and stripped her in public), continued with her five brothers (one of whom teaches her to pick pockets), and ends with Major Ross, who has sentenced her to death because he "don't like my mug" (240–41). Similarly, in *The Conduct of Life,* Maria Irene Fornes presents a male authority figure, the army lieutenant Orlando, who keeps a twelve-year-old girl locked in a warehouse as his slave. In Fornes's *Fefu and Her Friends,* Julia has internalized the voices of male judges, of whom she says, "They clubbed me. They broke my head. They broke my will" (33). Her crime is her womanhood, her woman's body: "He said that women's entrails are heavier than anything on earth and to see a woman running creates a disparate image in the mind. It's antiaesthetic" (33–34). Adrienne Kennedy's Negro-Sarah is guilty not only of womanhood but of her African heritage; as a result, she projects a prison in her mind, her imagined "funnyhouse" that precedes the moment of her suicide—a reflection of the white world that has rejected her and thereby caused her death.

In her depiction of the prison on stage, Wallace likewise challenges traditional definitions of crime and punishment, victim and abuser. However, while many twentieth-century women playwrights redefine the terms with their opposites, Wallace is more sophisticated in her equations. While others present their women characters as helpless victims of a patriarchal, white, oppressive society, Wallace creates situations in which blame is earned by all, and the criminals are often indistinguishable from the victims—who may or may not be women. Wallace asks her reader/audience to reconsider the stereotype of woman as victim and to examine how that image affects both the participant and the viewers/voyeurs of crimes. Using the symbol of the prison throughout her plays, she questions definitions of crime and punishment in our gender- and class-oriented society. She does so in such a physical manner in order to appeal to the audience members, who sympathetically align themselves with the prisoners, possibly feeling trapped themselves—out of politeness, perhaps, or out of having paid for tickets—along with the characters, in the theater. By focusing on issues of the passive watcher in her plays, she forces her audience to reexamine its own role in the theater and in society. Like Foucault, she parallels the theater with the prison, but she does so on stage, challenging her audience to recognize and transgress its own societal conscription.

Wallace's plays confine both characters and audience, who share the same suffocating or threatening space of her theater/prison as her reviewers are quick to note. Of *Flea,* Sarah Hemming writes: "Angela Davies's clever, understated set creates just the corner of a room, allowing the rest of the black box theatre to fill in the remainder and so trapping you with the characters in the claustro-phobic intensity of Wallace's play" (21). Charles Spencer compares William Wharton's novel with Wallace's telling of *Birdy,* focusing on the stage set that "undermin[es] the book's exhilarating sense of freedom" (23). By physically placing the prison on stage, rather than within the imagination, Wallace nec-essarily grounds it for the audience. And she always provides actions within her plays that frighten or surprise. For instance, of *Trestle,* Anita Gates writes that "[Lisa] Peterson is the sort of director who will not let the audience look away" (B9)—but the compelling action she cites as her example is Wallace's direction that two characters toss ceramic plates back and forth, their relation-ship symbolized by the imminent breakage which occurs simultaneously in the characters' and audience's worlds.[1] Such physicality aligns fiction with re-ality, creating prisons defined by place—physical prisons—that exist on both planes. Such spaces are inherently dramatic.

John Bender, in his syntactical analysis of the prison, *Imagining the Peni-tentiary,* explains that early English prisons were places of waiting, not places of punishment. In such prisons criminals awaited trial and sentencing, and "Death was the common penalty, though often commuted to transportation abroad" (Bender 11–12). Bender uses Victor Turner's language to describe the old-style prisons as ritual sites at which "prisoners were subjects who [. . .] underwent the 'liminal' experience of rites of passage." Prisoners were trans-formed by their experience, though not necessarily for the better: "The 'limi-nal' rite of passage enacts symbolic demise and takes for granted a randomness that, quite unpredictably, can bring about real death" (26). The act of waiting in itself then could effect real—though not necessarily positive—change. "Fi-nally, however . . . liminality does not posit change in personality but change in status; it fosters the outlook appropriate to new social standing" (27). Wallace draws on these theories in her dramas: Her prisons are places of waiting rather than places of physical punishment, but they are also liminal spaces in which characters change—often in reaction to or recognition of social status. Within such spaces, time itself proves an effective form of torture and an even more effective agent of social change. Bender explains how the modern prison mir-rors the narrative form: "The liminal prison became the penitentiary when, through a conflation of the legal and grammatical notions of a 'sentence,' randomness gave way to narrative order and 'sentences' came to be served rather than executed" (35). The prison thus effectively becomes a metaphor for itself, a dialectical space in which one is simply confined. Naomi Wallace explodes the metaphor by presenting it on stage, replacing its metaphorical qualities with physical presence.

One Flea Spare is set in the past—in fact, in two different pasts, one during and one following the London plague—so the play wavers between those times and our own time, ultimately suggesting, like Bender, an align-ment between imprisonment and time. As Julia Kristeva writes, "There is a massive presence of a monumental temporality, without cleavage or escape, which has so little to do with linear time (which passes) that the very word 'temporality' hardly fits: all encompassing and infinite like imaginary space" (191). Using Nietzsche's terminology, Kristeva distinguishes between two types of time, *cursive* and *monumental*: cursive time occurs linearly, and thus passes, while monumental time is ever-present, never changing, and thus "englobes . . . supra-national, socio-cultural ensembles within even larger entities" (189). By displacing and splitting the time periods of *One Flea Spare* and her other prison plays, Wallace clarifies that such imprisonment is monumental rather than linear, and that her concern is indeed with supra-national and socio-cultural ensembles. History repeats itself, eternally and helplessly, and thus time itself is the darkest prison, "without cleavage or escape." Time and space thus work together within Wallace's plays as conceptual warnings against almost inevitable repetition.

Kristeva defines linear time in terms of production and monumental time in terms of reproduction. As is characteristic of Wallace, she subverts these terms by placing her plays, historically, within times of nonproduction: pestilence, depression, war. Such periods themselves operate as prisons, more like places than times, yet Wallace's characters ultimately experience a release. Kristeva compares monumental time to "Kronos in Hesiod's mythology, the incestuous son whose massive presence covered all of Gea in order to separate her from Ouranos, the father." Indeed, Wallace's rendition of time includes such forced repression and focuses, likewise, on the sexual implications. But it also explores what Kristeva presents as another type of women's time, cyclic repetitions that evoke "unnamable *jouissance*" (191). Wallace likewise presents the flip-side by ultimately freeing her characters from their physical prisons.

One Flea Spare is framed by three scenes that occur after Morse's release from the Snelgrave home—after the Snelgraves have died, Bunce has presumably escaped, and the threat of the plague has lifted. The first and last scenes of act 1 and the last scene of act 2 take place "in an empty room or cell" in which Morse is locked (7). Like Fornes's Julia, Morse has internalized the voices of her inquisitors, and she delivers a series of monologues in which she both asks and responds to their questions. These questions suggest that Morse is suspected of murder: "What happened to the gentleman? [. . .] What happened to his wife? [. . .] Whose blood is on your sleeve?" (7). The answer begins with a poetic pastiche that unfolds into the rest of the play, positioning the other characters within the past tense as flashbacks. Wallace thus creates a series of prisons for Morse, who is trapped either in the past Snelgrave house or in the present jail. Her prior history also includes a prison, for Morse was born into servitude and abuse; her young mistress, a girl her own age, "had a fat stick that she kept in her trunk of toys and she would sneak up behind [Morse] as

[she] swept the floors and hit [her] across the back" (45). Her mother, upon showing signs of the plague, was locked in the basement by the master—who was probably Morse's biological father—without water or food and left to die. The only question about Morse is what her future might hold—and even that seems hopeless. Her final monologue begins with the question "Can I go now?"—but she hears no response and barely pauses to listen for one (73). For Morse, the past, present, and future are all very much the same, and though she is only twelve years old, she acknowledges, "I'm old on the inside" (22).

Morse defies a variety of stereotypes: She hardly seems like a child, but she does not seem like a murderer either, even when she drives a knife into Darcy's heart. Darcy has developed tokens of the plague and begs for death. Bunce admits, "I haven't the courage"; Morse, meanwhile, does the deed swiftly and without reflection, but first she asks, "What will you give me?" and settles for a pair of gloves to which she could easily help herself (71). She is Darwinian but not Christ-like in her suffering; she is self-educated in amorality. Her crime seems heroic to the other characters and to her audience, but not to her society, which condemns her to jail. Compared with Glaspell's Mrs. Wright, Morse is not tried by a jury of her peers, and her inquisitors are unlikely to sympathize with her motivation. Mrs. Wright will probably be released to return home and live out her remaining days in solitude, her neighbors eternally suspicious of her crime; she may not be found guilty, but she will never feel free. Morse, in contrast, may never leave prison, yet she seems perfectly content, even sanguine, in her final words, a recollection of a child's corpse floating in the river: "As I reached into the water to touch her, a ship hoisted its sail. A door slammed in the street. One, two, three voices called out to the other. A bell rang. And the city called out to one other. A bell rang. And the city came alive once more." She pauses to sing a song and remembers, "When I looked down in the water again for the body of the child, it was gone. And I was glad. I was glad it had gone" (73). Trapped in her cell, Morse almost happily reflects on life starting anew. She sees in the child's corpse her own lost self, but rather than regret the past, she is pleased to have survived. Her supposed crime may have landed her in jail, but her real punishments—the beatings she endured and the brutal death of her mother—render the cell harmless, almost safe. Morse's current confinement seems innocuous because her past is so horrible and also because she herself seems so detached. The framing device, coupled with the physical absence of Morse's inquisitors, causes Morse's present tense to feel removed from time and space. In fact, the present moment of the play seems peculiarly irrelevant in relation to the past. Morse's prison is not the jail cell she inhabits but the past she replays in her head: her history, her identity, her self. When she loses sight of the child's corpse, she symbolically lets go of her past, and in spite of her physical confinement, she becomes free. Morse's great strength is her ability to adapt. "I'm not a Braithwaite anymore, you know," she tells Kabe the watchman, meaning that although she has claimed to be the child of the aristocratic Braithwaites, she now leaves even that false identity behind.

Darcy too has been figuratively imprisoned for most of her life, although unlike Morse, she never manages to transcend her bonds. Sadder even than Morse's poverty is Darcy's marriage. Although an aristocrat, Darcy is poverty stricken by gender. At age seventeen, when she had been married to Snelgrave for two years, she was badly burned in a fire. Since that time—and she is now "an elderly woman" (4)—she has hidden her disfigurement with a long dress and white gloves. In his review of the New York production, William Over complains: "Diane Wiest as the wife seems immobilized by a heavy brocade dress—a character detail that might have been used to express the ineffectuality of her class facing the social breakdown, but instead the actor seems merely hampered" (256). That costume did not work, but Over's comment on its potential is revealing: The dress is a permanent shell, both prison and protection. When Morse asks Darcy early on, "Are you not hot in all that dress?" (Wallace, *Flea* 17), she responds, "No, child. I never wear anything but this sort of dress" (18), and when Bunce tells her, as she is dying, to take it off, she says, "Never" (68). She dies wearing the dress. She has been punished not for a crime but for a heroic attempt: She was trying to save her horse, a wedding gift. Snelgrave speaks of the incident with contempt (36); he has tormented her by refusing to look at or touch her since the time of the fire. She has lived in isolation within her dress, and ultimately she cleaves to her prison *as* protection; she would rather die than lose control—of her body or its cover.

When Bunce's thirteen-year-old brother was crushed in a coal mine, Bunce jumped on the master and "bit his ear in two." He remembers: "One of his guards popped a knife in my side. Never healed up right" (20). Darcy, fascinated with this age-old wound, compares him to Christ (53) and asks to touch it. Darcy and Bunce, both permanently wounded characters, have lost tactile feeling, yet both feel emotions intensely; "You don't feel with your hands," Bunce has learned (67). Like Darcy, Bunce finds himself shackled by his own body. One of his scars, a source of fascination for Snelgrave, who imagines it resulted from "Spanish Main pirates" or "a drunken brawl," was actually self-inflicted with a sail hook in order to avoid conscription: "To keep from the press, we'd cut ourselves a wound and then burn it with vitriol. Make it look like scurvy" (16). Although Bunce is male, he is poor, and therefore he too has been enslaved his whole life. He has served "the Spaniards [. . .] against the French [. . .] the Hollanders against the English, [. . .] the English [. . .] against the Hollanders [and finally the Turks] against the English, French, Dutch, and Spaniards and all Christendom" (55). By the end of the play he vows, "I won't sail for the Navy again. Ever. I'll kill somebody first, even if it's me" (50). Quite possibly, his only release, like Darcy's, will be in death.

"Is this not a poor man's plague?" asks Kabe the watchman, rhetorically (38). It is a poor man's plague in that, as Kabe explains to Morse, "All that's got wealth has fled" (22), with few exceptions such as the "unlucky" Snelgraves (23). But it is also the poor man's plague in the more positive sense that the poor have gained control. The plague has given Kabe power over the aristocrats, whom he hates, and he delights in his new role: He taunts Darcy about her "pretty white hands" and addresses her by her first name (12); he sells fake and disgusting medicines to Snelgrave at outrageous prices (40–41); and he refuses to allow the Snelgraves out of their home for any price (39). When Snelgrave dies, Kabe names Bunce "Mr. Snelgrave" and tells him how to escape. (65–66). He claims to dislike sailors, but clearly not as much as he despises the rich. Snelgrave accuses Kabe, "I smell a Leveller's blood in you" (41). (The Levellers of whom he speaks are members of "an English party that arose in the army of the Long Parliament [c. 1647] and advocated the leveling of all ranks and the establishment of a more democratic government" [Webster's].) Kabe denies the accusation in spite of its obvious truth. More ironic, however, is the fact that while the members of the party could not achieve their goal, the plague could level the ranks of everyone in its path—or better yet, as Wallace demonstrates, invert them. By act 2, Bunce not only ignores Snelgrave's orders (which he had unflinchingly followed in act 1), but he threatens Snelgrave with a stick, as Darcy and Morse tie the old man to a chair. There he watches Morse play a game with dolls, a child's fantasy of the world in reverse: "Even the rich had shoes" (56). Morse relates the tale of a fire angel who asks her young man to hold her as she burned—"and the young man came to her," she says. But Snelgrave contradicts her: "No. He didn't come to her. He was a coward, your man. [...] He walked away. [...] He turned his back" (57). Here he confesses his crime toward Darcy; this is his one sympathetic moment. In the next scene, he is punished as Morse blindfolds him and exits to the kitchen, leaving him to listen to his wife and Bunce making love. The following morning, Snelgrave is found dead—not of the plague, but of humiliation. For once, during the disordered world of the plague, crime and punishment form a viable equation.

Except for the aristocratic male, the characters in this play have been imprisoned for all or most of their lives, having endured the prisons of gender and class. Paradoxically, the plague frees them from these metaphorical manacles: When they are physically imprisoned, they are emotionally unfettered; in the absence of society, they unlearn society's rules. Dressed in each other's clothes, trying on new identities almost daily, the characters learn new rules based on the concept of survival of the fittest, which has nothing to do with the rules of their society. Snelgrave is in fact the least fit, and he seems to have no experience of the world, but he has always been in charge. He attempts to bond with Bunce over their common experience in the Navy: "I'm a rich man, Bunce, and you a common sailor yet—look at the two of us—we have the sea between us," and he sees no irony in the fact that he has never actually sailed: "But if I step my foot in a boat, the world goes black before my eyes" (15).

When he uses the pronoun *we,* he rarely means himself, especially if his words imply action. "We'll need to vinegar this room twice a day from now on," he tells Bunce, and this is clearly a command, not a commiseration (28). Yet for the first act of the play, Bunce follows Snelgrave's orders without question. Snelgrave's power lies completely in his social status, which is slowly over-turned by the plague. His rise to power—along with that of his class—seems random and inexplicable. Yet while Bunce realizes that the tables have turned and that his physical power far exceeds Snelgrave's hollow words, he also understands that this turn is merely momentary, and that once the plague lifts, all the norms will be reestablished. He never for a minute trusts Darcy, in spite of his attraction to her. As he prepares to escape, he tells Morse that if he were to stay, he would be hanged for Snelgrave's murder, and that Darcy, who is still alive at this point, would likely turn against him: "Who's to say she wouldn't be in the front row just to see me rise up in me britches after I drop down and into hell?" (67). Bunce is physically the fittest, but he is the most powerful only during the topsy-turvy time of the plague; otherwise, the rich—whose advantages seems random and cruel—rule. In the Snelgraves' room, which seems removed from the rest of the world, the characters and audience recognize the absurdity of society's norms, yet Bunce realizes this change is temporary. While Kabe promotes him to the aristocracy by addressing him as Mr. Snelgrave, Bunce does not seem anxious to occupy the position or to perpetuate the act.

While Bunce performs a series of actions, the Snelgraves, according to their class, simply observe. The stage directions specify that they "watch" him on three occasions: Once Snelgrave watches Bunce eat (16); once Snelgrave watches Bunce work (24); and once Darcy watches him attempt to bandage himself (28). Darcy stops watching and starts acting, beginning by helping Bunce with his bandage, which indicates a shift in her character. Snelgrave, however, remains an observer. When he is tied to his chair in act 2, until the poetic justice of his blindfolding, all he can do is watch, so the stage directions no longer need indicate that he does so. Seventeenth-century society is thus criticized for its detachment, for its privileged-observer status. But so is our contemporary society—because that is who comes to watch *One Flea Spare.* While the play's audience is encouraged to condemn Snelgrave for his inaction, it is aligned with him in observation: Like the aristocracy, the audience watches comfortably while the actors perform. Thus, the play implies a criticism of its own audience. And while Wallace is careful to draw distinctions between time periods and to present her play as an obvious fiction, her critique of capitalism extends well beyond the London plague and into twenty-first-century America. In fact, she wrote the play in response to the Rodney King incident in Los Angeles, with its echoes of random power and abuse. Time itself thus becomes a sort of prison—progress itself, a myth—as the world remains mired in unjustified and unjustifiable systems of abuse.

In *One Flea Spare,* Wallace presents a fairly clear divide between the victims and the oppressors, which she then complicates by compromising the innocence of her victims: Morse will turn on anyone and do anything for a modest fee; Bunce abandons Morse and is about to abandon Darcy before her death; Darcy sees nothing wrong with disciplining servants with "a piece of leg from a chair" (19); and Kabe gives Morse pieces of fruit in exchange for the privilege of sucking her toes. The villain Snelgrave himself becomes pitiable as he admits his guilt to Morse and dies of hearing his wife having sex with the sailor—both of whom thereby cruelly (again compromising their innocence) torture him. Wallace toys with stereotypes to keep the audience from becoming too comfortable with its assumptions. One of her finest inversions is having both Snelgrave and Bunce admit to cowardice with regard to Darcy: Snelgrave was too cowardly to face her after she was burned (57), and Bunce is too cowardly to perform her mercy killing (71). These admissions reinforce Darcy's martyrdom and Morse's courage, thereby making the female characters seem morally stronger than the men, whose money and physical prowess become meaningless. Not only are crime and punishment not equated, but they are not related—unless crime is defined as birth into a particular gender or class.

The Trestle at Pope Lick Creek bears many similarities to *One Flea Spare,* among them its challenge to gender stereotypes and its reliance on the prison as both theme and form. Like *Flea,* it takes place in two times, a past and a present, and the present depicts an adolescent locked in a jail cell. The difference is that Dalton Chance is male and that he has not killed anyone— even though he says he has. Furthermore, while in *Flea* the three present-tense scenes frame the past, in *Trestle,* past and present are spliced together, nearly alternating, and the past tense does not occur chronologically. Some of the scenes are out of order, giving the past a sense of taking place completely in Dalton's reluctant memory—except perhaps for one scene in which he is not present (but which he may well imagine [316–18]). The time (both past and present) is the Depression; the place is "somewhere in the U.S." (281). Set in the past, *Trestle,* like *Flea,* presents time as a continuum in which history helplessly, inevitably recurs.

While Dalton's past tense does not involve being trapped in a room, it does involve being trapped in a life: The Depression, a time period, is a prison. Dalton says he wants to go to college when he gets older, but Pace Creagan bluntly informs him: "You're not going to college. None of us are going to college" (289). When he asks Gin, his mother, what she wanted when she was fifteen, she responds: "Someone to look me straight in the face and tell me flat out that I wasn't going anywhere" (293). Gin cannot say those same words to her son, even when he asks her to; instead she strives to make them untrue. But she fights against incredible odds and with little hope, working in life-threatening conditions for little pay. Her husband gave up the fight long ago; he spends most of his time sitting in a dark room. He is free to go outside, but he prefers to sit alone. He was told when he was younger, "Dray, You are what you do." Now that he has no job, he is afraid he has become invisible: "I'm afraid. [...] That if I go out, they won't be able to see me" (324). In this fear, Dray voices the central theme of the play, an equation between seeing and being. The words "You are what you do" echo in his son's head as he reconsiders what he has done—or not done—what he has seen, and what he has therefore become.

The play chronicles Dalton's friendship with Pace Creagan, a seventeen-year-old girl fascinated by trains. Unlike Gin, who sees trains as "always taking someone away, never bringing someone back" (293), Pace sees them as 153 tons of molten steel. Her language, when she speaks of trains, is charged with sex, so much so that Gin asks her: "Cylinders, huh? Driving wheels. Articulated locomotives. If you're thinking to trick my son—" But Pace cuts her off: "Mrs. Chance, I'm not sweet on your son's locomotive system, if that's what you think" (300). What she is sweet on is danger and power. She drafts Dalton as her sidekick and dares him to race a train across the trestle. They finally agree to race the train together, after weeks of consideration and consultation, but in the end Dalton backs out. Pace runs alone, on the condition that Dalton watch her. But then he looks away. She, needing a witness, stops running the train and, instead, dives to her death. Pace's ghost rebukes him: "Bastard. I needed you to watch [...] Because we can't watch ourselves. We can't remember ourselves. Not like we need to" (337). Dalton's function is merely to witness, but he fails her by turning his head, invalidating Pace's life and thereby causing her death. According to his father's mantra—You are what you do—Dalton has murdered Pace. Dray is an older version of Pace in that he shares her desires, lamenting in old age, "All my life I wanted to say something that mattered" (330). Pace likewise wants to matter in a world where such a thing seems impossible. Her solution is to be seen—to prove that she exists.

Pace's ghost grieves over her own death: "I was going to be different. I don't know in what way. That never mattered. But different somehow" (317). She has already succeeded by defying her gender stereotype. Dalton explains: "You're loud. Your hands are dirty. You stare. [...] And you're not pretty, really" (295). In fact, she is stereotypically masculine—and she treats Dalton like a girl. She tells him what to do, sometimes threatening him with a knife, and he follows her orders, including undressing so that Pace can "look at" him. "Are you gonna touch me or what?" Dalton asks, and her answer is "No" (304). This realignment of their roles is at the root of their troubles; Dalton becomes sexually frustrated and ultimately mortified when he enjoys Pace's ten-second kiss to the back of his knee (312): The stage direction following that action indicates, "The potential for violence is evident" (313). Then, just before Pace's run across the trestle, he climaxes as she orchestrates their imaginary sex scene (341–42), emasculating him. He remembers, "Pace wanted to make the run that night. I wouldn't do it. I was afraid. No, I was angry" (336). In his humiliation, he refuses to run—and refuses to look—thus finally asserting himself as a man and destroying her altogether. In another gender-role reversal, Gin not only works while Dray sits home and broods, but she and other women decide to reopen the glass factory. Gin will risk her life working with glass (Dray describes his father's work at that factory: "Once glass hit him in the mouth. Long thin pieces of glass. He pulled them out of his cheeks with pliers, like pullin' fish bones out of a fish" [306]); she has already risked her health working with chemicals that have permanently turned her hands blue. If she were to behave as a traditional, submissive female, she and her family would starve. While breaking gender stereotypes has its dangers, both Dalton and Gin demonstrate that conforming to them could be even worse.

Two years earlier, Pace ran the train with Brett Weaver, the school track star who died that day. While the whole town thinks that Brett was drunk and alone, Pace tells Dalton a different story, one in which she played a pivotal role:

> 'Course Brett, he was faster. I expected to be running behind. But Brett was worried. About me. He was stupid like that. He turned to look over his shoulder at me and tripped. I thought he'd just jump up and keep going so I passed him right by. [...] I thought Brett was right behind me. [...] He didn't call out. He didn't say wait up. I didn't know. Why didn't he call out? (314).

Two years ago, Pace, like the rest of her world, operated according to stereotypes, expecting the male to be faster, trusting in his independence. The train that killed Brett taught Pace a different lesson. Brett did not call out because he knew Pace could not help him, and he could only hurt her. He behaved nobly, like a "man." To redeem herself for her role in his death, Pace wants to reenact the run and get another chance. She outlines the plan to Dalton:

> PACE. You might trip. Anything's possible. We got to be ready for it.
> [...] And then there I am at your side.
> DALTON. No. I'd slow you down and you know it. You just pass me by.
> [...] You've got to save your own skin.
> PACE. Yeah, but I can't just leave you there.
> DALTON. Yes you can.
> PACE. You'll be killed.
> DALTON. I'll be torn apart.
> PACE. So I put my arm around your waist and start to drag you down the tracks with me. It's hard going. We've only got fifty feet or so 'til we're clear. [...]
> DALTON. So you drop me. [...] You drop me and run. You run for your life.

PACE. No. I don't leave you. I—[. . .] I drag you with me.
DALTON. [. . .] And then? And then you hear me scream.
(Dalton lets out a terrible scream. At the same time Pace screams:)
PACE. I save you! (302–3)

Pace needs to replay the events of Brett's death to choreograph a better ending. She casts herself in Brett's former role, outlining the instructions, issuing the dare, and ultimately playing the martyr. Having witnessed the train's raw power, Pace has spent the past two years studying trains and worshiping them. Not coincidentally, the train is feminized. Pace always refers to it as "she," a traditional pronoun usage, but for a non traditional reason: Pace relates to the train as a killer. She sees herself as responsible for Brett's death, which is why she needs to redeem herself for her sin through Dalton. When Dalton admits to having killed Pace, he has in effect become Pace, inheriting the guilt that was her driving force. Instead of rousing him to relive the events, however, his guilt merely lands him in jail, where he accepts the hatred heaped on him by his society.

Dalton's jailer is Brett's father, Chas, a pathetic and cruel man who sees in Dalton all that Brett could have been and all that Dalton has thrown away. With Chas as jailer, Dalton's world seems increasingly small, his imprisonment intensified. Chas's emotions suffocate Dalton: Chas taunts Dalton about his sentence ("When they hang you the last thing you hear is your own neck break" [290]), watches him sleep (319), and even dares Dalton to kill him (322). In prison, Dalton does not find peace. Finally Dalton turns on Chas and calls Brett "a fucking loon" (334), forcing Chas to admit that he had hit his own son. He also tells Chas that Pace had seen him hit Brett, regularly, and that Brett had liked for Pace to watch. Brett had enjoyed having a witness: "Brett would take Pace aside and ask her if she saw it. Of course she saw it. She was standing right beside him! But Brett wanted to make sure" (335). Then, in a strange turn of events, Brett began to hit himself each morning, as if to save his father the trouble, and Chas remembers: "I just watch" (335). Thus the abuser becomes the witness, the victim the abuser. The witness, Pace, becomes the victim. Yet she is also the abuser, forcing Dalton into a life he does not want. In this play, every character plays nearly every role, and as the number of roles seems finite, even society itself seems a prison. These characters attempt to fill new roles as a sort of escape from the old, but they find themselves instead repeating cycles. These roles are random and not ultimately fulfilling; in the end, Dalton leaves jail to become someone else, but his life already seems spent. Quoting Victor Turner, John Bender defines the old-style prison in words that parallel Wallace's play: "The essential feature of these symbolizations is that the neophytes are neither living nor dead from one aspect, and both living and dead from another. Their condition is one of ambiguity and paradox, a confusion of all the customary categories" (qtd. in

Bender 26). This condition is not as much that of Dalton's jail cell as of his Depression-era world.

The title character of *Birdy,* Naomi Wallace's stage adaptation of William Wharton's novel, is confined but not to a jail cell: his prison is a psychiatric ward. Unlike Morse and Dalton, this young man is not the protagonist of the play; while he exists in a nearly catatonic state, squatting like a bird in the center of his room, his childhood friend Al Columbato visits and relives their past, reminding Birdy of the trials of their teenaged years in an ultimately successful attempt to "bring him back" (10). Both Birdy and Al are split into two characters on stage, younger and older versions of themselves—Young Al and Young Birdy, Sergeant Al and Birdy—each played by a different actor. The young characters are somewhat troubled, but they remain hopeful, while the older characters are damaged, quite possibly beyond repair. Interestingly, however, Birdy's cell is not his real prison, as he explains toward the end of the play: "When I decide to get out of here, I'll go" (68). His human body confines him. Birdy realizes in his youth that he does not want to be human; he wants to be a bird. He falls in love with his pet pigeon, Perta, and dreams of her. He tries to train himself to fly. Act 1 ends with a monologue in which Young Birdy recalls a dream in which he entered a cage and lived like a bird: "In my dream, I'd been living in this flight cage with the other males. I could talk to them. And I made sounds like a bird. I ate seed. In my dream, in the cage, I learned to fly the way I've always wanted to" (40–41). In the cage of his dream, Birdy, for the only time in his life, feels completely free. Society defines prison as a cage. For Birdy, however, the cage symbolizes freedom. As with Morse and Dalton, society is the real cage, the one that requires him to behave in ways antithetical to who he is.

That same happy dream, however, also foreshadows Birdy's future troubles. Within the dream, he sees himself as a bird in the cage but also as a boy, sitting, watching himself, outside the cage: "Me, out there, doesn't seem to know about me in the cage, hanging on the wire. How can I see myself in two places at once?" (41). This disconnectedness proves to be the root of his problem: He cannot integrate his fantasies into his real life, and he cannot feel complete except in his dreams. "I am not alone, not separate": Young Birdy utters these words to his birds in his fantasy (58); his reality is just the opposite, except for his friendship with Al, which dwindles. Meanwhile, Young Al suffers from the same issues, as his older self reminds Birdy of a diving helmet he once made out of an oil can: "The helmet worked perfectly. It didn't leak. [. . .] Something else happened. Big, strong, streetwise, tough-talking Al panicked. It was a grave down there. I kind of blacked out. [. . .] The air bubbles were plopping out of the bottom and I had enough air but I went completely ape" (58–59). Isolation drives both characters "completely ape," each in his own way. Al becomes a violent soldier who cannot trust anyone, and

Birdy becomes a mental patient, unable to communicate with human beings at all. Both characters crave contact, yet neither seems able to make the connection.

Like Birdy, Al finds himself imprisoned in his body, and like Birdy, he tries to deny who he is, though in a less poetic manner. Young Al's mother resents how much he eats, his father beats him, and he dreams of payback. When his older self meets Birdy's psychiatrist, Dr. Weiss instantly recognizes Sergeant Al as a classic victim of abuse. When Sergeant Al and Young Al are together on stage, Dr. Weiss can literally see only the older version, who remains polite and tells white lies; he seems to sense Young Al, however, who is honest and rude. The older self has grown around the younger one, like a hardened tree trunk or a permanent mask—or a prison wall. His physical prison is symbolized by the bandages he wears around his face, the result of a recent brawl with authority, one that led to a summary court-martial. Sergeant Al admits his own falsehood to Birdy, "I don't want to see anybody who knew me the way I used to be. I know I'm not me any more and I don't want to do any more pretending than I have to" (63).

As Sergeant Al remembers his friendship with Birdy, he experiences a range of emotions from passion to guilt. Renaldi, an orderly, suggests that Al "loved" Birdy—"I mean loved him, like loved him" (15)—and Sergeant Weiss, in response to Al's statement, "We were friends," counters, "It seems there was more to it than that" (46). Sergeant Al tells Renaldi, "What you and Weiss want to know is did we get it on together, did we do the hokey-pokey. Does it matter? No. It doesn't" (16). The issue of homosexuality is suggested but muted; rather than labeling the relationship, the play probes its intensity. The scenes in the present remind Sergeant Al of scenes in the past—moments of extreme emotion, all involving physical connections: Young Birdy hanging for his life from a tank, begging, "Hold me, Al" (2); Young Al, his tongue frozen to a railroad track as a train approaches, commanding Young Birdy, "Piss on my tongue or I'll beat the crap out of you!" (15); Young Al saving Birdy's life after the two have fallen through ice (47); Young Birdy screaming, "I won't hit you!" while "raining blows on Al in a frenzy" (54). These moments of connection are times of life and death. The more mundane episodes, however, pull the characters apart, leaving Young Al unable to comprehend Birdy's obsession with birds, and Young Birdy likewise unable to relate to Young Al's obsession with girls. Sergeant Al remembers, "Nobody else I've ever known had such a close friend; it was like we were married or something" (13). Their closeness to each other quite possibly scared them, making them feel different from everyone else. Having conformed, Sergeant Al realizes, "I have the feeling we haven't had anything to do with making our own lives. [. . .] It's terrible to see how easy it is for them to make us like everybody else" (56). He feels as if he and Birdy have been cast in plaster molds, another variation on the prison theme.

Young Birdy suggests, when he finds himself uncontrollably hitting his best friend, that life itself is a prison: "It doesn't matter. [...] The earth turns and we're caught" (55). Again the prison theme is characterized by a lack of control of one's own actions or destiny. When his older self awakens from catatonia, he speaks a similar line to his old friend: "Don't you know time pins everybody anyway?" (71). But with this nod to the prison of monumental time, he suggests that they not simply accept defeat. Al has been successful in his assignment to "make some kind of contact" (5), and as such, both characters rediscover the connection they have lost. The ending takes a positive twist as Birdy envisions Al's emergence from his physical prison as if from a cocoon: "You reach over your head to the back of your neck. You start pulling and it's a giant zipper. You unzip over your head and across your face, your neck, over your stomach down to your crotch. [...] Then you step out of your hot-shot Al suit. You stand there in the sunlight. And you're beautiful" (71). Birdy's prophecy ends with Al taking flight.

In spite of the ever-present message of doom, all three plays end on notes of vague hope. Wallace makes destiny pose a threat, but she does so in an effort to shake the audience out of its comfortable seats and into action. History is inevitable only if the audience/society simply sits and watches. If, instead, the audience were to question the social order, then political change might ensue. Reviewing *One Flea Spare,* Tony Brown concludes: "History has been diverted if only for a moment, but a moment is long enough to change the future forever" (D15). And that is Wallace's goal. Her plays provide such moments, such diversions, which is why she sets them not only in history but in "moments of crisis." She explains: "I do tend to choose eras where there is that pressure on people and society in general. Because those are times when, however it turned out, there were usually more options that things could've gone in different ways" (qtd. in Hurwitt D1). As the plague in *One Flea Spare* causes the characters to doubt the established rules of their society, so Wallace's plays force the audience to pose the same questions about our own world. In this way, Wallace perfectly realizes the parallel posed by Antonin Artaud in his essay "The Theatre and the Plague": "Like the plague, the theatre is a formidable call to the forces that impel the mind by example to the source of its conflicts" (Artaud 30). Her concern is less with the individual mind than with the collective mentality, but such a mentality is in fact at the root of individual conflicts. Such a mentality is exactly what Kristeva means when she defines monumental time in terms of "supra-national, socio-economic ensembles"—the powers that rule society—which is why Wallace's plays always (even when not literally about prisons) occur within monumental time. Her physical prisons, in fact, become unimportant, vestiges of linear time, when compared with the true prison of her play—the threat of stagnation.

Kristeva writes of a new generation of feminists who encompass "an attitude of retreat from sexism (male as well as female) and, gradually, from any kind of anthropomorphism":

> This process could be summarized as an *interiorization of the founding of the socio-symbolic contract,* as an introduction of its cutting edge into the very interior of every identity whether subjective, sexual, ideological, or so forth. This in such a way that the habitual and increasingly explicit attempt to fabricate a scapegoat victim as foundress of a society or a counter-society may be replaced by the analysis of the potentialities of *victim/executioner* which characterize each identity, each subject, each sex. (210)

This passage defines Wallace's writing. "The interiorization of the founding of the socio-symbolic contract"—the reason that, in *One Flea Spare,* Snelgrave rules and no one questions his authority for most of his life until act 2 of the play; the reason that Pace can assuredly tell, by looking at Dalton's shoes, that he will never attend college—is the theme, in fact the culprit, of every Wallace play. Birdy refuses such interiorization and is therefore deemed insane. Wallace, like Kristeva, poses an alternative to the scapegoat mentality but not one that—like those of many other women playwrights—simply inverts the equation: She examines the "potentialities of *victim/executioner*" within every character. And that is why she tends to set her plays in prisons—where victims and executioners so closely and ambiguously exist.

For Wallace, John Donne's poem would be too personal—the simple longing of a man for a woman—if not for the poverty implied by the flea. Compared to Donne, Kathleen Foley explains, "Wallace's metaphoric intent is hardly so playful. Even in the 'enlightened' London of the mid-1600s, the poor were viewed as little more than vermin" (F30). Wallace appropriates the image for its grotesque sexuality, but she recontextualizes it as a statement as much about politics as about love—two topics she finds indistinguishable. She explains: "My plays are about who has it, who doesn't and why. I'm also interested in looking at how our personal lives are connected with history and culture" (qtd. in Weiss). Thus she always entwines the personal with the political, presenting sex within the context of history, against the backdrop of the social order; thus she sets her plays within Donne's "living walls" (15), the walls created by the flea's random suckling. Wallace presents the prison as a dialectical metaphor—a complex and seemingly contradictory symbol, more of freedom than of restriction. Each of her characters is—like the audience—a prisoner and even a jailer, thus implying that all of society is victim to age-old and unquestioned systems of rules. Only when they are physically imprisoned do Wallace's characters recognize and overcome their restrictions. Thus the prisons themselves become liberating—escapes from a society which itself has become more restrictive than shackles or bars. Naomi Wallace inverts the common symbol of the prison in drama and presents the converse situation: characters who are free to soar in spite of their imprisonment.

Notes

I am grateful to Middle Tennessee State University's Faculty Research and Creative Activities Committee for the grant that gave me time to write this essay. I also wish to thank the MTSU English department for enabling me to attend the Naomi Wallace Festival in Atlanta.

1. For a discussion of how Wallace aligns character and audience through physical action, see "Dialectic and the Drama of Naomi Wallace," in *Southern Women Playwrights: New Essays in Literary History and Criticism* (Tuscaloosa: University of Alabama Press, 2002), Barnett 159–60.

Works Cited

Artaud, Antonin. *The Theater and Its Double.* Trans. Mary Caroline Richards. New York: Grove, 1958.

Barnett, Claudia. "Dialectic and the Drama of Naomi Wallace." *Southern Woman Playwrights: New Essays in Literary History and Criticism.* Ed. Robert L. McDonald and Linda Rohrer Paige. Birmingham: University of Alabama Press, 2002. 159–160.

Bender, John. *Imagining the Penitentiary: Fiction and the Architecture of the Mind in Eighteenth-Century England.* Chicago: University of Chicago Press, 1987.

Brown, Tony. "Disturbing Look at the Dark Side of Life's Mirror." Rev. of *One Flea Spare,* Cleveland Public Theatre. *Cleveland Plain Dealer* 17 Sept. 2001: D15.

Donne, John. "The Flea." *The Norton Anthology of English Literature.* Ed. M. H. Abrams et al. 4th ed. Vol. 1. New York: Norton, 1979. 1068–9.

Foley, Kathleen. "Flea with a Bite." Rev. of *One Flea Spare,* Studio Theatre, Whittier, Calif. *Los Angeles Times* 18 June 1998: F30.

Fornes, Maria Irene. *Fefu and Her Friends.* 1978. New York: PAJ, 1990.

Foucault, Michel. *Discipline and Punish: The Birth of the Prison.* Trans. Alan Sheridan. New York: Vintage, 1979.

Gates, Anita. "In Dullsville, Playing Chicken with Life." Rev. of *The Trestle at Pope Lick Creek,* New York Theater Workshop. *New York Times* 3 July 1999: B9.

Hartigan, Patti. "Playwright Mixes Politics and Romance." *Boston Globe* 9 March 2001: C9.

Hemming, Sarah. "Shades of the Servant—London Fringe Theatre." Rev. of *One Flea Spare,* Bush Theatre, London. *Financial Times* 1 Nov. 1995. Arts p. 21.

Hurwitt, Robert. "Teen Angst against Depression Woes: Wallace's play *Trestle* to open at Aurora." *San Francisco Chronicle* 7 Jan. 2002: D1.

Kristeva, Julia. "Women's Time." Trans. Alice Jardine and Harry Blake. *The Kristeva Reader.* Ed. Toril Moi. New York: Columbia University Press, 187–213.

"Leveler." Def. 3. *Webster's New World Dictionary of the American Language.* 2nd College Edition, 1986.

Over, William. Rev. of *One Flea Spare,* Joseph Papp Public Theatre, New York, 14 April 1997. *Theatre Journal* 50.2 (1998): 254–57.

Spencer, Charles. "A Great Flight of the Imagination." Rev. of *Birdy,* Comedy Theatre, London. *Daily Telegraph* 7 May 1997: Arts 23.

Taylor, Paul. "What the Plague throws into relief about class-division and the nature of human intimacy comes under a scrutiny both sensitive and beadily comic." Rev. of *One Flea Spare,* Bush Theatre, London. *Independent* 3 Nov. 1995: Arts 16.

Wallace, Naomi. *Birdy.* London: Faber and Faber, 1997.

———. *One Flea Spare* (1995). *In the Heart of America and Other Plays.* New York: TCG, 2001. 1–75.

———. *The Trestle at Pope Lick Creek* (1998). *In the Heart of America and Other Plays.* New York: TCG, 2001. 277–342.

Weiss, Hedy. "She's a Free Woman: MacArthur Grant Winner Charts Her Own Course." *Chicago Sun-Times* 11 July 1999: Show 1.

Wertenbaker, Timberlake. *Our Country's Good* (1988). *Timberlake Wertenbaker: Plays 1.* London: Faber and Faber, 1996.

11

No Exit and *Waiting for Godot*: Performances in Contrast

LOIS GORDON

To be enwrapped in a perpetual care for judgments and actions which you do not want to change is a living death. . . . No matter what circle of hell we are living in, I think we are free to break out of it. And if people do not break out, again, they are staying there of their own free will. So that of their own free will they will put themselves in hell.

—JEAN-PAUL SARTRE

When Jean-Paul Sartre's three figures from *No Exit* arrive in hell, they encounter no torturers, flames, repulsive smells, or any of the traditional paraphernalia associated with the netherworld. Their eternal imprisonment will take place in a Second Empire drawing room outfitted with useless and unsightly objects, befitting the irresponsible and vulgar nature of their lives, and, as they soon discover, their immortality will be spent in the dual role of the tortured and torturer. The lights in their windowless room will forever remain on, their eyes will never blink, and they will never sleep: there will be no escape from the judgment, the "gaze," of each upon the other. Condemned by their lifetime acts of inauthenticity or bad faith, they will perpetually repeat the evasions, lies, and cruelties that defined their lives. Their hell is one of their own making.

Although when they first arrive, they offer rationalizations or deceptions about their pasts, including how they died, they eventually describe their lifetime activities of moral turpitude both in thoughts and deeds ranging from indifference to premeditated criminal acts; it soon becomes apparent that, directly or indirectly, each has caused the death of an avowed loved one. As they reluctantly enumerate these acts, they continue to deny responsibility for them, disclosing at the same time how their cunning deceptions permitted their crimes to go unpunished or even unobserved during their lifetimes. Finally, they reveal that one motivation alone prompted all of their actions, the most venal sin in the Sartrean universe: the compulsion to define themselves and seek validation through the eyes of Others. The play makes clear that within the Sartrean universe, one must engage in a life of action based on personal choice originating in one's distinct subjectivity. Subjectivity is thus both the starting and end point from which one's life—one's actions—takes on meaning.

As the play progresses, the characters have visions of life continuing on earth, Sartre's ingenious device for revealing their deepest (unconscious) awareness of who they are, and they face the horrific discovery that the world has either been indifferent to them or passed condemnatory judgments upon them, rather than the exalting designations they had wished for themselves. This leaves them, in the present time of the play, in Sartre's word, naked—at the mercy of their fallen brethren for judgment. That they still depend on the Other for verification condemns them forever. Hell is indeed other people.

When we first meet Sartre's three figures, they only appear to be distinctive, in terms of nationality, class, profession, and lifestyle. In fact, they are very much alike. Each, for example, has taken pleasure in cultivating dishonest relationships with supposed lovers. Garcin has not only been cruel and condescending to his wife, but he has also tortured her by flaunting his many infidelities in front of her. His stubborn contempt for women is apparent in his use of women for sexual pleasure and as objects of false pity. He repeatedly boasts of how he saved his wife from her lower station in life ("[I] picked her up out of the gutter").

The vain, insipid Estelle rationalizes that her only crime was marrying and living with a wealthy older man in order to provide for her sickly brother. But Estelle deceived her husband with an extramarital affair, conceived a child with her lover, and drowned the child, after which the lover killed himself. Of his suicide, she says, it "was absurd of him, really; my husband never suspected anything."

While Garcin and Estelle are guilty of inauthenticity, of continuously rationalizing the truth of their acts, the lesbian Inez has a lucidity the others lack. Although she chooses to pursue a life of bad faith, Inez is the only character who articulates Sartre's moral position ("It's what one does, and nothing else, that shows the stuff one's made of"; "You are—your life, and nothing else"; "Hell is other people"), but she is entirely loveless. She has chosen a life based on "twisted and corrupted" social relationships, and the combination of her knowledge regarding the moral imperative of authenticity and her incapacity to feel makes her the most forlorn, if not despicable, of the three figures. During her lifetime, Inez seduced another woman (Florence) away from her husband, convinced her that she was responsible for his death (although he died in an accident), and drove her to suicide.[1] Inez makes clear that throughout it all she never loved Florence. She had the same contempt for her that Garcin had for his wife. In her affair with Florence, and one assumes in all her relationships, her lovelessness has been lethal. Inez knows exactly who she is, admitting: "Human feeling. That's beyond my range. I'm rotten to the core."

In addition to their aberrant sexual lives, other moral transgressions bind the characters in peculiar relationships. The pacifist journalist Garcin, for example, initially says that he died for his political ideals; only much later does he confess that he was shot as a deserter during wartime. We finally learn that he broke down at his execution and died a coward—the reverse of his lifetime self-image as a hero. An arrogant idealist, the macho Garcin twisted reason throughout his life to rationalize his actions both as a husband and political activist. Now dead, everyone can judge him as a coward, and he can do nothing about it, except—since this is hell and time is endless—exploit the weaknesses of his cellmate-judges by wooing the indifferent, narcissistic Estelle and condemnatory Inez on their own terms. This involves his understanding each of the women's needs and weaknesses and manipulating them to his ends.

Conceited and sex-obsessed Estelle is an easy target. Garcin remains contemptuous of women, but this is of no concern to Estelle as long as he succumbs to her nymphomaniacal needs, even in front of Inez. And succumb he will, because he knows Estelle will say whatever he wishes regarding his manhood and courage—with Inez in attendance to note Estelle's verbal as well as sexual corruption. Inez, on her own behalf, can similarly woo Estelle by acting as her mirror: She can tell Estelle how beautiful she is, which reinforces Estelle's identity as much as Estelle's flattery sustains Garcin's. But since Inez wants to have Estelle to herself, she both courts and tortures Garcin. She says to him, a man of ideas and a misogynist: "She doesn't count. She's a woman"—a statement he might make; at the same time, she refuses to validate Garcin's self-image as a hero as Estelle has. Inez is tortured by Estelle's attempted lovemaking with Garcin, because Estelle's rejection of her is both a humiliation to her personally and an insult to her lifestyle generally.

All of the characters are hypocritical and loveless and would use or even destroy the other(s) without a moment's hesitation. When Garcin first sees Estelle and Inez, he tries to ignore them, since as women they have not been the Others to whom he has looked for validation. Later, when the men on earth call him a coward, he puts himself at the mercy (gaze) of the women for validation: first the vapid Estelle, who makes him feel guilty—a poetically just punishment for a man who has mistreated women—and then the lesbian Inez, who sees through him, which unnerves him.

Inez's hatred of everyone is most palpable. She thinks that her hatred of men caused her to turn to women, but she finally admits that she enjoys the suffering of women as much as the suffering of men. In a cold and precise statement she says: "I can't give and I can't receive." But Estelle and Garcin might say the same, and as the tension builds, the serial manipulations of the separate couples are designed to annihilate the third person and, depending on the moment, to weaken the partner in that particular encounter.

Each thus becomes a victim and a victimizer. Inez, Estelle, and Garcin continually seduce and reject each other—for sexual and nonsexual ends. As they deceive and are deceived by the other (always prompting the third character on stage to plan the next move, each character further imprisoned by his or her self-serving purposes), a series of combinations and permutations develop in the rapidly but subtly changing relationships that provide the play its most dramatic moments. It is difficult to keep apace of each character as tortured or torturer, as Self or Other, because at each moment of rejection or victory, each becomes the Subject or the Object.

No Exit divides into in three movements. In the first, the characters arrive; they lie, rationalize, deceive, and juggle facts and impressions regarding why they are here. In the second, incapable of following Garcin's suggestion that they remain quiet, they make forced and incomplete confessions about their lives. They judge one another and flirt with the idea of helping one another. In the last and longest section of the play—in actions that will continue long after the curtain falls—they desperately seek validation from one another. In so doing, they demonstrate their superior skills at torturing each other, as well as the growing intensity of their own pain. In forever rejecting responsibility for their lives and in evading self-evaluation, they have failed to learn Sartre's central moral imperative—that one's acts during each moment of existence define one's being:

> Man is nothing else but what he makes of himself.... Man will be what he will have planned to be,... responsible for what he is.... Life has no meaning a priori. Before you come alive, life is nothing; it's up to you to give it a meaning, and value is nothing else but the meaning you choose. There is no universe other than a human universe, the universe of human subjectivity." [2] (Being and Nothingness xlvi)

For those who have spent their lives catering to or dependent on the world of Others, hell is indeed, and appropriately, other people,[3] with an emphasis on "other." Of passing interest, the play was originally printed as *The Others*,[4] a direct, uncomplicated definition of hell; the revised *No Exit* is more provocative, focusing on the door that opens at the end of the play and is useless to any of the characters, because each is still tied to the Other[s] for moral definition.

In the existential universe, as Sartre defined it, one is not born "good" or "evil," with a specific "human nature," or "essence," as Christianity assumes in the concept of original sin. To Sartre, man is "nothing"—not even Locke's *tabula rasa* or possessing Camus's innate sense of "innocence." As Sartre writes:

> Man exists, turns up, appears on the scene, and only afterwards, defines himself. If man, as the existentialist conceives him, is indefinable, it is because at

first he is nothing. Only afterward will he be something, and he himself will have made what he will be. Thus, there is no human nature, since there is no God to conceive it. Not only is man what he conceives himself to be, but he is also only what he wills himself to be after this thrust toward existence.[5] (Being and Nothingness 20)

Nor should one seek a moral judgment from others. One moves through life by means of conscious acts (one "exists"), which alone define the quality of one's life (one's "essence"). Hence Sartre's famous proclamation: "Existence precedes essence."

The terror of Sartre's vision, almost glimpsed by Garcin, lies in the paradox of human experience: the obligatory yet ultimately meaningless nature of good acts, the necessity to perform benevolent acts in the absence of metaphysical verification. Sartre writes: "At every moment I'm obliged to perform exemplary actions," at the same time he says, "Man is condemned to be free. . . . There is no universe other than a human universe, the universe of human subjectivity. . . . This means that no limits to my freedom can be found except freedom itself or, if you prefer, that we are not free to cease from being free" (Being and Nothingness 439).

One lives in a concrete world having come from nothing, and eventually one returns to the void. All the same, one yearns for meaning and direction; one demands justification, and one remains intensely mystified. Nevertheless, even in this mystified state one is obliged to perform good actions: "There is not a single one of our acts which does not at the same time create an image of man as we think he ought to be." This makes the individual the creator of his or her own existence and essence, the author of his or her moral imperatives, despite the awareness that ultimately everyone will rejoin the metaphysical nothingness that precedes and follows human existence. Sartre continues: "Man makes himself man in order to be God, and selfness considered from this point of view can appear to be an egoism; but precisely because there is no common measure between human reality and the self-cause which it wants to be, one could just as well say that man loses himself in order that the self-cause may exist" (Being and Nothingness 626).

Samuel Beckett's *Waiting for Godot* is another example of human imprisonment—of characters on a road with only a rock and tree—as one hears repeatedly their statement, "Let's go," always followed by the stage directions "(*They do not move.*)." However, apart from their imprisonment on a road that comes from and goes nowhere—the playwright's emblem of the existential or absurd world in which they live—Beckett's vision is entirely different from Sartre's. Beckett's two couples in *Waiting for Godot* are among literature's most authentic characters, and they function as exemplary figures of good faith. In addition, unlike Sartre's characters who never contemplate the human condition, Beckett's couples are obsessed with it, and they have all they can do to distract themselves from continuously posing metaphysical questions that they can never answer. Fully aware of the truths Sartre propounds, Beckett's figures have created the best way of surviving from day to day in a universe they will never comprehend.

They are, to be sure, aware of the paradox of their condition—demanding purpose, meaning, or validation for their ultimately purposeless and meaningless lives—and as such, they are heroic models in the very fact of their survival. While they often speak of the difficulty of living, which of necessity involves waiting for direction, they face and contend with the only two alternatives that the existential or absurd anguish allows: They can commit suicide (which in their ridiculous attempts they reject) or they can construct a lifestyle whose purpose is to bury their darkest dread in the deepest recesses of their mind. They choose the latter, in constructing a relationship with one another that allows them Beckett's single imperative: survival. As a result, in the midst of all their travails, they enjoy moments of tender caretaking ("Like a carrot?" one asks his hungry partner), warm camaraderie, and even the joy their silly games provide. They also find occasions when they can undertake acts of kindness and generosity to strangers. It is in such moments—of sheer survival, as well as of altruism—that they are like Sisyphus, as he rolls his rock to the top of his mountain, certain that it will fall down but defiant in enjoying the texture of his rock and the blue of the sky. Beckett's characters similarly surmount their fate. They carry as best they can their own burdens of existence in the face of inevitable death and oblivion. At the end of the day, given their options, one might well say of them, as Camus says of Sisyphus, that they are "happy." They are alive.

Of course Beckett's characters have more opportunity for happiness than Sisyphus, for each partner of Beckett's two couples has another person, both to care for and to be taken care by. Beckett goes so far as to illustrate that companionship and camaraderie not only permit moments of distraction and affection, but they also provide a mechanism with which to challenge the finality of inevitable annihilation. In those moments when Beckett's couples perform acts of kindness and altruism, they show the possibilities of human nature to confront the boundaries of the human condition.

Beckett's characters are imprisoned not by their own actions, as are Sartre's, they are imprisoned by the human condition. The world, limited as it is on this barren road, is at their disposal, and they evoke and react to the gamut of emotions known to all humankind. Sartre's characters, blind or at best disinterested in the human condition, are trapped by their own bad choices, condemned by their indifference to the value of life and the power they have in creating a worthy life. Sartre's condemned people lack any sense of the possibilities life permits, of the human freedom that precedes metaphysical oblivion. On the other hand, Beckett's heroes are artists, fully aware of their freedom within their limited universe, conscious that their every act is an invention or a creation—their only evidence of being alive.

Playing to the Others: Sartre's "Actors" in a Scriptless, Directionless, Universe

The arrival of each character in hell reveals the personality and moral style of a lifetime. Garcin arrogantly inquires of the valet: "Do you know who I was?" and later requests of him that he be "more polite." Glancing at the hideous furniture in the room, Garcin admits: "I had quite a habit of living among furniture that I didn't relish, and in false positions. I'd even come to like it." Not entirely unaware of his inauthenticity, he evaluates his last remark: "Bogus in bogus." In a playful reversal of Subject and Object, Sartre personifies the objects in the room—in a "capricious" bell, for example—which is appropriate for a group of people who, like mechanical objects, were assigned identities by Others. The objects in hell are also reflections of their inmates' useless lives: a paper knife can neither cut nonexistent books nor kill the threatening Others who are already dead. Even Garcin's (and the others') language is bogus or inauthentic. He speaks of hell as "this—er—residence" and observes without commentary the absence of mirrors. All the room's new inhabitants have flattered themselves by depending on mirrors for their identities, either literally (although they have seen only the superficial in what technically has been a reverse image of themselves) or in what Sartre calls the "gaze" or "eye" of other people. Then, using a visual image that anticipates many that follow in the play, Garcin says: "*I'm facing* the situation," although his next remark reveals the hypocrisy of his statement: "I won't have it springing up on me *from behind* [italics mine]." On some level aware of his self-deceptions, he is distressed when he realizes that he lacks eyelids and will never sleep again: "Then how shall I endure my own company?" His dependence on an Other is reiterated in his fear of remaining alone when the valet is about to depart: "You're going . . . Wait."

When the post office clerk Inez enters, her first question is "Where's Florence?" followed by a remark similar to Garcin's to the departing valet: "Tortured by separation." Observing Garcin, her first response betrays her rigid sexual stereotyping: "Well, as far as I'm concerned, you won't get anywhere." She next expresses her fear of isolation at the same time she ridicules the person she misses—Florence, the "tiresome little fool." Addressed as "Mrs." she promptly corrects Garcin: "I'm not married" and in a rather obtuse fashion, admits, by identifying with Garcin, that she has been a torturer. That is, first observing his pain, she associates him with the devil; then projecting *her* pain on to him as a torturer/devil (and incorporating the complicated meaning of the mirror) she says: "I know what I'm talking about. I've often watched my face in the glass."

To Garcin's repeated "I want to think things out," she expresses horror, because, as she explains, he is twisting his mouth. Again, connecting her Self to the Other, she says: "You've no right to inflict the sight of your fear on me." Unlike Garcin, however, she believes "My life's in order. It tidied itself up nicely of its own accord." True enough, Inez has lived according to her ideal of independence even if she has neglected to take her partners' needs into account. It is clear that these two will torture one another when Garcin says: "We should make a point of being courteous to each other," and Inez replies: "I'm not polite."

When Estelle arrives, she also sees Garcin as an Other. She confuses him with her dead lover: "Don't look up," she says, "I know you've no face left." Like Garcin she uses language inauthentically, acknowledging their present status as "absentees"—an ironically accurate measure of their withdrawal from a meaningful life. However, unlike either Garcin or Inez, Estelle admits, "I never could bear the idea of anyone's expecting something from me." Lacking Garcin's rationalizing and Inez's cold calculating skills, she says: "Everything that goes on in one's head is so vague, isn't it? It makes one want to sleep."

Estelle believes it must be "a mistake" that she is here. She and Garcin then condone the shame of each other's life (although the questions they pose to each other are half-truths). Was it a crime, Estelle asks, living with an older man to save her brother and then having a lover? Garcin asks if one should live by his principles. Each one's mindless affirmation condones the other's illusion. Each, in effect, becomes a mirror to the other. Estelle's blind affirmation even prods Garcin to lie about his death and describe it as an act of courage and resignation, and he brags about the moment he was shot.

Inez who recognizes their hypocrisy and also acknowledges her own bad faith—her hypocrisy and cruelty—makes two remarks about their present whereabouts that change the direction of the play:

> They've thought it out. Down to the least detail. Nothing was left to chance.
> This room was all set for us.

And she adds:

> If only each of us had the guts to tell.
> . . .
> We're all tarred with the same brush. . . . We are criminals—murderers—all three of us. . . . There have been people who burned their lives out for our sakes—and we chuckled over it.

From this point on, the subterfuges multiply, apparitions from the living world multiply, and the three are stripped of their excuses. It becomes clear that they have all tried to legitimize their individual cruelties with excuses of self-sacrifice. Although Garcin suggests that they remain quiet in "self-communings," after a long silence, Estelle, incapable of introspection, seeks her usual way of affirming her existence, through a mirror and an Other: "When I can't see myself I begin to wonder if I really and truly exist. . . . Somehow it kept me alert, seeing myself as the others saw me." Inez, clearly her opposite, says: "I'm always conscious of myself—in my mind. Painfully conscious." Neither the person of total feeling nor of total mind will survive Sartre's demands.

Inez, who also breaks the silence, flaunts her lesbianism and flirts with Estelle, offering her eyes as a looking glass ("You're lovely, Estelle"). Estelle, a nymphomaniac who has never liked women ("I don't make friends with women very easily"), also says: "You scare me rather," but Inez continues to court her. Estelle cannot control her attraction to Garcin ("I wish he'd notice me"), but he is consumed by his own thoughts ("I know I begged you not to speak," he says to her). Estelle's continued interest in Garcin provokes Inez to remark that Estelle's face is blemished. To this Estelle utters one of the play's many hilarious lines: "A pimple? Oh, how simply foul!" The nature of Estelle's existence is defined.

If Inez and Garcin are battling over Estelle and Garcin gains the upper hand, Inez reminds Garcin of his cowardice (which does not distress him since he venerates only the judgment of his male colleagues on earth), and she exhorts him about Estelle's nymphomania. This, she says, would prompt Estelle to say anything he wants. But the desire for her affirmation, rather than sex, is Garcin's sole reason for turning to Estelle.

In the course of these and the following activities, each enacts in a heightened way the sadistic roles of a lifetime. Inez, who correctly assesses Estelle's need for flattery, tortures her: "Suppose I covered my eyes. . . . All that loveliness of yours would be wasted on the desert air." Estelle, increasingly needy of a man, endures Inez's criticism of men and her (accurate) remark that Garcin is not interested in her: he's more concerned with his peers on earth. With each one's struggle for attention, followed by rejection and exposure, Garcin says: "We may as well stop. . . . We're between ourselves. And presently we shall be naked as—newborn babes." If indeed this is so, he suggests, they could all make "a clean breast of it" because, as he speaks for Sartre: "We know nothing. Nothing that counts."

What follows is *almost* each one's confession, but a few salient details are reserved until the end of the play. Garcin begins, although Inez already knows he is a "deserter." This important matter, however, seems only peripheral to him, and he chooses just to admit his cruelty to his wife: "Night after night I came home blind drunk, stinking of wine and women." His wife said nothing but she judged him when "only her eyes spoke." Garcin has no sense of regret; the most he can admit is that he was "a well-beloved brute." He has yet to admit his greatest deception, in terms of what has most mattered to him, his cowardice.

Inez admits that she was "a damned bitch" with Florence, allowing her no identity of her own: "I crept inside her skin, she saw the world through my eyes." She recalls Florence's abandonment of her husband: "I had her on my hands. . . . I'm rather cruel really." Inez was as sadistic to her partner as Garcin was to his wife and Estelle to her husband and lover. Inez even admits: "I can't get on without making people suffer." Although Garcin fails to mention his cowardice, Inez fully admits her lies to Florence—telling her that both of them caused her husband's death (in fact, he was run over by a tram), after which Florence gassed both herself and Inez. In Estelle's confession, she admits that "it pleased [her lover] no end" to have a child and that after she drowned the child, he shot himself.

In the last part of the play Inez says: "Well, Mr. Garcin, now you have us in the nude, all right," to which he replies: "Suppose we start trying to help each other." The dramatic intensity of the play reaches a peak as Inez expresses the truth about all of them: "I can't give and I can't receive." This becomes the motif of the play's powerful last section, where the seductions accelerate not just for personal need but for moral approval. That is, whatever the characters appear to do for one another is in fact an overture toward self-justification. As Garcin says: "We're chasing after each other, round and round in a vicious circle. . . . That's part of [the] plan, of course." In the manifest efforts at enticing the Other, that Other is in the act of beguiling someone else. Sartre's stage directions are magnificent:

> Inez has come up and is standing behind Estelle, but without touching her. During the dialogue that follows she speaks almost in her ear. But Estelle keeps her eyes on Garcin, who observes her without speaking, and she addresses her answers to him, as if it were he who were questioning her.

Inez and Estelle's visions of life on earth reinforce the meaninglessness of their previous lives: a man and woman are about to rent Inez's house and make love in it; Estelle's young lover is dancing with another woman and calling her by the endearments once reserved for Estelle. Inez's remark shapes the conclusion of the play: "Nothing of you's left on earth—not even a shadow. All you own is here." She again speaks for Sartre.

Sartre is relentless in the condemnation of his characters. To the extent they may have admitted their crimes, they still fail to take responsibility for them. As such they are trapped, as though by choice, in old patterns that will forever involve an alternation of assault and rejection and, finally, a sense of torture greater than any they have known before. Thus, as Inez tries to seduce Estelle again, Estelle is flirting with Garcin, who is still trying to hear himself proclaimed a hero by those on earth. Garcin then tells Estelle to talk to Inez ("But she doesn't count," says Estelle: "She's a woman"), and Estelle makes clear that she will take Garcin on any terms. Even though he says: "I shan't love you," she admits that doesn't matter.

They begin touching each other in Inez's presence. Garcin will return to Estelle if she confirms his heroism. Their insincerity at this delicate moment is comical:

> GARCIN: Will you trust me? . . . You *must* give me your trust.
> ESTELLE: What a quaint thing to ask! . . . I'm giving you my mouth, my arms, my whole body. . . . My trust! I haven't any to give."
> [. . .]
> GARCIN: Am I a coward?
> ESTELLE: How can I say?
> GARCIN: I can't decide.
> [. . .]
> ESTELLE: You've a twisted mind, that's your trouble. Plaguing yourself over such trifles!
> GARCIN: I wanted to make a stand. But was that my real motive?

Inez is proficient in moralizing for others:

> Exactly. . . . Fear and hatred and all the dirty little instincts one keeps dark— they're motives too. . . . Try to be honest with yourself—for once.

Although Garcin boasts that he has given his life over to introspection, he remains unable to stop rationalizing and to admit his cowardice. In the midst of his pseudo-dark night of the soul, Estelle continues her seduction efforts, once more admitting her code of morality: "Coward or hero, it's all one—provided he kisses well." At that point, Garcin finally hears the Others' judgment from on high (the earth), a truth he has avoided throughout his life, one that Inez has been repeating throughout the last few minutes of the play: "Garcin's a coward." Estelle continues trying to gain his attention: "Why trouble over what those men are thinking. . . . Touch me," she commands.

Garcin begs Estelle to have faith in him, but she can only laugh at him, playfully call him a coward, and direct all her energy to her own needs. "You think too much. That's your trouble," she remarks as the moral gap between them widens even further. Sartre's comic talent dominates the moment as Garcin says to Estelle:

> A thousand of them are proclaiming that I'm a coward, but what do numbers matter? If there's someone, just one person, to say quite positively that I did not run away, that I'm not the sort who runs away, that I'm brave and decent and the rest of it. . . . Will you have . . . faith in me? Then I shall love you and cherish you for ever.

Estelle's response, "I'd love you just the same, even if you were a coward," forces Garcin's "You disgust me, both of you." He asks Estelle to leave (to go where?), as though she could rob him of his (nonexistent) identity: "Go away, You're even fouler than she. I won't let myself get bogged in your eyes. You're soft and slimy. . . . Like a quagmire."

The door opens and everyone remains in hell. Garcin gives as his reason his hope that he can still convince Inez of his authenticity: "It's because of her I'm staying here. . . . If you'll have faith in me I'm saved." Admitting that he lived his life to be a hero, he now breaks all of Sartre's rules: He wants confirmation that he is better than his acts. Inez again speaks for the author, although the words remain her (the Other's) reflection, not Garcin's:

> It's what one does, and nothing else, that shows the stuff one's made of. . . . One always dies too soon—or too late. And yet one's whole life is complete at that moment.

Inez reminds him of the significance of his actions: "You are—your life, and nothing else." Aware that he still lacks authenticity and is dependent on her judgment, she cruelly adds: "You're a coward, Garcin, because I wish it," and, "I am a mere breath on the air, a gaze observing you, a formless thought that thinks you." Incapable of assuming responsibility for his life and asserting his freedom, now or before, Garcin will remain dependent on the gaze of Others and spend eternity trying to persuade Inez and Estelle to accept his view of himself.

Estelle, witnessing his pain, runs to him: "Revenge yourself. . . . Kiss me, darling," to which Inez makes her judgment: "What a lovely scene: coward Garcin holding baby-killer Estelle in his manly arms. [But] I'll never let you go." The two- and three-person games will forever continue, each forever tortured and torturing in seeking and withholding absolution from the other. "Well, let's carry on then," says Garcin at the end.

Waiting for Godot

Beckett's *Waiting for Godot* is another dramatization of human imprisonment, its characters repeatedly saying: "Let's go," with their declaration always followed by "(*They do not move.*)." Their imprisonment is Beckett's poetic construct of the human condition within Sartre's existential world. However, with the exception of the world in which they are placed—an eternally incomprehensible universe—the characters and dilemmas posed in Sartre's and Beckett's plays could not be more dissimilar. Sartre's people are like cardboard figures who are artfully manipulated according to the playwright's philosophical paradigms of good and bad faith. Beckett, who insisted throughout his life that he was no philosopher, creates lifelike characters who occupy a world their author only vaguely intuits—an inscrutable universe similar to Sartre's but one without his strict demands regarding good faith and authenticity. All the same, Beckett's people are thoughtful, endowed with reason and a passion to understand, and well aware of the meaninglessness of human events and the fact that their survival merely marks their progress toward ultimate oblivion.

Beckett, with compassion for the human need to live with at least the illusion of hope, focuses on how Vladimir and Estragon, despite their conclusions about the inscrutability of the universe, nevertheless manage from day to day, as though some answer might be forthcoming "tomorrow" (a word used frequently in the play)—regarding their purpose on earth and their whereabouts after death. That is, Godot will appear, and the emptiness in their hearts and the anguish of their souls will diminish.

Camus's remarks from "Absurd Freedom" are applicable to Vladimir and Estragon:

> I can negate everything of that part of me that lives on vague nostalgias, except this desire for unity, this longing to solve, this need for clarity and cohesion. . . . I don't know whether this world has a meaning that transcends it. But I know that I do not know that meaning. . . . And these two certainties—my appetite for the absolute and for unity and the impossibility of reducing this world to a rational and reasonable principle—I also know that I cannot reconcile them. . . .
>
> If I were a tree among trees, a cat among animals, this life would have a meaning, or rather this problem would not arise, for I should belong to this world. I should *be* this world to which I am now opposed by my whole consciousness. . . . This ridiculous reason is what sets me in opposition to all creation.
>
> . . . The absurd man . . . feels innocent. To tell the truth, that is all he feels—his irreparable innocence. (Camus 38–39)

In surviving from day to day—that is, in waiting for Godot—Beckett's figures convey both the profound need for purpose or direction in life and the emotional fragmentation that accompanies that need. This differentiates them from Sartre's characters, but even more distinctive is their courage when they step away from their ordinary activities and engage in acts of gratuitous compassion and altruism. This makes them heroic by any standards in the existential or absurd universe.

That Vladimir and Estragon persist in a world where, as Beckett writes in the first line, there is "Nothing to be done," defines their stoicism:

ESTRAGON: I wasn't doing anything.
VLADIMIR: Perhaps you weren't. But it's the way of doing it that counts, the way of doing it, if you want to go on living.
ESTRAGON: I wasn't doing anything.

VLADIMIR: You must be happy too, deep down....
ESTRAGON: Would you say so?...
VLADIMIR: Say, I am happy.
ESTRAGON: I am happy.
VLADIMIR: So am I.
ESTRAGON: So am I....
[...]
VLADIMIR: Wait ... we embraced.... We were happy ... happy. What do we do now that we're happy ... Go on waiting ... waiting....

The paradox of Camus's Absurd, like Sartre's Existentialism, involves a tension between engagement and impotence, and between logic and absurdity. But the fact of life's ultimate meaninglessness must be repressed from consciousness, allowing one to live fully and without anguish in a random and disordered universe.

The minimization of anxiety in Beckett's world is accomplished through the creation of rituals and partnerships that enable his characters to survive the hours and years—that is, to live or to wait. Vladimir and Estragon, while free to devise any sort of relationship, reject an alliance based on power and submission, unlike Beckett's second couple in the play, Pozzo and Lucky. However even for a "master" like Pozzo and a "servant" like Lucky—a dictatorial sadist and a submissive masochist—there is comfort in companionship: "The road seems long when one journeys all alone." Vladimir and Estragon, however, choose a more humane partnership where one assumes the more rational and philosophical role (Vladimir), and the other, the more emotional and sensual one (Estragon): Thus, they aspire to a friendship with egalitarian stability. In this way, they hope to pursue a relatively peaceful and predictable coexistence. The overarching imperative in their relationship is that each distract the other from despair over the human condition.

For example, Estragon intentionally avoids answering Vladimir's provocative question, "Do you remember the Gospels?" He knows that discussing the two thieves might—and later does—provoke a discussion of their own questionable redemption, a subject they must avoid. So Estragon answers in a private, nonresponsive way, connecting the Gospels with their geographical origins: "I remember the maps of the Holy Land. Coloured they were. Very pretty. The dead sea was pale blue...." To maintain their relationship and distract Vladimir from his serious contemplations, he concludes his remarks with the non sequitur "We'll be happy."

Similarly, to disguise his own acute disappointment when Pozzo tells them that he is not Godot, Estragon responds only to the alliterative quality of Pozzo's name: "You're not Mr. Godot? ... Bozzo ... Bozzo." When Vladimir advises that he "calm" himself, Estragon's answer is once again private and seemingly incoherent. It is based on the sound quality of "calm"—"Calm. calm. The English say cawm"—rather than the logical meaning of Vladimir's statement.

Estragon's lack of memory and of time and space distinctions help the couple avoid their most profound concern, salvation:

> VLADIMIR: . . . the two thieves. Do you remember the story?
> ESTRAGON: No.
> VLADIMIR: Shall I tell it to you?
> ESTRAGON: No.

Vladimir urges Estragon to listen to his story, because "It'll pass the time." But his tale is again about life, death, and redemption. Although the continuously forgetful Estragon tries to distract Vladimir with "Our what?" or "Saved from what?" taboo subjects *are,* at moments, raised, and the game seems at risk. Estragon says, "Who am I to tell my private nightmares to if I can't tell them to you?" to which Vladimir replies, "Let them remain private. You know I can't bear that." Some comments are almost intolerable, especially those relating to time and their meeting with Godot:

> VLADIMIR: Where were we yesterday . . . ?
> ESTRAGON: How would I know? In another compartment. There's no lack of void.

Until they recover a familiar cue, such as "charming spot," their resolve is weakened.

The beginning of the play clearly establishes their assignments. Beckett places the two men in opposing postures. Estragon is seated on his rock at stage front. He faces the audience with his head down and hands cupped before him. Vladimir, near the back of the stage, stands with his back to the audience. His hands are at his side, and his head is turned toward the sky.

A debilitated Vladimir advances with "short, stiff strides [and] legs wide apart." He walks toward Estragon and sees his friend who, exhausted by his attempts to pull off his boots, says: "Nothing to be done" (a refrain always stated in the passive voice). Estragon is responding solely to his boot, since his assigned role requires concrete thinking. That is, by projecting his spiritual suffering onto his boot and foot, he can conceal his inner pain. Their game is begun, and the intensity of Estragon's suffering—the matter of greatest consequence to him—is held in abeyance. Vladimir, as the man of reason also committed to minimizing their common condition, intentionally ignores both his own and Estragon's pain. He responds in an impersonal, logical, and abstract manner. As if he were deep in thought, he circumvents Estragon's *concrete,* personalized "Nothing to be done" (and following "Help! . . . It hurts!")

with a seemingly casual, *general* remark, which seems directed more to the audience than to Estragon:

> I'm beginning to come round to that opinion. All my life I've tried to put it from me, saying, Vladimir, be reasonable, you haven't yet tried everything. And I resumed the struggle. (*He broods, musing on the struggle. Turning to Estragon.*) So there you are again.

Although the subject of pain never surfaces, Vladimir demonstrates both the effectiveness and shortcomings of their role assignments. He understands (and shares) what Estragon is saying, but he responds as if he were a philosopher contemplating the nature of human activity ("I'm beginning to come around to that opinion"). Unlike Estragon, Vladimir can survey the past ("All my life ... "), and in so doing he confesses that his lifetime of philosophical contemplation has left him where he began. He has tried to put aside Estragon's "opinion" ("Nothing to be done") by waging an intellectual, as opposed to Estragon's physical, "struggle" (a word that reverberates throughout the play: "No use struggling ... / No use wriggling ... "). And this leaves him in the mental state of "brooding," parallel to Estragon's physical state of "exhaustion" after wrestling with his boots. Facing Estragon for the first time, his concluding remark places Estragon back on track. Estragon's response, "Am I?" and Vladimir's, "I'm glad to see you back. I thought you were gone forever," ends this interaction, with Vladimir abstractly mentioning their common "struggle" but in fact not comforting Estragon.

If the setting of *No Exit* is a room furnished with a few useless and unsightly objects, *Waiting for Godot* encompasses a sparse natural world—of animal (man), vegetable (Vladimir's tree), and mineral (the road and Estragon's mound or rock). Lacking a social history, *Godot*'s Everymen are "being"—existence without essence. They define themselves anew each day in their relationship with one another, and they relate to each other in such a way as to keep their fears to a minimum, to comfort and amuse each other, and, most importantly, to give validation to the other's existence. That Vladimir and Estragon necessarily share the most profound life goal—of determining a purpose for living—is clear in the very name of their quest—Godot. This may refer to (a diminutive) God from the external world (cosmic or natural) who would provide them with a sense of direction (the "Mr. Godot" they await). But "Godot" is virtually a contraction of their nicknames, Gogo and Didi. Thus, each one of them may provide the other with a daily sense of cohesion in his life. When they are in despair over the possibility that an external solution will never arrive, they say, "Let's go." But they find it equally convincing that if they return to their daily routines—and subsist on whatever each gets from the other—their hopelessness will pass, and thus their "Let's go" is always followed by, "They do not move."

The paradox of purposeful action and ultimate meaninglessness pervades the play. A deceptively simple boot routine is rationalized as purposeful activity:

> VLADIMIR: It'd pass the time.
>   (ESTRAGON hesitates.)
>   I assure you, it'd be an occupation.
> ESTRAGON: A relaxation.
> VLADIMIR: A recreation.
> ESTRAGON: A relaxation.
> [...]
> We don't manage too badly, eh Didi, between the two of us? ... We always find something, eh Didi, to give us the impression we exist.

Their goal remains the ambitious: "to try to converse calmly" according to their well-performed script:

> ESTRAGON: So long as one knows.
> VLADIMIR: One can bide one's time.
> ESTRAGON: One knows what to expect.
> VLADIMIR: No further need to worry.
> ESTRAGON: Simply wait.
> VLADIMIR: We're used to it.

On occasion, they acknowledge the true subject of their game:

> VLADIMIR: Now what did we do yesterday ?
> [...]
> ESTRAGON: Yesterday evening we spent blathering about *nothing* [emphasis mine]

But Vladimir and Estragon are exemplary in the elasticity of their accommodation to the Absurd. Among the mysterious, erratic, or uncontrollable forces of the universe are their several adversaries, including logic. Logic only *appears* to be more discrete and manageable than fateful events, such as physical debilitation, the intrusion of strangers, or any event that might change their routine. Logic, after all, gives the impression of cohesion and viability and helps one in the pursuit of survival. It dictates coherence: pointing to this, rather than that, course of action. In addition, logic can provide one with a sense of comfort, for it is a natural state of mind. And thus, Vladimir and Estragon's most everyday routines, including their silly vaudeville exchanges and bowler hat jostling, depend on the mechanics of logic, on continuity and causality.

Most of their interactions depend on memory, which also depends on continuity and causality. All the same, should their games fail, they have established emergency measures that depend upon their knowledge of one another and their anticipation of the other's behavior. Although a good deal of the play's humor arises from their failure to do simple tasks, like removing shoes and buttoning pants, habit continues to demonstrate one's logic and provides the hope of linear and predictable behavior—all of this in a random and chaotic universe.

The characters often insist on the "truth" or "validity" of their actions—for example, Vladimir: "That's right", "It is true"; or Lucky's assurance that the content of his monologue is "established beyond all doubt." But Vladimir and Estragon's major logical problem is why their designated appointment with Godot never materializes. Ultimately, Vladimir and Estragon doubt; therefore, they exist, and in their every activity they are pawns of an undefined fate that determines the erratic efficacy of causality and any of logic's other manifestations.

Another adversary and dimension in the paradox of the Absurd is sensory experience. One would assume, as in the case of logic, that sense perception is natural and reliable. Yet when Estragon is given a turnip, Vladimir says: "Oh pardon! I could have sworn it was a carrot." Their most basic assumptions regarding the simplest of sense perceptions are uncertain. For example, although Estragon is traditionally portrayed as the heavier of the two men, their conversation about the rope that might hang them suggests the reverse:

ESTRAGON: Gogo light—bough not break—Gogo dead. Didi heavy—bough break—Didi alone. . . .
VLADIMIR: But am I heavier than you?
ESTRAGON: So you tell me. I don't know. There's an even chance. Or nearly.

The simplest use of language reveals the extent of human limitation. That words cannot communicate the most urgent of situations is underscored when each man cries for help and is answered as though he had asked for the time of day. "Help me!" evokes the response, "It hurts?"

Time is perhaps the most terrifying and least comprehensible of their adversaries. Despite all their efforts, Vladimir and Estragon cannot deal with either mechanical or cosmic time. They cannot change themselves; they cannot change the world that operates independently of them. To do the former would necessitate a goal or sense of purpose, but since the latter is indifferent in providing these, Vladimir and Estragon know well one of Beckett's axiomatic truths: in the absence of attainable goals or ideals, nothing, in a concrete way, *can* change.

Nevertheless, *Godot* appears to move linearly—toward a future when Godot will arrive. The play is filled with traditional terms like "tomorrow" or "yesterday," the colloquial or exaggerated "a million years ago," and specifics like "in the nineties." These, however, function either in personal or abstract terms, appropriate within the existential universe. In *Godot*, days, months, and years pass in an instant; the tree blooms overnight; in what they think is the next day, Pozzo and Lucky age; Pozzo is blind; Lucky, dumb. "When! When!" laments Pozzo, "Have you not done tormenting me with your accursed time?" Beckett's figures play out their lives before us existentially.

Time (and space) thus bends and contracts throughout *Godot*, and each figure plays out his life against a complex counterpoint of mechanical time (in which one ages and moves to death and obliteration) and cosmic time (in which one's acts have no function whatsoever). In the end, as Camus's Mersault in *The Stranger* discovers, one's life is enacted within a universe that is both indifferent and autonomous—mysterious and stable, decaying and regenerative—a world of entropy and eternal renewal.

The idea of human achievement performed in the face of mortality and cosmic indifference is inherent in Existentialism and the Absurd, and it is given its most extensive expression in Lucky's monologue ("Given the existence ... "). The speech, in three divisions, is a chaotic worldview of a one-time philosopher-poet. In the first part, Lucky expostulates on the universe as ruled by an enigmatic, capricious deity: "Given the existence ... of a personal God ... who from the heights of divine apathia divine athambia divine aphasia loves us dearly with some exceptions for reasons unknown." In the second section, he describes the human creature who "wastes and pines" in spite of all the "strides" and "labors of men"—intellectual, social, and physical. In the last section Lucky speaks of how, in the end, just a stony, indifferent earth survives. After all labors are "abandoned" and "left unfinished" a landscape remains scattered with decayed bones—"the skull the skull"—the relics of human habitation.

Almost every word and activity in the play repeats Lucky's remarks on human achievement and ultimate decay. Each speaker gains Lucky's wisdom and in fact becomes like him, a modern-day Atlas—a spiritually and emotionally burdened innocent—bearing the world's hopes on his shoulders. Lucky is a maddened Sisyphus whose heavy bags are filled with the rubbish of intellectual endeavor and with disintegrated stone and sand, a reminder of the end that awaits humanity. Nevertheless, Lucky continues and "waits" in his own fashion. The day the tree blossoms, he becomes speechless. Like the other figures in the play, Lucky endures as he demonstrates the human inability to comprehend the entropic yet undiminishing energy of human endeavor and natural event.

Even Pozzo reaches Lucky's wisdom. Pozzo believed he could control his life, but "one day" (words he often repeats), he realizes and concretely demonstrates the blindness of his ways. Having stretched human freedom to social, economic, and political excess as a landowner, the sightless Pozzo eventually reaches Lucky's conclusion regarding the futility of human accomplishment in the face of an indifferent, if not malign, ruling force (which he addresses as the same undefined "they" who beat Estragon). Pozzo follows a long line of literary archetypes who take good fortune for granted and learn too late the blindness of their ways.

Yet Pozzo persists and, in the end, achieves a redemptive innocence—not from fate, an intervening God, or Godot, but from the audience which, like Vladimir and Estragon, comes to pity him and identify with his plight when, as he puts it, life passes from day to nighttime in an instant. His speech, paralleling Lucky's at the climactic point of act 1, is the most dramatic moment in the play's rising conclusion. It is of interest that Beckett intended for Pozzo to be portrayed as a needy character and "not be played as a superior figure (as he usually is.)" Beckett goes on to explain that Pozzo "plays the lord—magnanimous, frightening—only because he is unsure of himself" (qtd. in McMillan and Fehsenfeld 141).

Pozzo tells us that he has been educated by Lucky—the mad, child-like, one-time poet, who states that the end result of all human endeavor is excrement—in Lucky's words, "waste," "defecation," "caca" ("acacaca-cademy," the end product of study). But as Lucky has taught Pozzo about human limitation and time, Pozzo's blindness and his remarks on time propel Vladimir toward his own epiphany near the end of the play. His conclusion and some of his words are even identical to Pozzo's:

POZZO: They give birth astride of a grave. The light gleams an instant, then it's night once more.
VLADIMIR: Astride of a grave and a difficult birth. Down in the hole, lingeringly, the gravedigger puts on the forceps.

Before and after these speeches, Pozzo and Lucky function as catalysts that release Vladimir and Estragon's frustration and hostility, muted during their games of camaraderie. Only after observing that Pozzo and Lucky are debilitated, do Vladimir and Estragon become more aggressive toward their guests, now hostage to their benevolence. After a brief show (or release) of hostility, Vladimir repeats Pozzo's words ("They give birth astride of a grave ... ") in his "Astride of a grave and a difficult birth ... ," and with the vertical intersecting with the linear, each character begins to articulate a similar understanding of himself, as well as of the human condition. Each regains a measure of primal innocence and, as Beckett alludes to in the dialogue, assumes a kinship with Adam, Cain, Abel, and a suffering, unredeemed Christ.

Beckett's vision would seem to be of a humanity more sinned against than sinning. In Vladimir's terms, we are a "species" condemned not to hell but to death: We are gratuitously fallen through the mere act of birth, and we possess only the illusion of salvation. The reality of undeserved suffering and death is our only birthright. Underlying our every effort to seek salvation or direction is the haunting lament: "My God, My God, why hast Thou forsaken me?" Blindness, like Pozzo's, and silence, like Lucky's, are humanity's only recompense—accumulative images of the ultimate wasting and pining of body, mind, and spirit, the nonredemptive suffering to which all are condemned.

Beckett's vision may evoke our terror, in its portrayal of human suffering, but it arouses our pity as well, as it renders humanity in a state of stoic survival and in gratuitous acts of kindness. It is this last element, the act of altruism as an act of free will or free choice, that grants Beckett's figures their heroic, if not tragic, status. In the face of inevitable suffering and oblivion, Beckett's characters have choices: to capitulate, to endure the frustrations of life, or to perform acts of kindness. Beckett would seem to be saying that stoicism and altruism may be unredemptive in terms of a responsive cosmic agency, but they surely offer moments of personal regeneration.

In an early speech, Vladimir steps outside of his prescribed role—"Let us not waste our time in idle discourse"—and calls for generosity to others, specifically demanding that he and Estragon uplift the fallen Pozzo and Lucky. He remarks that the moment is unique: "It is not every day that we are needed.... Let us make the most of it, before it is too late!" Despite Vladimir's awareness of the questionable moral worth of the human "species", he affirms the imperative of going beyond one's meanest urges toward altruistic action: "Come, let's get to work!" In effect, Vladimir is asking, "To be or not to be," in his own terms: "What are we doing here?" and in the silence occasioned by the question, he rejects aggression both toward himself (suicide) and toward others. At the same time, he embraces the only viable life alternative: their waiting and their acceptance of their waiting, "We are not saints, but we have kept our appointment." Implied is his understanding that since "the readiness is all," he must make the best of whatever fortune bestows in the act of passing the time.

In a subsequent speech, "Astride of the grave...," Vladimir echoes Pozzo's and Lucky's comments. The conflicting impulses of action and inaction, of acceptance and despair, alternate. He begins by asking, "Was I sleeping while the others suffered?" and evokes, "The tears of the world are a constant quantity," Beckett's exquisite statement about the alternation of tears and laughter in the human experience. Once more he states his earlier imperative that one must care for others, but he is overwhelmed by despair ("I can't go on."). Nevertheless, while this may be the dark night of his soul, he repudiates capitulation: "What have I said?" Reverting to his earlier negativism, he realizes that not only may his lifelong philosophical questions remain unanswered, but he may also lack verification that his ordinary daily activities have meaning or, for that matter, have even occurred: "To-morrow when I wake, or think I do, what shall I say of to-day? That with Estragon my friend, at this time, at this place, until the fall of night, I waited for Godot? That Pozzo passed, with his carrier, and that he spoke to us? Probably." And of this, he adds, "What truth will there be?"

Vladimir looks at Estragon and ponders the futility of his inquiries. Estragon is dozing again, and Vladimir, who has revered reason as a means of reaching truth, says of Estragon: "He'll know nothing," unaware perhaps that, as Democritus thought, nothing ("naught") is "more real than nothing," and, in Beckett's world, that truth lies beyond reason. Indeed, Estragon may be the wiser one in understanding that reality is entirely irrational, an intellectual void, a nightmare, or just a dream, as he describes life.[6] Once more reverting back to the more positive extreme, Vladimir returns to the one area of human activity that is meaningful, even if it makes little sense on a spiritual level and is forgotten the next day. One can find meaning by caring for others: by listening to the childlike cries of men lamenting the blows they received, by offering them pacifiers, like carrots, or by momentarily altering the balance of tears and laughter that mark the human experience. "[Estragon will] tell me," Vladimir says, "about the blows he received and I'll give him a carrot." Returning to his rational inquisitions, he wonders if, in the end, there is any purpose in any of these activities. Perhaps another figure—a person, Godot, or God—looks upon him as he looks upon Estragon and concludes that nothing matters: "At me too someone is looking, of me too, someone is saying He is sleeping, he knows nothing, let him sleep on."

Instead of repeating "I can't go on," Vladimir modifies Pozzo's and his own birth and grave speeches. In stating, "We have time to grow old," and, "The air is full of our cries," he affirms not only their waiting but the virtue of how they wait, with their self-made games and rituals, which are an anesthetic to the pain of being: "But habit is a great deadener." And so the game resumes, with Vladimir's "brooding," Beckett's description of him at the beginning of the play. Vladimir and Estragon are ready to greet Godot's messenger, and their repeated "Let's go" and "They do not move" recapitulate their return to wavering between hope deferred (Augustine) and hope maintained (Matthew). The refrain again underscores the paralysis inevitable from an inconclusive knowledge of the self and universe—and once more, like Lucky's speech with its absence of a final independent clause—their defining, if inconclusive waiting.

If we leave Sartre's characters with a sense of contempt for their frivolous indifference to the rewards of an active, humane approach to life, we depart from Beckett's couples inspired by the nobility of their perseverance as they endure on this mysterious road we all travel.

Notes

1. Florence turned on the gas, and both she and Inez died.
2. Sartre begins with the phenomenology of Husserl and Heidegger and their discussion of the "relative absolute." He also writes, "We can...reject the dualism of appearance and essence. The appearance does not hide the essence, it reveals it; it *is* the essence. The essence of an extent is no longer a property sunk in the cavity

of this existent; it is the manifest law which presides over the succession of its appearances; it is the principle of the series" xlvi.

3. One recalls the famous keyhole metaphor in *Being and Nothingness* about the Self and Other, 347–50, and Sartre's comment on mutual guilt in relationships: "I am guilty when first beneath the Other's look I experience my alienation and my nakedness as a fall from grace which I must assume.... Again I am guilty when in turn I look at the Other, because by the very fact of my own self-assertion I constitute him as an object and as an instrument, and I cause him to experience the same alienation which he must now assume" (351).

4. The play was apparently dedicated to an anonymous woman who told Sartre she wouldn't want to be judged by the actions of her lifetime. See Thody 80.

5. Sartre writes: "Human freedom precedes essence in man and makes it possible; the essence of the human being is suspended in his freedom" (Being and Nothingness 25).

6. Jack MacGowran once said: "I think sometimes the roles are reversed. I think Estragon is the one who has read and known everything and thrown it away. . . . Vladimir, who appears to be the brighter of the two, is, in fact, the half-schooled one madly trying to find out answers, pestering Estragon the whole time. . . . Estragon has read everything and dismissed it" (Quoted in Kalb 26).

Works Cited

Beckett, Samuel. *Waiting for Godot.* London: Faber and Faber, 1956.

Kalb, Jonathan. *Beckett in Performance.* (Cambridge: Cambridge University Press, 1989).

McMillan, Dougald, and Martha Fehsenfeld. *Beckett in the Theatre.* (New York: Vintage, 1948).

Sartre, Jean-Paul. *On Theatre.* Trans. Frank Jellinek (New York: Pantheon, 1976).

———. *Being and Nothingness: An Essay on Phenomenological Ontology.* Trans. Hazel E. Barnes (New York: Philosophical Library, 1956).

———. *No Exit and Three Other Plays.* Trans. Stuart Gilbert (New York: Vintage, 1948).

Thody, Philip. *Jean-Paul Sartre: A Literary and Political Study* (London: Hamish Hamilton, 1960).

Contributors

Claudia Barnett is an Associate Professor of English at Middle Tennessee State University, where she teaches courses in contemporary drama and playwriting. Her essays have appeared in *Modern Drama, Theatre Journal,* and the recent collection, *Southern Women Playwrights: New Essays in Literary History and Criticism.* She is also editor of *Wendy Wasserstein: A Casebook.*

Pamela Cooper, an Associate Professor of British and American literature at the University of North Carolina at Chapel Hill, is author of *The Fictions of John Fowles: Power, Creativity, and Femininity.* Her recent research interests include a book on postcolonial fiction, which applies aspects of post-structuralist theory to representations of the body in literary texts.

Thomas Fahy currently teaches at California Polytechnic State University in San Luis Obispo. He is co-editor of *Peering behind the Curtain: Disability, Illness, and the Extraordinary Body* (Routledge), and his recent work has appeared in several journals, including *Style, Mosaic, Prospects,* and *Shofar.*

Rena Fraden is Professor of English at Pomona College. She is the author of *Blueprints for a Black Federal Theater, 1935–1939* and *Imagining Medea: Rhodessa Jones and Theater for Incarcerated Women.*

Lois Gordon, Professor of English and comparative literature at Fairleigh Dickinson University, has written numerous books on contemporary American and British writers and on American culture. Her most recent books include *Reading Godot, The World of Samuel Beckett, 1906–1946, American Chronicle: Year-by-Year through the Twentieth Century,* and *Harold Pinter: A Casebook.* She wrote the first book on Harold Pinter to be published in the United States.

Robert F. Gross is the author of *S. N. Behrman: A Research and Production Sourcebook* and the editor of *Christopher Hampton: A Casebook* and *Tennessee Williams: A Casebook*. He has written articles on a range of modern playwrights, including August Strindberg, Eugene O'Neill, John Guare, Howard Brenton, and Harry Kondoleon. He teaches theatre at Hobart and William Smith Colleges.

Ann C. Hall, Ph.D., is currently serving as president of the Harold Pinter Society and English department chair at Ohio Dominican College. She has published widely on modern drama, literature, and feminism.

Christopher C. Hudgins is Professor of English at the University of Nevada, Las Vegas. He has written numerous articles on Stanley Kubrick, David Mamet, and Harold Pinter, and is the co-editor, with Leslie Kane, of *Gender and Genre: Essays on David Mamet* (2001). Hudgins is nearing completion of his long-term project, a book on Harold Pinter's filmscripts. He is a board member of City of Asylum, Las Vegas, an International Parliament of Writers' program supporting residencies for politically persecuted writers, and the recent recipient of the Governor's Award for Service to the Humanities.

Kimball King is Professor of English at the University of North Carolina at Chapel Hill. He is general editor of Routledge's Studies in Modern Drama series. His book-length publications in drama include *Twenty Modern British Playwrights* (1977), *Ten Modern Irish Playwrights* (1979), and *Ten Modern American Playwrights* (1981), as well as *Sam Shepard: A Casebook* (1989).

Tiffany Ana Lopez is Associate Professor of English at the University of California, Riverside, where she teaches courses on Latina/o literature, prison issues, children's literature, and American drama. She is editor of the anthology *Growing Up Chicana/o* (1993) and author of the forthcoming critical book, *The Alchemy of Blood: Critical Witnessing and Violence in Latina/o Literature.*

Fiona Mills is a Ph.D. candidate and teaching fellow in the English department at the University of North Carolina at Chapel Hill. Her recent articles have appeared in *Safundi* and *Americana: The Institute for the Study of American Popular Culture.* Currently, she is co-editing a book of collected essays on Gayl Jones.

As a playwright, director, actor, and poet, **Harold Pinter** has written twenty-nine plays, including *The Birthday Party, The Homecoming,* and *Betrayal,* twenty-one screenplays, including *The Go-Between* and *The French Lieutenant's Woman,* and several volumes of poetry and prose.

Index